THE OLD TESTAMENT AND PROCESS THEOLOGY

THE OLD TESTAMENT AND PROCESS THEOLOGY

AND

PROCESS THEOLOGY

ROBERT K. GNUSE

Chalice Press®

St. Louis, Missouri

Biblical quotations, unless otherwise noted, are from the *New Revised Standard Version Bible*, copyright 1989, Division of Christian Education of the National Council of Churches of Christ in the United States of America. Used by permission. All rights reserved.

Cover art: Detail from Michelangelo's *Creation of Adam,* Sistine Chapel
           ceiling frescoe
Cover design: Wendy Barnes
Interior design: Wynn Younker
Art direction: Elizabeth Wright

This book is printed on acid-free, recycled paper.

Visit Chalice Press on the World Wide Web at
www.chalicepress.com

10 9 8 7 6 5 4 3 2 1   00 01 02 03

Library of Congress Cataloging–in–Publication Data

Gnuse, Robert Karl, 1947–
    The Old Testament and process theology / Robert K. Gnuse.
        p.   cm.
    Includes bibliographical references and index.
    ISBN 0-8272-2713-2
    1. Bible. O. T. –Hermeneutics. 2. Process theology.   I. Title.
    BS476 .G68   2000   00–010042
    230' .0411–dc21

Printed in the United States of America

Contents

Abbreviations

AB	The Anchor Bible
ABD	*The Anchor Bible Dictionary*, ed. David Noel Freedman
AnBib	Analecta biblica
ASORDS	American Schools of Oriental Research Dissertation Series
BA	*Biblical Archaeologist*
BASOR	*Bulletin of the American Schools of Oriental Research*
BibB	Biblische Beiträge
BibOr	Biblica et orientalia
BTB	*Biblical Theology Bulletin*
CBC	Cambridge Bible Commentary
CBQ	*Catholic Biblical Quarterly*
CBQMS	Catholic Biblical Quarterly–Monograph Series
Conc	Concilium
HR	*History of Religions*
HSM	Harvard Semitic Monographs
HTR	*Harvard Theological Review*

HUCA	*Hebrew Union College Annual*
IDB	*Interpreter's Dictionary of the Bible,* ed. George Buttrick
IDBSup	*Interpreter's Dictionary of the Bible, Supplement,* ed. Keith Crim
Int	*Interpretation*
IRT	Issues in Religion and Theology
JBL	*Journal of Biblical Literature*
JNES	*Journal of Near Eastern Studies*
JQR	*Jewish Quarterly Review*
JSOT	*Journal for the Study of the Old Testament*
JSOTSup	Journal for the Study of the Old Testament Supplement Series
KD	*Kerygma und Dogma*
NICOT	New International Commentary on the Old Testament
OBO	Orbis biblicus et orientalis
OBT	Overtures to Biblical Theology
OTL	Old Testament Library
QD	Quaestiones disputatae
SBLMS	Society of Biblical Literature Monograph Series
SBT	Studies in Biblical Theology
SHANE	Studies in the History of the Ancient Near East
SJT	*Scottish Journal of Theology*
SWBA	Social World of Biblical Antiquity

TS	*Theological Studies*
VT	*Vetus Testamentum*
VTSup	Vetus Testamentum Supplements
WMANT	Wissenschaftliche Monographien zum Alten und Neuen Testament
ZAW	*Zeitschrift für die alttestamentlichte Wissenschaft*
ZDPV	*Zeitschrift des deutschen Palästina-Vereins*

Introduction

I

In the intellectual advance of the Judeo-Christian tradition there has been significant development in the human perception of God, even though, for the most part, Christians often have been oblivious to this evolution. All theologizing is done within a worldview or philosophical system; this is true for both biblical theologians and later Christian theologians. The use of the reigning worldview may be conscious or unconscious by the spokespersons of the faith, but it most certainly is present in the way ideas are formulated and in the choice of vocabulary for religious expressions. Religious belief always must resynthesize the inherited theological traditions of the past "creatively and faithfully," to speak to the present spiritual needs of people in a way that may be "disturbing" to them, and to prepare for future needs that may be even more "problematic" than the present ones.[1]

Historians of thought have spoken of the three significant worldviews through which thought and philosophical articulation have developed in the Western tradition. The first is that of the ancient world, which has been described as mythic or mytho-poetic due to its sense of an organic universe full of life forces and its portrayal of reality in symbolic and story form.[2] Northrop Frye, in his highly respected work *The Great Code: The Bible and Literature,* speaks of this age as the "metaphorical" era in human development. At this time in the ancient Near East there was little separation

---

[1]Thomas Raitt, *A Theology of Exile* (Philadelphia: Fortress Press, 1977), 6.
[2]Henri Frankfort, "Myth and Reality," in *The Intellectual Adventure of Ancient Man,* ed. Henri Frankfort (Chicago: University of Chicago Press, 1946), 3–27; and Mircea Eliade, *Myth of the Eternal Return* (Princeton, N.J.: Princeton University Press, 1954), 3–162.

of subject and object in the minds of people; both were linked by power—
words in themselves had power.[3]

The second age is that of ascendant Greek philosophy, which emerged
in classical Greece and ultimately became the foundation for Western
thought. This worldview is characterized by its dedication to logical and
rational arguments, which can be either deductive or inductive. The result
is often a grand philosophical system that attempts to organize thought
and ideas into some rational system. Christian historians often point to
Augustine and his use of Neoplatonic thought as mediated through Plotinus
as the quintessential synthesis of biblical thought and classical Greek
philosophy. Frye characterizes this age as the "metonymic" era, wherein
language was individualized to be an outward expression of inner thought,
or texts and ideas were seen to reflect universal images, as in Plato's
philosophical system.[4]

Finally, ideational historians speak of the rise of the scientific-empirical
mode of thinking, which finds its roots already in the late medieval world[5]
but comes to fuller fruition in the early modern period. Frye envisions this
to be the "descriptive" age, wherein philosophers spoke of the distinction
between the subject and the object as the human being became a distinct
observer of the physical objective realm around him or her.[6] Presumably,
it is this third era in which we currently live, especially in light of our
contemporary emphasis on logical, empirical, and scientific thought, which
demands primarily physical evidence (rather than rational and abstract
deductions) as an adequate proof for an argument.

There are confident theorists today, too numerous to mention, who
speak of an emerging fourth age that is being brought forth by the
revolutionary understandings of the twentieth century in physics and
astronomy. In this age people will view the universe in organic and holistic
terms once more, as in the very first age, only with greater depth of
understanding. Process thinkers speak of their worldview as the harbinger
of this age philosophically, for Whitehead attempted to view the world in
philosophical categories that were dynamically organic and in the
contemporary mode of scientific discourse. Frye likewise speaks of a new
age of thought wherein human language and literary metaphor once more
are seen as having power.[7]

---

[3]Northrop Frye, *The Great Code: The Bible and Literature* (New York: Harcourt, Brace,
Jovanovich, 1982), 6; and Ronald Farmer, *Beyond the Impasse: The Promise of a Process Hermeneutic,* Studies in American Biblical Hermeneutics 13 (Macon, Ga.: Mercer, 1997), 52–53.

[4]Frye, *Great Code,* 7–12; and Farmer, *Impasse,* 52–54.

[5]Henning Graf Reventlow, *The Authority of the Bible and the Rise of the Modern World* (Philadelphia: Fortress Press, 1985), 9–38.

[6]Frye, *Great Code,* 13–14; and Farmer, *Impasse,* 54–56.

[7]Frye, *Great Code,* 15–18; and Farmer, *Impasse,* 56–58.

A corresponding religious perception of the gods or God might be associated with each age. The first age is the era of polytheism and pantheism, wherein the Divine is closely connected to the forces of this world in early neolithic farming communities and river valley civilizations of the old world. The second age is one of classical theism, wherein monotheism arises with Zoroastrianism, Judaism, and Christianity in Western Asia, and monism emerges in the thought of the Greek philosophers and in the late Vedas and Upanishads of India.[8] In the third age the possibility of agnosticism or even atheism becomes plausible under the aegis of strict scientific reductionism promoted by European deists and rationalists. Finally, in the newly emerging stage, "panentheism," a popular notion advocated by process thinkers and even some scientists, might be a potentially ascendant perception of the Divine. Herein the Divine is seen as entering into a dynamic relationship with the universe and especially conscious human beings. This, of course, is a brief generalized summary, and many might quibble with the facile distinctions here presented. But it is not our purpose to do a history of philosophical thought.

Theologizing in the Judeo-Christian tradition might be said to have gone through a parallel development. The biblical literature emerged late in the period of mythic and poetic thought and shared much in common with those intellectual assumptions. Biblical texts were formulated at the end of that intellectual age and already show some of the assumptions of the later worldviews. Perhaps one might even say that biblical thought mediated through the ancient church fathers together with Greek philosophy actually helped to give rise to the next stage of human intellectual endeavor in the West. Nonetheless, when one seriously looks at the biblical text and inquires after the intellectual and cultural assumptions of the persons who are therein portrayed as acting in meaningful religious and political modes of behavior, it becomes quite evident that they were people of a primitive age. The biblical writers may have been more sophisticated than those people whose actions they recalled, but one still must admit that the actions of those narrative personages reflect where the intellectual mind-set of that age is to be located by our analysis. Most of the literary plots in biblical narrative are explicable with the insight that the people of that time were in the first stage of intellectual development, and even some of the reflective theology implied by the later authors and editors of the text has to be seen in the same light. This comes through in their portrayal of God, human actions, human moral response, and the everyday social-political response of citizens. What interests us most at this point is their perception and portrayal of God.

---

[8]Robert Gnuse, *No Other Gods: Emergent Monotheism in Israel,* JSOTSup 241 (Sheffield, U.K.: Sheffield Academic Press, 1997), 129–76.

II

The God of the biblical text was portrayed in dynamic fashion, as a deity with human emotions whose mind could change. Numerous narratives in the Hebrew Scriptures especially testify to this phenomenon, but it is often the tendency of Jews and Christians to ignore these stories and to place the ideas expressed by the narratives into our modern thought forms. We dismiss too many images of God as symbolic and crude anthropomorphisms, especially the capacity for the divine mind of God to change and also the apparent pain experienced by God over the rebellion of the chosen people.[9] But these passages will not go away, and the sincere reader of the biblical text cannot ignore them. Gerald Janzen cleverly observes that we may initially hunt for texts to support a classical view of God, but the biblical language forces us to acknowledge that a process perspective more easily can apprehend the imagery of the Bible. For centuries church fathers forced themselves to interpret these dynamic biblical images of God as metaphors and anthropomorphisms, so they could ignore the implications for theology. But their forced inversions of these dynamic biblical texts over the years are really evidence for the true nature of the biblical testimony about God.[10] Historians of Christian thought have spoken of how the ancient, medieval, and early modern Christian interpreters of the biblical text subordinated the clear testimony of the text regarding the suffering of God to their own philosophical assumptions inherited from classical Greek philosophy.[11]

If we refuse to dismiss these passages as merely ancient and primitive ways of speaking or as literary anthropomorphisms (God portrayed in human form) and anthropopathisms (God portrayed with human emotions), and then we permit them to speak to us with all their vivid power, we might find that they address us in meaningful ways for our modern age, even though we live two thousand years removed from the mytho-poetic worldview of the first millennium B.C.E. Hence, it is helpful to look more closely at the stories to appreciate the different worldview from which these accounts originated. We may discover that in some regards their ancient worldview shares more with our modern worldview than we do with the intervening ages between us. We need to return to our intellectual roots in the power of the biblical text before we have the necessary assumptions to make a leap forward into a new age of intellectual articulation and theological confession.

---

[9]Lewis S. Ford, *The Lure of God: A Biblical Background for Process Theism* (Philadelphia: Fortress Press, 1978), 29.

[10]Gerald Janzen, "Metaphor and Reality in Hosea 11," *Semeia* 24 (1982): 7–44.

[11]T. E. Pollard, "The Impassibility of God," *SJT* 8 (1955): 353–64; Lester Kuyper, "The Suffering and the Repentance of God," *SJT* 22 (1969): 257–77; and Ford, *Lure,* 131.

III

For concrete illustration let us turn to a few examples from the biblical text. In 2 Kings 20 Isaiah twice gave oracles to Hezekiah, first proclaiming the king's imminent death and then proclaiming the prolongation of the king's life. In between these two oracles Yahweh came to Isaiah, as the prophet walked in the courtyard of the king, with the message that Hezekiah's prayers and tears had been effective in changing the divine will. Although this may sound like divine fickleness to the modern mind, and even if Christian theologians engage in mental gymnastics to explain the divine *volte-face,* nonetheless, the biblical text indicates that Yahweh's mind was changed by human petition, in this case the prayer of pious King Hezekiah. The image of God's mind being changed by human response in this particular narrative accords well with process theology but not classical theism.[12]

In the book of Ezekiel we observe what appear to be unfulfilled oracles by the prophet. In Ezekiel 26:7–14 the prophet clearly declares that Nebuchadrezzar of Babylon will attack and destroy the city of Tyre ("I will make you a bare rock," Ezek. 26:14). However, in Ezekiel 29:18–20 the prophet declares that Yahweh has decided that Nebuchadrezzar will not conquer Tyre, but will take the country of Egypt instead. Yet we know that Egypt was never conquered by Nebuchadrezzar, and the biblical audience probably knew that as well. Hence, two questions arise. Did these two oracles truly not come to pass? The answer is obviously yes. To appeal to a later conquest by Alexander the Great as fulfilling these oracles, as some biblical literalists attempt to do, is cheating. Why did the editor include two failed prophecies by Ezekiel and make the prophet look like a false prophet? Perhaps a more important issue than the prophet's integrity was at stake. The biblical authors did not believe in a predetermined universe in which events could be foreseen by divination, as was the custom throughout much of the ancient world. The oracle went unfulfilled not because Ezekiel was a false prophet, but because Yahweh's mind could change—and the prophet would be notified appropriately. If the divine will could change, then the universe was not fixed and predetermined, and human will could make significant decisions to affect the outcome of events in history. This affirmation of freedom in the cosmic and historical unfolding of events and the corresponding significance of human free will, as well as the responsibility that came with it, was for the biblical authors a significant theological statement. Temporarily sacrificing the apparent image of Ezekiel, or any other prophet, as a true prophet on a few short oracles is a small price to pay by the authors of the prophetic books in order to make these other theologically revolutionary statements.

---

[12]Lewis S. Ford, "Contingent Trinitarianism," in *Trinity in Process: A Relational Theology of God,* ed. Joseph Bracken and Marjorie Suchocki (New York: Continuum, 1997), 56.

These accounts may twist our concept of the immutable will of God and predestination into a knot, but they were theologically significant for the biblical authors. It was for them a powerful statement of divine grace and responsiveness to the human creatures' prayer and worship. It also affirmed the significance of human response to the Divine and the importance of free will in the choice of moral actions. In turn, this called upon humans to take their decision-making processes seriously and to steadfastly strive to live the moral life of obedience. This made the importance of the Torah great, ultimately greater than the role of ritual and sacrifice. Biblical authors were fighting for significant insights with these notions, and their ultimate victory on these theological issues helped lay the foundations for the way we think philosophically and religiously in the Western tradition. We should not squirm at the theology in these texts but recognize that this is an earlier mode of speaking about God, which we do not share today. Further, it was a necessary mode of thinking in a stage of evolution that would lead to our way of thinking today.

IV

In the early church new philosophical modes of thought were merged together with biblical thought. Greek philosophy was married to biblical theology; the culmination of this convergence is demonstrated best in the writings of Augustine in the fourth and fifth centuries C.E. This synthesis of thought has been the foundation for Christian theology until this century.

In this stage of human thought, Christian theologians symbolically envisioned God in the absolute categories proposed by Greek philosophy. Hence, God was omnipotent, omniscient, and omnipresent, the famous omni-terms that every confirmand has had to learn at some stage in religious education. In addition, other adjectives were spawned by thinkers to characterize the nature of God, including eternal, immutable, indivisible, and so on. These absolute terms were deemed worthy human expressions to be used of the transcendent God worshiped by Christians. But they were not the language of the Bible. Biblical language was more dynamic and human in its portrayal of God. Fortunately, this language, too, was retained in our religious discourse, so that words like loving, gracious, merciful, and even angry are also terms dutifully memorized by generations of youthful confirmands. But it was the absolute language of the philosophers that impressed itself most on our minds, and even on the theologian's craft.

Although the absolute language of the philosophers was good, it had its limitations. To speak of God's being omnipotent simply made the great question of the origin of evil even more painful, for it suggested even more surely that God had to will also the evil things that happened to humanity. As Jon Levenson has so adeptly demonstrated, the biblical portrayal of God as almighty is quite different from the Western Christian description of God as omnipotent.[13] Under the perception of God's might one could still envision metaphorical images about evil forces that must be confronted and defeated by God. That image of the divine defeat of evil, sin, and death is certainly at the heart of discourse about Jesus Christ's death and resurrection. But because of our overreliance on the metaphor of divine omnipotence, we unwittingly compromise the portrayal of the significance of the death and resurrection of Jesus as well as clear images in the Hebrew Scriptures that speak of Yahweh's defeat of evil. Hence, as Christians after the time of the early church began to use Greek philosophy and profit thereby, they also compromised aspects of their theology. This is testimony to the finitude of any human worldview or philosophical system that is used by Christians in the articulation of their beliefs.

The modern era has seen the traditional assumptions of Greek philosophy challenged by critical contemporary philosophers in the twentieth century. The Greek philosophical system appears to have collapsed and with it the foundation for much of the language we have used in our formulation of systematic theologies, confirmation manuals, and even devotional literature. Christian theologians and authors are now seeking to discover new idioms and modes of discourse to communicate our message to the faithful believers. In the late twentieth century several new philosophical modes of discourse were proposed, but as of yet no one way of conceptualizing religious thought has gained a consensus among theologians.

What we need is a new mode of interpreting the biblical text that can capture the spirit of the original authors without suppressing it in the philosophical categories of a later age. We need a hermeneutic that will not use the interpretative devices of dismissing anthropomorphisms as mere allegory, but rather will accept the language of the biblical text and use it sincerely and boldly to address contemporary existential needs. We need a hermeneutic that will offer us "a current thought and language within which we may interpret along the metaphorical grain, and not against the grain" of "those Hebrew Bible portrayals where God's passionality and mutability are either asserted or assumed."[14]

V

A contemporary mode of philosophical discourse arose within the past century that is associated with Alfred North Whitehead. His metaphysical system has been titled *process philosophy,* and those Christian thinkers who attempt to express Christian thought utilizing his philosophical concepts

---

[13]Jon Levenson, *Creation and the Persistence of Evil* (San Francisco: HarperCollins, 1988), 3–156.

[14]Janzen, "Metaphor," 19.

are called *process theologians*. What this volume seeks to contribute is the blending of process theological categories with themes taken from the Hebrew Scriptures or the Old Testament. Previous authors have undertaken similar discussions, most notably Gerald Janzen[15] and Terence Fretheim.[16] The work of Lewis Ford, which addresses not only the Hebrew Scriptures but biblical theology in general, also has been most helpful.[17] But no one has attempted to articulate a wide range of specific themes from the Hebrew Scriptures in Whiteheadian terms. This short work will attempt to undertake such a task in cursory fashion to give inspiration to other biblical theologians who wish to engage in the same quest.

When Christian theologians in general, or biblical theologians in particular, weave what they consider to be significant religious themes together into an organized synthesis for presentation to the readers, they use some established philosophical system of thought, either consciously or unconsciously. The great systems of thought available to the Judeo-Christian tradition historically have been the philosophical paradigms of Plato and Aristotle. When religious thinkers draw on such systems of thought, they do not take the entire philosophical system into their religious discourse. They select modes of thought, particular images, and ways of speaking most appropriate for their theological task, and they often ignore significant portions of the greater metaphysical system not relevant to their theological needs. Often philosophical systems delve into great detail in regard to issues of epistemology and ontology, which provide more philosophical jargon than is necessary for the theologians who imbibe of the system.

Furthermore, theologians sometimes will contradict certain parts of the philosophical system that they use, because their themes, taken from either the Bible or their particular religious tradition, require a certain articulation that may be in tension with the logical extensions of the metaphysical system. A theologian begins with the primary premise of the existence of God in the generation of a theological system, although for a philosopher the existence of God is an issue for discussion, not a foundational assumption with which one begins. Thus, the theologian, of necessity, cannot take the philosophical system of any thinker without adjustments. This is commonplace in the Jewish and Christian traditions and must be accepted by any thinker who seeks to use a philosophical system in his or her religious discourse. Medieval and early modern Christian thinkers of the Roman Catholic and Protestant traditions frequently used the categories of thought provided by Aristotle. But at times

---

[15]Ibid., 7–44; and "The Old Testament in 'Process' Perspective," in *Magnalia Dei–The Mighty Acts of God,* ed. Frank Cross et al. (Garden City, N.Y.: Doubleday, 1976), 480–509.

[16]Terence Fretheim, *The Suffering of God,* OBT (Philadelphia: Fortress Press, 1984), 1–166.

[17]Lewis S. Ford, "Biblical Recital and Process Philosophy," *Int* 26 (1972): 198–209; and *Lure,* passim.

they had to confess traditional dogmas in ways other than Aristotle's categories would permit simply because they were received articles of faith.

Religious discourse, by necessity, must reconcile themes and ideas taken from the sacred texts, the creeds of the religious traditions, and the respected teachers of the tradition with not only the reigning philosophical system but also the social-historical context within which the author writes and the particular existential needs of the religious community addressed by the author.[18] The philosophical system is not the most important component in this theological task; presumably, the sacred texts and the creeds are. The philosophical system provides the format into which the raw materials of the received tradition are placed. The philosophical system provides the vehicle for expression of religious thought; it is not the system of religious thought itself. The sacred traditions provide the content, which is then placed into the philosophical vehicle. Or again, one might say that the philosophical system provides language by which the beliefs of the tradition may be expressed in an intellectually respectable and contemporary idiom for the audience of the theologians. Therefore, theologians must use the philosophical system in a rather pliable fashion and mold it for the sake of the theological traditions.

Alfred North Whitehead knew this. He understood full well that those who might seek to use his system would change and modify his language and his paradigms. He provided not a fixed metaphysical system of thought, but rather suggestive paradigms that attempted to do justice to our modern scientific understandings. He hoped that his suggestions would inspire later thinkers who would not be afraid to tinker with his system of thought, especially if they achieved the agenda that Whitehead himself sought—the creation of a philosophical worldview that incorporated the dynamic understandings of the universe provided by modern science. Elizabeth Kraus says it well:

> Whitehead would be utterly inconsistent if he had intended PR [*Process and Reality*] as the formulation of an ultimate metaphysics to be at worst slavishly parroted and at best explicated and commented on by a narrow coterie of adoring followers. To be a genuine Whiteheadian is to see his thought as seminal, as tentative, as demanding the kind of development, rethinking, and revision which results from the confrontation of a theory with its application to broad-spectrum practice.[19]

Whitehead himself had a distrust of language in terms of its ability to communicate great thought and the nature of reality in precise fashion. He

---

[18]Edward Farley, *Ecclesial Man* (Philadelphia: Fortress Press, 1975), passim.
[19]Elizabeth Kraus, *The Metaphysics of Experience: A Companion to Whitehead's Process and Reality* (New York: Fordham University Press, 1979), xii.

was distrustful even of his own language, which frequently had many neologisms that of necessity he had to create. He saw his system as "metaphorical and elliptical," that is, designed to inspire others to engage in the same task as he did without feeling obligated to clone his language, for his work is a "continual plea for the imaginative leap from language to meaning."[20] Philosophy is an attempt to poetically envision the universe, and it cannot be dogmatic about the formal terminology that is used.

Norman Pittenger, who ranks as a significant process theologian, observes that one cannot use process philosophy in its pure form for theology. Theologians may draw only some of the key elements from it for their task. Above all, process categories must be subordinate to Christian ideas. Pittenger reminds us that this was how Augustine used Plato and Plotinus and how Thomas Aquinas used Aristotle.[21] We must be mindful of this theological requirement or else we shall straightjacket our theology into a philosophical system. In a similar vein, Gerald Janzen states that process thought cannot be reconciled with the theology of the Hebrew Bible simply and completely, but biblical theologians may use the presuppositions of process thought in their analyses of the text. If this is done properly, then a "new fundamental imagery" from the Hebrew Bible will emerge for biblical theology and Christian theology in general.[22]

John Collins provides us with a valuable warning, however. He demands that biblical theologians who correlate the biblical text with process thought must move beyond the mere quoting of passages from the Bible that sound similar to process concepts. Rather, they must seek the deep underlying assumptions that may bind the two together. In response to Collins, we must admit, of course, that this will not be easy, for we are comparing the biblical thought of the first millennium B.C.E. with the scientific philosophy of the modern (or even postmodern) age. But it is indeed necessary to make a correlation between biblical thought and process thought on a wide range of issues and in a deeper fashion to justify the use of these philosophical categories in the discourse of biblical theology. Furthermore, Collins declares that biblical theologians must determine the character of the Bible as a revelatory work before they can weld it together with metaphysical systems of thought. Should the Bible be treated as revelation from a divine "other," thus making it a source superior to philosophical logic, or is it a record of the human experience of the Divine, thus making it a source equal to philosophical reflection?[23] This latter request may be virtually impossible for biblical theologians to accomplish. Nonetheless, despite the stern warnings of Collins, I believe it is a worthwhile

---

[20]Kraus, *Metaphysics,* 8.

[21]Norman Pittenger, *The Divine Triunity* (Philadelphia: United Church Press, 1977), 115–17.

[22]Janzen, "Process Perspective," 497–98.

[23]John Collins, "Process Hermeneutic," *Semeia* 24 (1982): 115.

task to undertake an analysis of Hebrew Bible themes with process categories, if only for a few humble insights we might gain into theologizing, preaching, and teaching of these biblical materials. If the way in which we present the meaning of biblical texts and images is changed a little, and for the better, then the quest is worthwhile.

Hopefully, I am a true Whiteheadian in the use of categories. By that I mean the attempt to use the language of process thought in a creative synthesis with biblical categories, especially those taken from the Hebrew Scriptures. By its very nature, discourse received from the Hebrew Scriptures cannot be systematically woven together with the entire system of thought provided by Whitehead. Nonetheless, the use of some of the Whiteheadian categories may be most meaningful in the rearticulation of the biblical thought into expressions and perceptual paradigms compatible with the modern way of thinking.

A reader deeply immersed in the thought of Whitehead may be somewhat disappointed by the use of process categories in this volume. Other Christian theologians, as well as New Testament scholars, have used Whitehead's categories of thought in more detailed fashion than this work will be able to demonstrate. Much of that is due to the nature of the Hebrew Scriptures and the era from which they came. There is a tremendous gap between the worldview of the ancient Near East out of which the Hebrew Bible arose and the modern worldview that is the intellectual arena of process thought. Process categories can be merged with themes from the Hebrew Bible only in general and limited ways without artificially forcing the modern intellectual categories on the ancient texts. (Perhaps I may have done a little of that too.) One must be cautious when using modern intellectual paradigms on biblical texts, so as not to swallow them up into the modern philosophical system. Therefore, my use of process thought with the Hebrew Scriptures of necessity will be limited. But I hope that my synthesis is valid, and, more importantly, that it will give insight and inspiration to those who read it.

VI

This volume will explore some avenues suggested by previous authors who have ventured into this field. Past authors have paid special attention to the biblical doctrine of God and the related question of divine suffering, and these topics will be treated here from the particular perspective of the Hebrew Scriptures. Because process thought is extremely concerned with temporality and explaining the concepts of development and the temporal flow, the significance of process thought for the scholarly biblical concept of *Heilsgeschichte* is worth consideration.[24] Other biblical themes may be

---

[24]Ford, "Biblical Recital," 198–209; and *Lure,* passim.

addressed from new perspectives. Creation in process thought differs from the biblical and Christian view of creation, especially the absolute model of creation out of nothing. Whitehead himself very clearly rejected notions of static creation and the Christian idea of *creatio ex nihilo*. But this monograph will stress the actual continuity between Whitehead's thought and the real biblical views of creation. This volume also will attempt to discuss the relationship of process thought and specific biblical themes such as covenant, prophecy, and Law. Finally, scholarly understandings of how biblical authors reinterpreted ancient thought, as well as the traditio-historical process in biblical literature and the canon, may be understood from process perspectives. The short chapters dedicated to each of these topics are not meant to be detailed expositions; they are speculations designed to inspire others. This work is an intellectual endeavor still in process, and others are welcome to join in its development.

1

Recent Scholarship and the Need for a New Theology

I

In the past generation a great shaking of the foundations has occurred in the area of Hebrew Bible scholarship. The paradigms of a former age have been critiqued and new models have been proposed with significant implications for biblical theology. The older models of doing biblical theology are still valuable, but there is a sense that newer paradigms are needed.[1] In a previous work I submitted that recent scholarship in the Hebrew Scriptures suggests the use of evolutionary and processual approaches to the articulation of biblical theology.[2] Two areas of research that point in this direction are the evaluation of Israel's settlement process and the emergence of Israel's religious beliefs, especially monotheism. Formerly, we viewed both these phenomena as dramatic occurrences in Israel's social and intellectual history, but more recent scholarship indicates that the emergence of Israel's social-political identity and monotheism came more gradually than we heretofore suspected. I believe our new insights encourage the use of process paradigms to organize and give expression to those biblical beliefs in a meaningful contemporary idiom. To illustrate this, it would be helpful to review the contemporary scholarship that seeks to rewrite our biblical introductions.

---

[1]Janzen, "Process Perspective," 480–509, advocated the use of process theological categories as early as 1976.

[2]Gnuse, *No Other Gods,* passim. This chapter is a brief summary of two chapters from that book that review recent theories on the conquest and emerging monotheism, 23–128.

II

Evaluation of the conquest or settlement process of ancient Israel in the Iron Age I period (1200–1050 B.C.E.) provides insight into the origin of the Israelite social-political and religious ethos that subsequently inspires our theology. For example, the theory of an Israelite invasion or internal revolution suggests that biblical thought was distinctive and morally superior to the cultures surrounding Israel in that age. The revolutionary theory also has inspired liberation theology for the past generation. Theories stressing peaceful infiltration or peaceful settlement from within the land emphasize the evolutionary nature of Israel's cultural and religious development.

In this century three significant theories have been advocated to explain the emergence of Israel in Palestine. (1) The theory of a gradual, peaceful infiltration of Palestine by seminomadic Israelites was proposed by German scholars Albrecht Alt, Martin Noth, Manfred Weippert, and other historians and archaeologists from the 1920s through the 1970s.[3] (2) William Foxwell Albright, George Ernest Wright, Yehezkel Kaufmann, John Bright, and other archaeologists in the 1940s and the 1950s declared that the conquest was a unified, military invasion by Joshua that may have been more extensive than the biblical book of Joshua indicates. Destruction at Canaanite sites at Debir, Lachish, Luz/Bethel, and Hazor were attributed to this late thirteenth-century B.C.E. Israelite invasion.[4] (3) Out of this last school there arose in the 1960s and 1970s the theory of internal revolution explicated by George Mendenhall, Norman Gottwald, and others. Poor Canaanites oppressed by Egyptian taxation and oppressive city-states revolted and fled to the highlands to create an egalitarian state. Perhaps a small group of Yahweh worshipers from Egypt united in covenant with the parasocials (bandits or *'apiru*) already in the highlands and the peasants from the lowland cities.[5]

All three theories have been criticized extensively, and this, in part, led scholars to search for a new paradigm. The peaceful infiltration model was criticized for the inability to demonstrate that a large number of Israelites originated outside the land of Palestine, for an inadequate understanding of nomadism, and for the failure to see commonality between Israelite

---

[3]Albrecht Alt and Martin Noth wrote several articles, and longer works include: Noth, *The History of Israel,* trans. Peter Ackroyd (New York: Harper and Brothers, 1960), 53–84; and Manfred Weippert, *The Settlement of the Israelite Tribes in Palestine,* trans. James Martin, SBT 2d ser. 21 (London: SCM Press, 1971), 1–146.

[4]William Foxwell Albright and George Ernest Wright wrote a number of essays and book chapters, including Wright, *Biblical Archaeology,* 2d ed. (Philadelphia: Westminster Press, 1962), 69–85.

[5]George Mendenhall, *The Tenth Generation* (Baltimore: Johns Hopkins University Press, 1973), 1–226, and other articles; and Norman Gottwald, *The Tribes of Yahweh* (Maryknoll, N.Y.: Orbis Books, 1979), 3–916, and numerous articles.

culture and late Bronze Age Palestine (1550–1200 B.C.E.). The violent conquest proponents were chided for their belief that archaeology could be used so readily to verify biblical texts, when material data from the ground is so often ambiguous, and for failure to admit that the cities in Palestine more likely were destroyed by Egyptians, Canaanite war lords, or migratory Sea Peoples. The destroyed cities fell at different times, and several cities mentioned in the biblical text were not inhabited during the conquest (e.g., Jericho and Ai). The social revolution model failed to provide concrete evidence for a peasants' revolt, did not understand clearly the relationship between pastoral and sedentary lifestyles, and appeared driven by dated social scientific theories and old biblical hypotheses (e.g., amphictyonic league and early covenant ceremonies).[6]

New theories have been proposed for the Israelite emergence in Palestine. Excavations of highland villages since 1980 have impressed archaeologists with the continuity between lowland urban Canaanite and highland village Israelite culture, especially in regard to pottery, farming techniques, tools, and building construction. The peaceful nature of the villages became evident, and the rapid population growth from 23 to 114 villages with quick agricultural intensification implied that farmers migrated from the lowlands to the highlands. Pottery, particularly the collar-rimmed jar, once described as specifically Israelite, were seen to be derived from late Bronze Age Canaanites. Farming techniques appear to have been learned in the lowlands, especially constructing lime-coated cisterns and hill terraces to hold runoff water. Canaanite construction techniques included the manufacture of certain bronze tools (chisels, axes, and mattocks) and building construction (casemate wall, the four-room house, and pier technique in roof supports). Canaanites evolved into Israelites with the decline in the late Bronze Age culture and the deterioration of city life caused by Egyptian campaigns, excessive taxation, and perhaps even climate change.[7] There are, however, different models for this process.

Peaceful Withdrawal

In the early 1980s archaeologists who made these observations, such as Joseph Callaway and Lawrence Stager, proposed that people simply withdrew peacefully into the highlands to avoid economic stress in the

---

[6]Weippert, *Settlement*, 46–132; C. H. J. de Geus, *The Tribes of Israel* (Amsterdam: Van Gorcum, 1976), 120–92; Niels Peter Lemche, *Early Israel*, VTSup 37 (Leiden: Brill, 1985), 1–297, 411–35; and Robert Coote and Keith Whitelam, *The Emergence of Early Israel in Historical Perspective*, SWBA 5 (Sheffield, U.K.: Almond, 1987), 49–80, 173–77.

[7]Joseph Callaway, "Village Subsistence at Ai and Raddana in Iron Age I," in *The Answers Lie Below*, ed. Henry Thompson (Lanham, Md.: UPA, 1984), 51–66, and "A New Perspective on the Hill Country Settlement of Canaan in Iron Age I," in *Palestine in the Bronze and Iron Ages*, ed. J. N. Tubb (London: Institute of Archaeology, 1985), 31–49; Lawrence Stager, "The Archaeology of the Family," *BASOR* 260 (1985): 1–35; and other scholars.

valleys. David Hopkins' evaluation of highland Israelite agriculture in Iron Age I (1200–1050 B.C.E.) implied a peaceful movement concurrent with agricultural intensification of the land. Cooperation on the clan level and optimal use of labor to diversify crops and animals spread the risk of agricultural disaster over more people and lessened its likelihood.[8] Gösta Ahlström found evidence for continuity between Canaanites and Israelites in pottery and technology, and also in his assessment of the biblical text (e.g., the name Israel is compounded with the divine name of El, a Canaanite god). People retribalized in the highlands, and perhaps foreigners entered the land bringing the worship of Yahweh.[9]

Symbiosis or Internal Nomadic Settlement

Other scholars recognized the cultural continuity between Israelites and Canaanites but observed certain phenomena, such as the elliptical shape of the village (like a pastoralist camp) and the four-room house, as indicative of Israelite pastoral origins. C. H. J. de Geus suggested that Israelites were ethnically united, sedentary tribal highlanders who lived between the areas of urban control, interacted with the cities so as to become acculturated, and thus experienced "cultural symbiosis."[10] Volkmar Fritz used the word *symbiosis* to describe the settlement process, and Israel Finkelstein characterized it as an "internal nomadic settlement." Continuity, or symbiosis, is exemplified by not only pottery but also the Israelite four-room house, an evolutionary culmination of Canaanite architectural forms combined with nomadic tent design. Familiarity with livestock breeding, metalwork, and pottery implies Israelites were not true nomads but had intensive contact with farmers. Israelites were "culture-land nomads" or "enclosed nomads" throughout the late Bronze Age (1550–1200 B.C.E.) who moved about in the plains around cultivated land and traded with townspeople. When the cities declined, pastoralists developed horticultural (fruit and olives) and agricultural (grain) skills to compensate for commodities no longer available from trade.[11]

Peaceful Transition or Transformation

Some scholars believe that the existing settled highland population was sufficient to create Israel by human reproduction, with lower mortality

---

[8]David Hopkins, *The Highlands of Canaan,* SWBA 3 (Sheffield, U.K.: Almond, 1985), 15–275.

[9]Gösta Ahlström, *Who Were the Israelites?* (Winona Lake, Ind.: Eisenbrauns, 1986), 6–97, *A History of Ancient Palestine* (Minneapolis: Fortress Press, 1993), 282–390, and various articles.

[10]de Geus, *Tribes,* 123–87, 210–12.

[11]Volkmar Fritz, "The Israelite 'Conquest' in Light of Recent Excavations at Khirbet el-Mishâsh," *BASOR* 241 (1981): 61–73, and "Conquest or Settlement?" *BA* 50 (1987): 84–100; and Israel Finkelstein, *The Archaeology of the Israelite Settlement* (Jerusalem: IES, 1988), 237–356, and other essays.

rates made possible by improved agricultural conditions. A "peaceful transition" of power occurred, which shifted the center of human activity from the valleys to highlands. This led to national unification, because whereas valley regions were isolated from each other by highlands, highland regions were more likely to interrelate economically and politically. Niels Peter Lemche concluded that Canaanites became Israelites without any ethnic transformation by virtue of a socioeconomic transformation from valley agriculture to highland agriculture.[12] William Stiebing proposed that dry climatic conditions in the Mediterranean area between 1250 and 1200 B.C.E. caused population decline, drought, and urban deterioration from Mycenaean Greece to Palestine, which ended the Bronze Age and resulted in "cultural collapse." This led to "widespread population shifts," such as the movement from the Palestinian valleys to the highlands, with subsequent population increase.[13] Robert Drews suggested that Sea Peoples were professional mercenaries who turned their fighting skills on the great cities. As social systems collapsed and urban centers were destroyed, social control shifted to those highlands, where population then increased.[14] Robert Coote and Keith Whitelam proposed that hinterland or highland regions develop in periods of prosperity to provide more food and to relocate surplus valley population, while in times of economic decline they can absorb population withdrawing from lowlands. Trade decline causes highlanders to engage in "risk reduction" forms of agriculture and herding. This is "realignment" and "transformation" rather than collapse or revolution.[15]

Peaceful Amalgamation or Synthesis

Some theorists stressed that highland Israel arose as a synthesis or amalgamation of several different groups of people, including urban refugees, bandits, highland pastoralists, and those who entered the land. Baruch Halpern believed that bandit elements and people from outside the land (from Egypt and Syria) merged together because of common economic concerns and the need to maintain trade after the disappearance of Egyptian control. The exodus group from Egypt brought the sacred name of Yahweh, and groups from Syria created the name of Israel in the

---

[12]Lemche, *Early Israel,* 1–435, *Ancient Israel,* Biblical Seminar 5 (Sheffield, U.K.: JSOT, 1988), 75–172, *The Canaanites and Their Land,* JSOTSup 110 (Sheffield, U.K.: JSOT, 1991), 13–173, and numerous essays.

[13]William Stiebing, "The End of the Mycenean Age," *BA* 43 (1980): 7–21, and *Out of the Desert?* (Buffalo: Prometheus, 1989), 189–97.

[14]Robert Drews, *The End of the Bronze Age* (Princeton, N.J.: Princeton University Press, 1993), 3–225.

[15]Robert Coote and Keith Whitelam, "The Emergence of Israel," *Semeia* 37 (1986): 119–42, and idem, *Emergence of Early Israel,* 22–80, 129–66.

land during the thirteenth century B.C.E.[16] James Flanagan, Gloria London, and William Dever alluded to a symbiosis of various population elements (urbanites, bandits, people from outside the land) with an existing highland population, who redefined themselves in opposition to the old lowland culture. The Israelite four-room house, collar-rimmed jar, characteristic pottery, terracing, and other material differences are merely economic adaptations to hill life taken from lowland culture as people moved from urban society in the valleys to village-familial life in the highlands. Agriculture and pastoralism are separate subsistence strategies by the same people.[17] Thomas Thompson observed that the same people move from towns to highlands according to economic needs. Townfolk rely on cereal grains, fruit, and wine, while highlanders resort to a combination of herds and grains. Indigenous folk in the highland villages during Iron Age I were augmented by lowlanders, non-sedentary highlanders, and outside pastoralists.[18]

In conclusion, the past twenty years have been revolutionary in terms of interpreting the Israelite settlement with new archaeological information. New models emphasize Israelite settlement as peaceful and internal, having continuity with predecessor societies of the late Bronze Age. Older models were exciting springboards for biblical theology, for one could speak of the contrast between Israelite religious and political values and those of the Canaanites, as well as the rest of the ancient Near East. We could theologize about God's dramatic presence in history. But now those old Israelite conquest themes are inappropriate for biblical theology.

What are the implications of these new models of settlement for biblical studies and biblical theology? They tell us that Israelites were part of their environment, and their social and religious beliefs had more continuity with their milieu than we have acknowledged in our biblical theology and textbooks. If Canaanites slowly evolved into Israelites, this would explain the condemnations of the classical prophets and Deuteronomic reformers. They correctly accused the Israelites of polytheism, because Israelites were really Canaanites in the process of evolving into Israelites. Classical prophets and Deuteronomic Reformers were not calling people back to a pure Yahwistic faith; they were part of the continuing process of transformation.

---

[16]Baruch Halpern, *The Emergence of Israel in Canaan,* SBLMS 29 (Chico, Calif.: Scholars Press, 1983), 47–261, and "Settlement of Canaan," *ABD* 5: 1120–43.

[17]James Flanagan, *David's Social Drama,* SWBA 7 (Sheffield, U.K.: Almond, 1988), 119–88, 288–89; Gloria London, "A Comparison of Two Contemporaneous Lifestyles of the Late Second Millennium B.C.," *BASOR* 273 (1989): 42–52; and William Dever, *Recent Archaeological Discoveries and Biblical Research* (Seattle: University of Washington Press, 1990), 39–81, and other essays.

[18]Thomas Thompson, *Early History of the Israelite People,* SHANE 4 (Leiden: Brill, 1992), 1–422, and other essays.

III

Contemporary biblical scholarship also portrays the emergence of monotheism as a later and more gradual phenomenon than has been assumed. This critical viewpoint has arisen due to recent archaeological discoveries and a reassessment of the biblical narratives. Only a small minority of preexilic Israelites were developing monotheistic ideas, and they probably went through various stages of evolution until they became consistent monotheists in the Babylonian Exile. A few critical scholars suspect that this evolution may have been totally a postexilic phenomenon. In addition, Israel's intellectual continuity with the ancient world is now emphasized instead of a contrast between the Israelite ethos and ancient Near Eastern thought.

Late nineteenth-century scholars, such as Julius Wellhausen and William Robertson Smith, influenced by Darwinian scientific evolution, described gradual Israelite religious evolution through several stages until sophisticated ethical monotheism was attained.[19] Subsequent biblical scholars, including William Foxwell Albright, George Ernest Wright, John Bright, and Yehezkel Kaufmann, reacted against evolutionary paradigms and proposed a Mosaic revolution that introduced monotheism very early. Israelites were mono-theistic, except for superstitious folk, who occasionally slipped back into a syncretism combining Yahweh worship with Canaanite polytheism. At those times prophets and reformers called for a return to the old Mosaic religion.[20]

Contemporary biblical scholars affirm that Israelite or Jewish religious development evolved in progressive stages or "leaps" in the pre-exilic period until its culmination in the monotheism of the Babylonian Exile (586–539 B.C.E.). A large number of scholars, most notably Morton Smith, V. Nikiprowetsky, Fritz Stolz, Bernhard Lang, Gerd Theissen, Baruch Halpern, and Ranier Albertz, focus on certain periods in Israel's religious experience when these leaps might have been made. Nikiprowetsky and Lang provide the following outline[21]: (1) Yahweh was a typical West-Semitic deity elevated over other local gods by David. (2) Elijah and Elisha in the ninth century B.C.E. opposed the importation of the Tyrian Baal into Israel by the Omride dynasty in an economic and political struggle. They united Yahweh devotees

---

[19]Julius Wellhausen, *Prolegomena to the History of Ancient Israel,* trans. Allan Menzies and J. Sutherland Black (Gloucester: Peter Smith, 1973 [1878]), 1–548; and Robertson Smith, *The Religion of the Semites,* 2d ed. (New York: Schocken, 1972 [1889]), 1–492.

[20]William Foxwell Albright, *From the Stone Age to Christianity,* 2d ed. (Garden City, N.Y.: Doubleday, 1957 [1940]), 1–403; George Ernest Wright, *The Old Testament Against Its Environment,* SBT 2 (Chicago: Regnery, 1950), 9–112, and *God Who Acts,* SBT 8 (London: SCM Press, 1953), 11–128; and Yehezkel Kaufmann, *The Religion of Israel,* trans. and abridg. Moshe Greenberg (New York: Schocken, 1972), 1–451.

[21]V. Nikiprowetsky, "Ethical Monotheism," *Daedalus* 104, no. 2 (1975): 68–89; and Bernhard Lang, *Monotheism and the Prophetic Minority,* SWBA 1 (Sheffield, U.K.: Almond, 1983), 13–59, and numerous essays.

and El devotees into a common cause, and this set in motion a tendency toward monolatry and the merger of Yahweh and El. (Elijah's name may mean Yahweh is my El, a sign of this alliance.) (3) Classical eighth-century B.C.E. prophets demanded exclusive devotion to Yahweh. Hosea especially attacked some traditional aspects of Yahwistic piety as inappropriate (e.g., calf or bull veneration and ritual Yahweh prostitutes). (4) The reforms of Hezekiah in the late eighth century B.C.E. centralized worship in Jerusalem, encouraged exclusive devotion to Yahweh, and perhaps introduced the reforms found in the Book of the Covenant (Ex. 21–23). The elevation of Yahweh as the high god in times of crisis was "temporary monolatry," which could evolve into "permanent monolatry." (5) Josiah's reform in the seventh century B.C.E., inspired by laws in Deuteronomy 12–26, appears monotheistic with its closing of shrines and bitter attack on many forms of ritual behavior. (6) Sixth-century B.C.E. exilic theology, especially the oracles of Second Isaiah, declared that other gods do not exist. Perhaps Zoroastrian religious beliefs influenced Jews in the Babylonian Exile. (7) Some postexilic Jews were still polytheists (e.g., Jews at Elephantine), but postexilic literature finally defeated the vestiges of polytheism (especially Asherah veneration). This theory of progressive development mediates between Albright's idea of revolutionary monotheism and Wellhausen's gradual evolutionary model by suggesting a series of intellectual revolutions over a period of years, which culminated in the exile. Scholars even use the words *evolution* and *revolution* together in their discussions.[22] Monotheism evolved, but it was neither gradual nor inevitable. The greatest crisis was the exile, and it caused the emergence of consistent monotheism.

These new theories have been augmented by recent archaeological discoveries that attest to extensive Israelite devotion to Asherah, the goddess of fertility, and other gods of Canaan, as well as to so-called pagan activities like sun veneration, human sacrifice, and cultic prostitution. A text from Kuntillet 'Ajrûd, a ninth- or eighth-century B.C.E. shrine located on a trade route in the Sinai wilderness, discovered in 1975, reads, "I bless you by Yahweh of Samaria, and by his Asherah," and "Yahweh of Teman and his Asherah."[23] At Khirbet el-Qôm, an eighth-century B.C.E. site near Hebron in Judah, a text reads, "Blessed be Uriah by Yahweh and his Asherah."[24] Many scholars believe that Asherah was revered as a goddess consort of Yahweh and that polytheistic Yahwism may have been the normative

[22]Othmar Keel, "Gedanken zur Beschäftigung mit Monotheismus," in *Monotheismus im Alten Israel und seiner Umwelt*, ed. Keel, BibB 14 (Fribourg: Schweizerisches Katholisches Bibelwerk, 1980), 21; and Lang, *Prophetic Minority*, 56.

[23]William Dever, "Asherah, Consort of Yahweh?" *BASOR* 255 (1984): 21–37; J. A. Emerton, "A New Light on Israelite Religion," *ZAW* 94 (1982): 2–20; Baruch Margalit, "The Meaning and Significance of Asherah," *VT* 40 (1990): 274–85; and other scholars.

[24]Ziony Zevit, "The Khirbet el-Qôm Inscription Mentioning a Goddess," *BASOR* 255 (1984): 39–47; Judith Hadley, "The Khirbet el-Qôm Inscription," *VT* 37 (1987): 39–49; and other scholars.

preexilic religion of Israel and Judah.[25] Older archaeological finds– are interpreted in retrospect as evidence of an ingrained polytheism among Israelites. One is the bull shrine in the highlands of Samaria from the early settlement period,[26] and another is the tenth-century B.C.E. cult stand unearthed at Ta'anach in 1968, which indicates that Yahweh was worshiped through the image of the sun.[27]

In the past such archaeological data was considered testimony for syncretism between Israelite and Canaanite religions, but now we believe that pure Yahwism may never have existed until the writings of the Deuteronomistic Historians. Biblical authors condemned actual practices– but not Canaanite intrusions into Yahwism; they really condemned early polytheistic Yahwism. Deuteronomistic Historians projected the values of reformed Yahwism into the past.

Contributions of Some Contemporary Scholars

Morton Smith stresses that the "Yahweh alone" party was a minority religious and political movement in the preexilic period. Most Israelites saw Yahweh as their high god but also worshiped other gods such as El, Baal, Gad, Anath, Am Yam, Zedek, Shalem, Asher, and Tsur. "Yahweh aloneists" emerged to oppose Omrides, and later prophets and Deuteronomic reformers brought practical monotheism to the masses. Only in the exile, when the people were surrounded by foreign religions, did they become monotheists.[28]

Gösta Ahlström uses the biblical text to discern that Asherah worship, the use of idols, worship of other gods, and even the iconographic portrayals of Yahweh were normal religious expressions. Israelite religion was a state cult under royal direction worshiping a high god, Yahweh, served by attendant deities, including Asherah, Baal, Shamash (sun), and Yerach (moon). Different regional interpretations of Yahweh at various shrines (Gibeon, Shiloh, Bethel, Dan, and Kuntillet 'Ajrûd) merged personality traits of other gods with Yahweh. Yahweh worship came into Palestine from Edom, rose to prominence with David, who merged him with

---

[25]Raphael Patai, *The Hebrew Goddess,* 3d ed. (New York: Avon, 1978), 16–58; David Biale, "The God with Breasts," *HR* 20 (1982): 240–56; Saul Olyan, *Asherah and the Cult of Yahweh in Israel,* SBLMS 34 (Atlanta: Scholars Press, 1988), 23–37; Dever, *Archaeological Discoveries,* 121–66; Susan Ackerman, *Under Every Green Tree,* HSM 46 (Atlanta: Scholars Press, 1992), 6–35, and "The Queen Mother and the Cult in Ancient Israel," *JBL* 112 (1993): 385–401; Wesley Toews, *Monarchy and Religious Institutions in Israel under Jeroboam I,* SBLMS 47 (Atlanta: Scholars Press, 1993), 151–72; and numerous other authors.

[26]Robert Wenning and Erich Zenger, "Ein bäuerliches Baal-Heiligtum im samarischen Gebirge aus der Zeit der Anfänge Israels," *ZDPV* 102 (1986): 75–86.

[27]Glen Taylor, *Yahweh and the Sun,* JSOTSup 111 (Sheffield, U.K.: JSOT, 1993), 24–37; and Judith Hadley, "Yahweh and 'His Asherah,'" in *Ein Gott allein?* ed. Walter Dietrich and Martin Klopfenstein, OBO 139 (Göttingen: Vandenhoeck und Ruprecht, 1994), 235–68.

[28]Smith, *Palestinian Parties,* 15–56.

El Elyon of Jerusalem, and was elevated by kings Hezekiah and Josiah in Judah for political reasons.[29]

Fritz Stolz believes that early pastoral Israel was polytheistic and could not inspire monotheism, for clan devotion to a single deity is really an attempt to use that deity as a mediator to a higher god. In advanced societies a deity may represent the fullness of the pantheon, as with El at Ugarit or Anu and Enlil in Mesopotamia. Jews became monotheists after Second Isaiah, when they portrayed God as both a distant creator and a personal deity and sought to control the Temple state in Jerusalem to implement their social ideology.[30]

Othmar Keel and his students focus on artwork and iconography, which reveals great continuity between Israelite art and symbolism and beliefs of neighboring cultures, particularly Canaan and Egypt. The prohibition against images did not prevent indirect portrayals of Yahweh in various forms, such as the solar disk. Monotheism arose only with Second Isaiah, although early contributions were provided by the royal courts in elevating Yahweh as a high god.[31]

Hermann Vorländer believes that Israelite and Canaanite religion are identical and that the emergence of Yahweh began only with David. Numerous deity figurines at Palestinian sites as well as biblical references indicate preexilic polytheism, and postexilic evidence at Elephantine in Egypt indicates that diaspora Jews still worshiped goddesses like Anat-Bethel, Haram-Bethel, and Babylonian deities—Bel, Nabu, Shamash, and Nergal. Exiles in Babylon turned to monotheistic religious self-definition to preserve their identity. Several factors assisted in this transformation: (1) The cult of Yahweh was imageless and easy to transplant to a foreign land. (2) The upper classes of Judah deported to Babylon had many of the intelligentsia ready to make a monotheistic transformation. (3) Jews were receptive to foreign ideas, including Babylonian beliefs concerning Marduk, Sin, and Nabu, as well as Persian Zoroastrianism. Vorländer dates Pentateuchal texts to the exile and later; thus, he finds monotheism in Yahwist, Deuteronomistic, and Priestly texts, all of which were inspired by Babylonian historiography.[32]

---

[29]Gösta Ahlström, *Royal Administration and National Religion in Ancient Palestine,* SHANE 1 (Leiden: Brill, 1982), 1–83, "The Role of Archaeological and Literary Remains in Reconstructing Israel's History," in *The Fabric of History,* ed. Diana Edelman, JSOTSup 127 (Sheffield, U.K.: JSOT, 1991), 116–41, and numerous essays.

[30]Fritz Stolz, "Monotheismus in Israel," in *Monotheismus im Alten Israel,* ed. Keel, 144–89, and "Der Monotheismus Israels im Kontext der altorientalischen Religions-geschichte," in *Ein Gott allein?* ed. Dietrich and Klopfenstein, 33–50.

[31]Othmar Keel, *The Symbolism of the Biblical World,* trans. Timothy Hallett (New York: Seabury, 1978), 7–356, and "Jahwe und die Sonnengottheit von Jerusalem," in *Ein Gott allein?* ed. Dietrich and Klopfenstein, 269–306; and Silvia Schroer, *In Israel Gab Es Bilder,* OBO 74 (Freiburg: Vandenhoeck und Ruprecht, 1987), 3–431.

[32]Hermann Vorländer, "Der Monotheismus Israels als Antwort auf die Krise des Exils," in *Der einzige Gott,* ed. Bernhard Lang (Munich: Kösel, 1981), 84–113.

Norbert Lohfink believes that latent monotheism or monolatry existed in the ancient Near East, but true monotheism did not emerge until the sixth century B.C.E.–in Zoroastrianism, among the Greek pre-Socratics, and among the Jews in exile. El and Yahweh merged in the minds of Israelites from the settlement period onward, and Yahweh merged with other deities by the time of Josiah because of his lack of connection to other gods in the Canaanite pantheon.[33]

Gerd Theissen suggests that monotheism emerged not in a gradual evolution, but as both revolution and evolution. Monotheism is an evolutionary mutation that "protests" natural selection, or brutal competition between peoples, and it calls for humanitarian universalism. Monotheism emerged with the teachings of Xenophon in Greece, Zoroaster in Persia, and Second Isaiah. Before the Babylonian Exile polytheistic Jews worshiped El Elyon, El Shaddai, Beth-El, Baal, Asherah, and the Queen of Heaven. From 1200 to 586 B.C.E. the exclusiveness of Yahweh was established, from 586 to 332 B.C.E. monotheism emerged, and from 332 B.C.E. onward a reaction against Greek philosophical monism caused Jews and Christians to declare their monotheism a unique revelation. In the preexilic era, Yahwism was a "temporary henotheism" during periods of crisis, but continual crises led to "chronic monolatry," which gave rise to the "consistent monotheism" of the upper class Jews in the exile.[34]

Mark Smith believes that Yahweh devotees "converged" Yahweh primarily with El and partially with Asherah and Baal. Beginning with the Baal conflict in the ninth century B.C.E., they eliminated certain customs in a process of "differentiation," including the cult of the dead, child sacrifice, sun worship, and worship at high places. Yahweh was elevated as the national high god by kings, especially Hezekiah and Josiah, so the state primarily was responsible for the emergent monotheism that triumphed in exile. Monotheism arose slowly out of polytheism (as an evolution), but differentiated itself radically from certain aspects (as a revolution).[35]

Ranier Albertz traces the development of "familial religion," or "popular religion," and its interaction with the official religion. The preexilic period had different forms of Yahwism in the various regions (state, local, and family religions), which were leveled out by exilic and postexilic biblical authors. Monotheism emerged out of social-religious conflicts and prevailed

---

[33]Norbert Lohfink, "Das Alte Testament und sein Monotheismus," in *Der eine Gott und der reieine Gott,* ed. Karl Rahner (Munich: Schnell und Steiner, 1983), 28–47, and "Zur Geschichte der Diskussion über den Monotheismus im Alten Israel," in *Gott, der Einzige,* ed. Herbert Haag, QD 104 (Freiburg: Herder, 1985), 9–25.

[34]Gerd Theissen, *Biblical Faith,* trans. John Bowden (Philadelphia: Fortress Press, 1985), 1–174.

[35]Mark Smith, *The Early History of God* (San Francisco: Harper and Row, 1990), xix–xxxiv, 1–167, and other essays.

during the exile, when Yahwism was separated from state support and emerged as a universalistic faith affirming human equality.[36]

Other more critical scholars in the so-called Copenhagen School (often called Minimalists) believe that monotheism emerged totally in the post-exilic era without preliminary stages of development in the preexilic period. Israelites were really the indigenous Canaanites, so that preexilic religion was a polytheistic, fertility religion with Yahweh as a high national deity. Postexilic Jews had little or no ethnic continuity with preexilic Israelites and Judahites, but they were new peoples settled in the land by the Persians, who assumed and revised the traditions of the preexilic inhabitants to legitimate themselves. Biblical texts were fictional creations from either the Persian (Thomas Thompson), Hellenistic (Niels Peter Lemche), or Maccabean (Philip Davies) era. The texts created stereotyped images of polytheistic Canaanite and monotheistic Israelite religion and culture, and they generated themes such as covenant, a righteous God, and ethical values. Yahweh was created out of a synthesis of preexilic deities (El, Elyon, Shaddai, Elohim, Shemesh–the sun god of justice, as well as the old Samarian deity, Yahweh) and foreign gods of the postexilic era (Elohe-Shamayim of Syria, the Zoroastrian Ahura Mazda, and Babylonian gods–Sin and Marduk). Intolerant monotheism emerged only in the Hellenistic era, and the other gods became angels serving Yahweh.[37] These authors receive their best audience in Europe, especially among Scandinavian scholars, who tend to date biblical texts very late, but American scholars are critical of this model.

Scholarly Contributions on Related Issues

Scholars have contributed numerous specialized studies on various aspects of Israelite religion that assume continuities between Israelite and Canaanite beliefs. Their conclusions include the following: (1) Infant sacrifice was part of the Israelite cult until Josiah's reform, and it may have involved the worship of an underworld chthonic deity of healing and fertility, Molek, in a cult of the dead (the Rephaim), or perhaps infants

---

[36]Ranier Albertz, *A History of Israelite Religion in the Old Testament Period,* 2 vols., trans. John Bowden, OTL (Philadelphia: Westminster Press, 1994), 1:1–94, 146–231, 2:399–426, and other essays.

[37]Lemche, *Early Israel,* 386–475, *Ancient Israel,* 155–257, *Canaanites,* 13–173, and numerous essays; Thompson, *Early History,* 13–24, 415–23, "How Yahweh Became God," *JSOT* 68 (1995): 57–74, and other essays; Giovanni Garbini, *History and Ideology in Ancient Israel,* trans. John Bowden (New York: Crossroad, 1988), 52–132; Herbert Niehr, "JHWH in der Rolle des Baalsamem," in *Ein Gott allein?* ed. Dietrich and Klopfenstein, 307–26, and "The Rise of YHWH in Judahite and Israelite Religion," in *The Triumph of Elohim,* ed. Diana Edelman (Grand Rapids, Mich.: Eerdmans, 1996), 45–72; and Philip Davies, *In Search of "Ancient Israel,"* JSOTSup148 (Sheffield, U.K.: JSOT, 1992), 11–161, and "Scenes from the Early History of Judaism," in *Triumph of Elohim,* ed. Edelman, 145–82.

were sacrificed directly to Yahweh.[38] (2) A cult of the sun was absorbed by Yahwism in Israel and Judah, especially in Jerusalem, to describe Yahweh as judge and protector of world order and to legitimate the status of the king.[39] (3) Yahweh's conflict with the primordial sea was significant in Israel's preexilic religion, and it reflects extensive Canaanite beliefs integral to Yahwism.[40] There are many general studies of Israelite religion and history, too numerous to mention, that assume that polytheism was the natural piety of Israel until the monolatry of the Deuteronomic reformers and the monotheism of Second Isaiah. They suggest that the religion of the biblical text has far greater continuity with the ancient world than we have acknowledged in the past, yet at the same time it reflects a sophisticated evolutionary advance over preexilic religion. The emergence of monotheism reflects six centuries of preexilic religious development out of polytheism crystalized by social and religious conflicts.

IV

What will be the shape of biblical theology as we articulate it with these new insights regarding the social origins of Israel and the evolution of monotheism? The older models of contrast and dialectical opposition dovetailed with the neo-orthodox theology of the early and mid-twentieth century; the social revolutionary hypothesis undergirded liberation theology and calls for social reform in our age. These newer models of development and continuity may inspire a different form of theology, one that affirms the developing traditions in Judeo-Christianity, one that senses that social reform and egalitarianism arise in a developmental process that unfolds for centuries, and one that uses the language of process theology.

---

[38] Alberto Green, *The Role of Human Sacrifice in the Ancient Near East,* ASORDS 1 (Missoula, Mont.: Scholars Press, 1977), 156–87; George Heider, *The Cult of Molek,* JSOTSup 43 (Sheffield, U.K.: JSOT, 1985), 1–408; John Day, *Molech* (Cambridge, U.K.: Cambridge University Press, 1989), 29–71; Ackerman, *Green Tree,* 101–63; and Jon Levenson, *The Death and Resurrection of the Beloved Son* (New Haven, Conn.: Yale University Press, 1993), 111–24.

[39] Hans-Peter Stähli, *Solare Elemente im Jahweglauben des Alten Testaments,* OBO 66 (Göttingen: Vandenhoeck und Ruprecht, 1985), passim; and Taylor, *Yahweh,* 19–265.

[40] John Day, *God's Conflict with the Dragon and the Sea* (Cambridge, U.K.: Cambridge University Press, 1985), 1–189; and Carola Kloos, *Yahweh's Combat with the Sea* (Leiden: Brill, 1986), 11–214.

2

Alfred North Whitehead
Philosopher of Process Thought

As theologians and religious thinkers creatively weave together images and ideas from the biblical text and the greater Christian tradition into some form of theological exposition, they must have an a priori set of systematic intellectual assumptions, or a philosophical system to create the framework of discourse into which they work their ideas. Within the past century one of those theological idioms that has attracted religious thinkers and authors, including me, is the mode of discourse called process philosophy, which traces its origins to the writings of Alfred North Whitehead. Its adaptation by theologians reflects a pattern attested to throughout Christian history. Certain assumptions and modes of discourse in this philosophical system do not accord perfectly with religious metaphors, so process theologians have adjusted some of Whitehead's ideas for their purposes. Thus, it is worthwhile to discuss not only the intellectual contributions of Whitehead, but also to consider some of the ideas of theologians indebted to his thought.

Alfred North Whitehead (1861–1947) taught mathematics at Trinity College in Cambridge University in England for twenty-five years. There he collaborated with Bertrand Russell in writing the famous work *Principia Mathematica* in 1910. After this he served for thirteen years at the University of London as a science professor and dean of the faculty. Upon retiring at age sixty-three he came to America to become a professor of philosophy at Harvard University, where he wrote a number of works, including his most famous volumes, *Science and the Modern World* (1925), *Process and Reality: An*

Essay in Cosmology (1929),[1] and *Adventures of Ideas* (1933). In these works he expressed his belief that science had developed to a stage that demanded a new scheme of ideas in the philosophical realm to reflect the new ideas in science. In addition to these works he also authored *An Enquiry Concerning the Principles of Natural Knowledge* (1919, 1925), *The Concept of Nature* (1920), *Religion in the Making* (1926), *Symbolism: Its Meaning and Effect* (1927), *The Function of Reason* (1929), and *Modes of Thought* (1938).

Influenced by his reading of Henri Bergson, Whitehead saw the analytic mode of thinking as inadequate. He believed that all things were inter-connected and that philosophy should see reality as an organic unity in opposition to science, which tended to isolate items. Newtonian physics was guilty of isolating parts of material reality for study and then committing the "fallacy of misplaced concreteness." By that Whitehead meant that science assumed "simple location" for everything, or that reality was composed of individual bits of matter existing concretely in space and time. He rejected simplistic notions of "simple location" and "substance attributes" as the mistakes of classical physics, and he strove for a "vision of the whole" or a comprehensive and holistic view of reality. The idea that something is an isolated bit of matter is an erroneous abstraction, for everything is tightly interrelated in the organic flow of space and time. Nor is reality smoothly continuous, as Newton assumed, but instead there is a complex sequence of experiential moments, or occasions, that are both objectively real yet subjective at the same time.[2]

Whitehead applied the deeper implications of the early twentieth-century scientific discoveries in quantum physics, electromagnetism, the theory of relativity, and biological evolution, and he grounded his metaphysical system in these modern sciences.[3] He described the units of reality differently according to their content and their relationship to each other. Whereas earlier philosophers, going back to the Greek philosopher Democritus, might have described reality as composed of things called

---

[1]The original edition of *Process and Reality* came out in 1929, but typographical errors and occasionally inconsistent use of language by Whitehead himself often lead commentators to use a critically corrected edition by David Ray Griffin and Donald Sherburne: Alfred North Whitehead, *Process and Reality: An Essay in Cosmology* (New York: Free Press, 1978).

[2]Whitehead, *Process*, 7–8; A. H. Johnson, *Whitehead's Theory of Reality* (New York: Dover, 1962; 1st ed., Boston: Beacon Press, 1952), 152; Nathaniel Lawrence, *Whitehead's Philosophical Development* (Berkeley and Los Angeles: University of California Press, 1956), 31–48, 85–103, 286–310, 322–33; Ivor Leclerc, *Whitehead's Metaphysics* (New York: Macmillan, 1958), 25; Victor Lowe, *Understanding Whitehead* (Baltimore: Johns Hopkins University Press, 1962), 17–20, 186–91; Samuel Enoch Stumpf, *Socrates to Sartre* (New York: McGraw-Hill, 1966), 396; William Beardslee, *A House for Hope: A Study in Process and Biblical Thought* (Philadelphia: Westminster Press, 1972), 31–32; and John Smith, *The Spirit of American Philosophy*, rev. ed. (Albany: SUNY Press, 1983), 161–86.

[3]Leclerc, *Whitehead's Metaphysics*, 4; and Lowe, *Understanding Whitehead*, 59–89, and *Alfred North Whitehead: The Man and His Work*, vol. 2 (Baltimore: Johns Hopkins University Press, 1990), 107–30.

"atoms," Whitehead preferred to describe the discrete unities of reality as "actual occasions," "actual entities," or "occasions of experience,"[4] and in his early writings he called them "event particles"[5] or "epochal occasions."[6] Whitehead laid the foundation for his discussion about "actual events" as both "events" and "objects" in his earlier work *An Enquiry Concerning the Principles of Natural Knowledge.*[7] These never exist in isolation but are related to the entire throbbing pattern of life. He suggested that such events might occur from four to ten times in a second of human experience. "Actual entities" might be said to include electrons, protons, atoms, and light waves or light particles. Of course, he viewed these subatomic phenomena with the eyes of a modern physicist who saw them not as particles, but as throbbing bits of energy or particles of experience that exhibited both wave-like and particle-like characteristics. They can be detected only by intense introspection or sophisticated scientific instruments, but not by everyday, commonsense observation. What we normally observe as objects or phenomena in the world are the groupings of such occasions or events. These insights, taken from contemporary physics, inspired the characterization of "actual entities" in his system of thought. Whereas previous perceptions of data in the universe were mechanistic, Whitehead strove for an organic view of reality that envisioned a "processive world" or a "world of evolutionary change."[8]

An "actual occasion," or "actual entity," is not so much a material object as it is an experience. It can be described as a simple drop of process, a pulse, a throb of existence, an event, a happening of value. Each one proceeds out of a previous actual occasion. An actual occasion does not truly exist; rather, it happens, it can be said to be in the process of becoming rather than existing. They are like "energy events" or "occasions of experience," which are not things in themselves, but exist in relationship to the other entities around them; these relationships produce what we call

---

[4]Whitehead, *Process,* 18, 73; Leclerc, *Whitehead's Metaphysics,* 53–59; William Christian, *An Interpretation of Whitehead's Metaphysics* (Westport, Conn.: Greenwood, 1959), 18–21; Donald Sherburne, *A Whiteheadian Aesthetic* (New Haven, Conn.: Yale University Press, 1961), 9, 13–14, 19–20; Lowe, *Whitehead,* 21–24, 36–56, and *Alfred North Whitehead,* 114–18; James Gray, *Modern Process Thought* (Lanham, Md.: UPA, 1982), 78; and Majorie Suchocki, *God–Christ–Church: A Practical Guide to Process Theology* (New York: Crossroad, 1982), 12–18.

[5]Alfred North Whitehead, *The Concept of Nature* (Cambridge, U.K.: Cambridge University Press, 1920), 172–74.

[6]Alfred North Whitehead, *Religion in the Making* (New York: Macmillan, 1926), 91–93.

[7]Alfred North Whitehead, *An Enquiry Concerning the Principles of Natural Knowledge* (Cambridge, U.K.: Cambridge University Press, 1919), 68–99, 110–27; and Lawrence, *Philosophical Development,* 1–140.

[8]Whitehead, *Process,* 387, *Adventure of Ideas* (New York: Macmillan, 1933), 149, 233, and *Modes of Thought* (New York: Macmillan, 1938), 219–20; Lawrence, *Philosophical Development,* 62–63; Norman Pittenger, *Alfred North Whitehead* (Richmond, Va.: John Knox Press, 1969), 21; and Lowe, *Alfred North Whitehead,* 118.

space and time.[9] To describe something as merely existing is to attribute to it a static reality and to imply that no change occurs for it– "actual entities are drops of experience, complex and interdependent."[10] These actual occasions happen, which is to say that a dynamic alteration occurs constantly as they interact with each other. No two actual entities are alike; each is unique.[11]

The subject and the objects perceived by the subject change continuously, so that the subject is transformed by the objects perceived on a constant basis. In our world the actual occasions are part of a pulsing organism called the universe, which is forever advancing creatively into the future. An actual occasion, or actual entity, represents each moment of existence for a segment of the universe. Actual entities are not permanent; they are always in the process of becoming something different as they transform from moment to moment. They are influenced by other actual entities and absorb them to come into existence. When an actual entity completes its self-creative process, it then perishes as it is absorbed by another entity. All actual entities transmit energy to the next actual entity, and in non-sentient objects, the data is transmitted unaltered; however, in "high grade entities," or sentient entities, the data is modified.[12]

As an actual entity moves forward into the future to become something new, it is for a brief time in a "moment of becoming" as it experiences an actual occasion. At that point it exists subjectively, but when it has become a fixed part of the past, to be used by future actual entities in their moments of becoming, it becomes objectively real. Hence, every actual entity is "dipolar"; that is, it is "potentiality" or has an "initial aim" as it is coming into existence, and it is "actuality" once it has taken concrete form. All of this sounds abstract, but it is a symbolic way to explain reality in a mode other than the Newtonian model, which describes the universe as concrete bits of matter. This system dynamically describes reality–the present "now" becomes a historical "then" to be taken into account by future "nows."[13] Whitehead described the temporal flow, something he believed previous philosophies had not accomplished adequately. Actual entities may also be seen as psychological concepts rather than bits of matter, so that an actual entity is not only the subject in a subject-object relationship but also an extension of the self.[14]

[9]Whitehead, *Nature,* 20–24, 33–40, and *Science and the Modern World* (New York: Macmillan, 1925), 106–7, 221, 253–55; Leclerc, *Whitehead's Metaphysics,* 71–75; Christian, *An Interpretation,* 17–38; Lowe, *Whitehead,* 21–24, 36–56; Kraus, *Metaphysics,* 2; Farmer, *Impasse,* 72, 201; and James Bacik, "Alfred North Whitehead," in *Contemporary Theologians* (Chicago: Thomas More, 1989), 210–11.

[10]Whitehead, *Process,* 18. Cf. Whitehead, *Religion,* 90, and *Modes,* 226.

[11]Whitehead, *Process,* 20, and *Modes,* 226; and Stumpf, *Socrates,* 397.

[12]Whitehead, *Modern World,* 221, *Religion,* 112–13, *Process,* 65, and *Modes,* 164; Leclerc, *Whitehead's Metaphysics,* 71–75; and Kraus, *Metaphysics,* 46.

[13]Whitehead, *Modern World,* 221; and Kraus, *Metaphysics,* 3.

[14]Johnson, *Whitehead's Theory,* 14–17.

On our human level we do not experience single actual occasions, nor would we be singular actual entities. We are societies or aggregates of many actual entities moving dynamically through time, the ongoing moments of becoming. Each of us is a "nexus" of many entities; we are "serially ordered societies" of occasions of experience. A nexus is a set of actual entities related and unified by their prehensions of each other. A nexus becomes social when similar elements or common traits among its members become important for the group as a whole and unify them coherently. A nexus with social order, serial order, or a personal order is a "society," and when that society takes on a personal order, it becomes an "enduring object." Something as small as a cell can be an enduring occasion. A "living society" is one in which there are a significant number of "living occasions" or a "dominant occasion" or a "presiding occasion." These dominant occasions unify sensory data about the external world for the organism and make the society sentient.[15]

There are gradations among actual entities, and Whitehead distinguishes four levels: (1) Some exist merely in empty space. (2) There are those in the "life histories of enduring non-living objects" such as electrons and simple objects. (3) Others exist in the "life histories of enduring living objects" such as vegetative and animal life. (4) Finally, there are those that exist in the "life histories of enduring objects with conscious knowledge," that is, people.[16]

II

Entities are united by the process called "prehension." Each entity arises by drawing forth or "prehending" its own composition from the actual entity that preceded it in the temporal flow. Each entity "grasps" the previous entity. A prehension also may be called a "feeling." Prehensions are either physical or conceptual as they grasp either another actual entity or a more abstract "eternal object" (an idea). The world is made up of actual entities, prehensions, and many nexus, and they are constituted not by being but by becoming, that is, the constant process of old entities evolving and arising out of new entities.[17] In the process of prehension the future is transformed into the present in the moment of becoming, and the form of causation is better described as a movement from the future to the present rather than from the past to the present. This means that future possibilities cause the present to arise more than the past determines actions. The future offers

[15]Whitehead, *Process,* 24, 34, 51, 73, 102, and *Adventure,* 258–61; Kraus, *Metaphysics,* 63; John Cobb and David Ray Griffin, *Process Theology* (Philadelphia: Westminster Press, 1976), 15, 19, 86; and Farmer, *Impasse,* 81, 239–41.

[16]Whitehead, *Process,* 177, and *Modes,* 214–15.

[17]Whitehead, *Modern World,* 105–7, and *Process,* 20, 22; Christian, *An Interpretation,* 14; Sherburne, *Aesthetic,* 43; and Lowe, *Whitehead,* 39–56.

the present moment options for becoming, and that potential gives rise to the present moment, not the past. The future causes the present by the "lure" of its possibilities. This has tremendous implications for talk about God, if God may be described as that future.[18]

Prehension describes how actual entities are connected and relate to their environment and the entire universe, as well as how the creative advance of time occurs. "Creativity" is the relationship of all the actual entities. There is mutual prehension in the universe as each entity is penetrated by and penetrates other entities, for entities are not discrete or insulated in self-contained monads. They affect others and are affected by others. When new things happen, entities link not only with the past but also with other entities in the contemporaneous world. Prehension involves drawing forth several components from the previous entities, though not all of them. What the actual entity prehends is predetermined, but how it prehends is not predetermined. In sentient beings or "high grade entities" the prehension would be called "freedom," but in objects it would be called "indeterminacy."[19]

An idea may be called a "conceptual prehension," and it constitutes the "mental pole" of an entity coming into existence, whereas a "physical prehension" constitutes the "physical pole" of an entity as it has come into existence. Every temporal entity originates from its mental pole, which implies that every entity originates in God, who gives an "initial aim" to all entities. All events or entities are dipolar; that is, the origination of the mental pole is from God (who offers potentiality) and the physical pole is in the world process (which is the actuality chosen by freedom).[20] In this manner Whitehead explained the relationship of the physical and the spiritual or mental realms that constitute our cosmos. He avoided extremes of reductionistic materialism, which pure science generates, or idealistic dualism, which philosophy or theology generates. Dipolarity was both a philosophical and a scientific metaphor for him.[21] Because prehension brings new entities into being and also brings entities into societies or aggregates in a constantly moving experience, the entities are best described as becoming rather than simply being. [22]

In every moment of becoming, new actual entities are formed out of the old entities by an activity called "concrescence." Each entity assists in the self-creation of another entity, and at the same time the new entity draws information out of the old entity. As new information comes together into a unity, it "grows together" (*concrescere*). In its moment of becoming,

---

[18]Ford, *Lure*, 7, 36, passim.

[19]Whitehead, *Process*, 22–24; and Lowe, *Whitehead*, 39–58.

[20]Whitehead, *Modern World*, 101–3, *Process*, 23, 36, 244, and *The Function of Reason* (Princeton, N.J.: Princeton University Press, 1929), 25–26.

[21]Gray, *Modern*, xi–xvii passim, addressed this extensively.

[22]Whitehead, *Process*, 25.

the entity is a subject presiding over its own origination. The movement from the old entities to the new entities can be called "objectification." Concrescence describes how the new entity absorbs or apprehends or prehends the data of the old entity. Whitehead spoke of concrescence as moving both like a wave and a particle, an analogy he drew from the movement of light.[23]

Concrescence or apprehension occurs in five stages: (1) There is an initial objectification of past feelings or data, which are called "conformal feelings" because they conform to the feelings of the previous entity. Different emerging entities prehend the previous feelings of a particular entity in diverse ways. A specific entity draws forth a multitude of compatible perspectives from the previous entity. (2) "Conceptual feelings" arise as the previous feelings are reproduced or are immanent in the newly emerging entity. Eternal objects drawn forth from the previous entity are used in the newly emerging entity in this "conceptual reversion" or "transmutation." The entity makes the new feelings its own by a process of "valuation." (3) "Physical purposes" occur as the process of concrescence ends and the data becomes fixed in the entity. Each simple physical feeling is integrated with a corresponding concept. (4) A certain consciousness of self occurs in the entity as "propositional feelings" or "intellectual feelings" arise. The former are physical purposes–feeling the data in diverse ways; the latter are conscious perceptions and judgments undertaken to determine whether the received data is of continuing value, whether it is true or false, or whether it is to be kept or discarded in the future. These characterize high-grade organisms in which consciousness or a flickering of consciousness is present, for therein affirmation and negation of data is a conscious process. (5) "Satisfaction" occurs as the many pieces of data become a concrete unity in the actual entity. Each new experience aims at the maximum enjoyment of the present moment, which occurs when the entities have absorbed the past into this moment of satisfaction via the process of feeling. They are now data for the future entities to prehend.[24]

The prehension of an old actual entity has three aspects. There is the subject that is prehending, the object or datum that is being prehended, and the subjective form or the subjective aim that characterizes how the subject prehends the object or datum. Therein the entity exhibits freedom as to what it shall become. There are "positive prehensions," which we would call "feelings," and there are "negative prehensions," which are called

---

[23]Ibid.; Johnson, *Whitehead's Theory,* 156–57; Leclerc, *Whitehead's Metaphysics,* 108–9, 156–62; Christian, *An Interpretation,* 12; Sherburne, *Aesthetic,* 41–71; and Farmer, *Impasse,* 73.

[24]Leclerc, *Whitehead's Metaphysics,* 142–44; Christian, *An Interpretation,* 12, 21–38; Sherburne, *Aesthetic,* 46–71, provides the best summary; Lowe, *Understanding Whitehead,* 349–60; Kraus, *Metaphysics,* 108, 124; Gray, *Modern,* 158; Bacik, "Whitehead," 216; and Farmer, *Impasse,* 204, 223–36.

"exclusions" because they eliminate feelings.[25] In other words, parts of the previous entity are accepted or remembered in the new present moment of existence (positive prehension), and parts of the previous entity are forgotten (negative prehension). Were we to diagram this process, we might draw a circle and divide it into four sections, with the sections being labeled A, B, C, and D. As the new entity prehends the old entity, it might take over elements A and C, but leave behind elements B and D. The first two are prehended positively, or remembered, and the latter two are prehended negatively, or forgotten. Completion of this process of prehension is called satisfaction. Satisfaction occurs when an entity is concrete, and this attainment is called "order." The entity may be used by future entities, and its effect on those future entities is its "objective immortality." Much data is brought together to make one actual entity, and then that entity becomes part of the future entities.[26] We might say that as history moves forward, some things are remembered and others are forgotten.

III

When an entity is apprehended by reason, it is called an "eternal object" (somewhat similar to Plato's notion of "ideal forms"). An eternal object is not real in the sense that Plato suggested; rather, it is a "pure possibility" of things as they might become in the unfolding future. There are potential ingredients or abstractions for what actual entities might become.[27] An attribute of an eternal object thus prehended is called an "abstract essence." Positive prehension by the succeeding actual entity involves "objectification" of the previous entity, "ingression" of that entity, and then "elimination" of nonusable data. This is "feeling," and it gives rise to our overall identity. Of course, negative prehensions or exclusions of data also contribute to our identity. Because eternal objects are appropriated differently by the process of "ingression" by the entities, this gives rise to the subjective differences in our universe, such as the diverse worldviews of people. Eternal objects give unity to all entities in the world.[28]

When concrescence occurs, there is a moment of freedom as each entity chooses what to prehend, and no two occasions have identical actual worlds. There is an "initial aim" that is provided to the emerging actual entity to give it a certain direction, but the entity has its own "subjective

---

[25]Whitehead, *Process,* 220; and Christian, *An Interpretation,* 12.

[26]Whitehead, *Process,* 23–24, 26, 84, 166; Johnson, *Whitehead's Theory,* 118; Christian, *An Interpretation,* 12; Stumpf, *Socrates,* 398–99; Kraus, *Metaphysics,* 62; Suchocki, *God,* 12–21; and Farmer, *Impasse,* 74, 204.

[27]Whitehead, *Modern World,* 228–30, and *Reason,* 24–26; Christian, *An Interpretation,* 13, 193–220 258–79; and Sherburne, *Aesthetic,* 25–34.

[28]Whitehead, *Process,* 52, and *Modern World,* 238, 248; and Johnson, *Whitehead's Theory,* 19–27.

aim," the way it seeks to appropriate the old data. These two aims in dialectic with each other create the tension between predetermination and freedom in every moment of the creative advance. In sentient beings the subjective aim is greater and the degree of freedom is more significant. Thus, an actual entity is in the dynamic process of self-creation or "achieved completeness," which lasts for a moment; then the entity goes out of existence as the following entity begins to prehend it.[29]

All actual entities, from the smallest entities to the larger aggregates of entities, are "social," that is, they interact with other entities both internally and externally. This social interaction connects all entities in the universe to each other in a process of change and organic interpenetration.[30] This strong social dynamic of Whitehead's philosophy has led process theologians, particularly John Cobb, to articulate the implications of process thought for social and political reform.[31] Process thought can generate a political philosophy that moves between liberalism's emphasis on the individual and conservatism's emphasis on society as a whole. It is "communitarianism," in which human rights are modified by a doctrine of social responsibility.[32]

The universe is a society of societies; there are "structured societies," which contain within them "subordinate societies." This model may describe a single organism or larger physical and biological systems in the world, for all organisms are societies of actual entities. There are four types of societies: (1) non-living, (2) vegetable, (3) animal, and (4) human. As one moves up through these four categories, there is an increased "depth of experience," "value," and possibility for "novelty." "Consciousness" emerges in the highest societies as a subjective form arising in the higher phases of concrescence. Once consciousness finally emerged in the creative advance, it became the means by which the higher forms of reality in the universe were "illuminated."[33] Said another way, intelligence evolved in the universe in order for the universe to reflect on itself and its development. Similar views were expressed by Stephen Hawking in his characterization of space and time in the universe.[34]

---

[29]Whitehead, *Process,* 27, 210, 283, 310, and *Modern World,* 248; Johnson, *Whitehead's Theory,* 40–43; and Lowe, *Whitehead,* 56–58. Cf. Farmer, *Impasse,* 73.

[30]Whitehead, *Process,* 90, and *Modes,* 226; and Pittenger, *Whitehead,* 26.

[31]John Cobb and Widick Schroeder, eds., *Process Philosophy and Social Thought* (Chicago: Center for the Scientific Study of Religion, 1981), 3–259; Cobb, *Process Theology as Political Theology* (Philadelphia: Westminster Press, 1982), vii–xvii, 1–158; and Randall Morris, *Process Philosophy and Political Ideology* (Albany: SUNY Press, 1991), 3–221.

[32]Douglas Sturm, "Process Thought and Political Theory: Implications of a Principle of Internal Relations," in *Process Philosophy,* ed. Cobb and Schroeder, 82.

[33]Whitehead, *Process,* 162, and *Modes,* 38–39, 214–15; Johnson, *Whitehead's Theory,* 52–55; and Gray, *Modern,* 78.

[34]Stephen Hawking, *A Brief History of Time* (New York: Bantam, 1988), 174–75.

IV

There is one actual entity that is timeless, and this is God. God is not a creator; rather, God is with all creation as the creative process occurs. God is not before or outside the process of creation; God is in the ongoing process of creation as the "chief exemplification" of the process, for God shares in all characteristics of the process. The world results from God's involvement in the creative advance; the actual world results from the immanence of God. People are in the "image of God" as a result of this divine immanence. God is the ultimate nontemporal principle providing all the possibilities for creative advance, the timeless "envisagement" of the multitude of future possibilities. God is the future, and God draws entities into the future.[35] This is the "primordial body of God" or the "primordial nature of God." God also remembers all the past moments of becoming, the old actual entities. This is the memory of God, or the "consequent nature of God," the "consequent body of God." It provides immortality for all the entities that have existed. In these two ways God provides both novelty and order for the universe, as well as direction for the universe to take, even though individual entities are free to deviate from that divine subjective aim. The subjective aim provides direction for biological evolution, a process that appears indeterminate because of the freedom of individual entities, but is ultimately part of God's offering of possibilities.[36] God is conscious (in regard to remembering the past) and has both mental and physical poles by virtue of divine self-involvement. God is dipolar, just as any other entity, for the mental side of God is the potentiality offered by the primordial nature, and the physical side of God is the actuality preserved in the "consequent nature."[37]

God exists as an organizer of the universe and also as a cooperating member of the active environment of actual entities. God provides a possible pattern to serve as the subjective aim for entities to follow; however, each entity in its freedom is responsible for the selection and use of this divine pattern. God orders the pure possibilities of future actual entities; God sets limits on what is possible and not possible; and God offers the initial aim to each entity. This aim also includes eternal objects, or ideals for potential achievement. An entity decides what to prehend from the previous moment; that is "valuation" of the external object prehended. One could speak of this on the molecular level as random movement, on the animal level as sentience, and on the human level as consciousness. At each level there is

---

[35]Whitehead, *Modern World*, 94–99, *Religion*, 90, 105, and *Modes*, 140–42; Leclerc, *Whitehead's Metaphysics*, 192–95; Christian, *An Interpretation*, 13; Sherburne, *Aesthetic*, 35–40; and Janzen, "Process Perspective," 499–500.

[36]Beardslee, *House for Hope*, 33–36, 144, 181.

[37]Johnson, *Whitehead's Theory*, 67; and Suchocki, *God*, 38–43, 85–86.

a degree of freedom, so that each entity in the universe is self-creative, not predetermined by God. There is a tension between what is willed by God and the freedom of the entities in the creative advance. On the molecular level it is indeterminacy; on the human level it is called freedom.[38] For Whitehead this explains the great debate of philosophers over whether the world is free or determined: the answer is found in the tension of freedom and determination. Because of this freedom, God's memory of the past, the "consequent nature," is not complete, for it receives the continual emergence of new actual entities. God is in process and is affected by the freedom of all entities in the creative advance. Thus, God and the entities together co-create the world.

The "primordial nature of God" is the unlimited conceptual realization of all potentiality. God is not before all creation, but with all creation. God is incarnate in the world process and yet transcends all the entities. The primordial aspects are the open-ended options of the future provided as choices to the actual entities as they move forward. God provides future choices to the entities and is the source of novelty, aiming at intensification of novelty for entities in the world. There is a temporal flow only because God "enjoys" novelty, or the new "insight" created by the interaction between God and the entities. This is the reason for the creative advance. God may be described as the "goad toward novelty," if stronger language is preferred.[39]

This gracious aspect of God lures the present into the future and provides hope for new options in the future. By providing an initial aim, God persuades or lures entities into a choice. The initial aim is provided to begin the movement of concrescence for each new entity. This lure is not compulsion or coercion, it is "persuasion" or "tenderness" or "love," and it is the primary force in the universe. God is not a "supreme agency of compulsion" but a "persuasive agency" in the cosmos. God may be thwarted at times, but God continues to offer possibilities to lure creatures "up the ladder of love." God creates by attracting, luring, and evoking—the same way that beauty creates. Whitehead admired Plato's belief that the Divine was a persuasive agency, and he despised what he perceived as the image of coercive force in the Bible.[40] The lure of God extends to the entire cosmos, not just human beings. God lures the evolutionary process to an ever richer complexity, increased freedom, and intensity of experience.

---

[38]Whitehead, *Modern World,* 232, *Religion,* 119–20, 151–53, and *Modes,* 140–42; Johnson, *Whitehead's Theory,* 60–63, 99; Leclerc, *Whitehead's Metaphysics,* 195–202; Christian, *An Interpretation,* 302–19; Sherburne, *Aesthetic,* 44–45; Kraus, *Metaphysics,* 57; Marjorie Suchocki, *The End of Evil: Process Eschatology in Historical Context* (Albany: SUNY Press, 1988), 67–68; and Farmer, *Impasse,* 79.

[39]Whitehead, *Process,* 67, 156–57, 343; Christian, *An Interpretation,* 373; Suchocki, *End of Evil,* 93; Gray, *Modern,* 159; and Janzen, "Metaphor," 17.

[40]Whitehead, *Process,* 185, 344, and *Adventure,* 213; Pittenger, *Whitehead,* x–xi, 25, 31; Kraus, *Metaphysics,* 161, 173; and Farmer, *Impasse,* 79–80, 217.

Other authors have spoken of God as the orthogenetic driving force behind biological evolution, bringing life to higher forms of consciousness. This idea was developed best in the writings of Teilhard de Chardin. From a theological or biblical perspective, it could be said that God creates the future in cooperation with the entities as they move forward in the process of becoming. This freedom of the entities is an important idea, for our understanding of the Divine affects our perception of human potential in the world and society.[41]

God is likewise consequent, or has a "consequent nature." Each prehension undertaken by every entity involves God, both as the primordial source of options and as a presence in concrescence. God is present in the life of all the entities, sharing with every new creation its actual world and its objectification as a novel element in God's consequent nature. God becomes each creature in the totality of creation; God is the personal order of divine occasions in a continual and a temporal way. The consequent nature of God also symbolizes the divine remembrance of the past. Once decisions of actual entities have been made and the creative advance moves beyond those decisions, they become fixed as the past. God is the "recipient of the world" who directs the process and absorbs the experience of every entity. God changes with the additions produced by the world process, so that positive developments enrich God, and negative developments cause pain for God. God's openness to the world is this physical pole of God; it is the temporal, ever changing aspect of God.[42]

This consequent nature of God is the "superjective nature" of God in terms of the potential it has for emerging future entities. Actual entities are taken into the consequent nature and are forever known by God; they are then used to bring about future possibilities. God remembers the past as the realization of the actual world in the divine nature and as transformed through divine wisdom.[43] This remembrance of the past is divine grace, for God recalls all that has happened, including the lives and experiences of people. Whitehead states, "[God] saves the world as it passes into the immediacy of [God's] own life. It is the judgment of a tenderness which loses nothing that can be saved."[44] God loves what is in the world by keeping it, so that genuine contributions made by that which perishes are not lost but are used for the furtherance of the creative advance. This is Whitehead's understanding of immortality.[45]

---

[41]Ford, *Lure*, 63; and Farmer, *Impasse*, 139–40, 218.

[42]Whitehead, *Process*, 345; Cobb and Griffin, *Process Theology*, 29; Christian, *An Interpretation*, 13; John Cobb, *A Christian Natural Theology* (Philadelphia: Westminster Press, 1974), 148; Janzen, "Process Perspective," 496; Kraus, *Metaphysics*, 163; Gray, *Modern*, 81; Suchocki, *End of Evil*, 84; Bacik, "Whitehead," 212–13; and Farmer, *Impasse*, 73, 80, 219–20.

[43]Whitehead, *Process*, 345; and Pittenger, *Whitehead*, 31–32.

[44]Whitehead, *Process*, 346.

[45]Pittenger, *Whitehead*, 15, 35; and Suchocki, *End of Evil*, 84.

God's attributes include awareness of the world, self-awareness, the capacity to relate, the ability to be influenced by the world, and freedom of choice. These are obviously not the characteristic views of God found in traditional Christian theologies. Whitehead envisioned God with "personal" and "relational" attributes, for God's perfection is not an abstract quality but is found in the divine capacity for relationships. The "divine power is relational rather than unilateral."[46] Whitehead, however, could use traditional language. He spoke of God as having purpose, wisdom, vision, knowledge, consciousness, and love, but of course, all of these are defined within the categories of process thought. He also used the classic dialectical language of Christianity, but the opposites he set in tension were of a different nature. God is permanent while the world is fluent, but God is also fluent while the world is permanent. God is one and the world many, but God is many and the world one. God creates the world, and the world also creates God. History and nature move toward a goal, which is the sovereign but personal rule of God. Whitehead's God is loving, faithful, and deeply involved in relationships with the world. However, there is no real physical end of time. In process thought there is an evolution that continues forever toward an enriched divine totality.[47]

In summary, Whitehead's God is immanent in the future as hopeful options, in the present as ongoing creative advance, and as the past in which all things are remembered. The former is called by him the "primordial nature," and the latter two are termed the "consequent nature." The consequent aspect of God is divine consciousness, and the primordial aspect of God is conceptual possibility. The consequent world is the "fluent world" become everlasting by an objective immortality in God, and the primordial future is where creative advance ever reestablishes itself with the subjective aim derived from God for the evolving world. Two notions appear to be significant in this vision: There is a "permanence of value achieved" ("consequent body of God") and an "ongoingness of value achievement" ("primordial body of God"). Just as the world acquires a future from God (primordial nature), in like manner God acquires a past from the world (consequent nature).[48] Whitehead could say, "It is as true to say that the World is immanent in God, as that God is immanent in the World."[49]

Students of Whitehead stress that Whitehead's God is compatible with the Christian God and Christian theologizing, for Whitehead removed the categories imposed on theology by Greek philosophy.[50] In this way

---

[46]Pittenger, *Whitehead,* 34–36; and Farmer, *Impasse,* 137.

[47]Whitehead, *Religion,* 154–58; Pittenger, *Whitehead,* 40; Cobb, *Natural Theology,* 147, 165; and Farmer, *Impasse,* 198.

[48]Whitehead, *Process,* 345–47; Kraus, *Metaphysics,* 3; and Ford, *Lure,* 40.

[49]Whitehead, *Process,* 348. Cf. Whitehead, *Religion,* 156–57.

[50]Charles Hartshorne, *Whitehead's Philosophy: Selected Essays, 1935–1970* (Lincoln: University of Nebraska Press, 1972), 63–110.

Whitehead's portrayal of God more closely approximates the biblical view of God, which is dynamic and speaks of divine interaction with the world. Whitehead would concur with this assessment, for he spoke of how the Western view of God had been created by the static philosophy of Aristotle— in particular, the image of God as the "unmoved mover," an absolute abstraction.[51] When this notion is combined with the traditional Christian perspective of God, it produces "the doctrine of an aboriginal, eminently real, transcendent creator, at whose fiat the world came into being, and whose imposed will it obeys." This "is the fallacy which has infused tragedy into the histories of Christianity and Mahometanism [sic]."[52] Whitehead hoped that his metaphysic would provide a new image for God that was more compatible with Christian theology. At the end of his volume he concluded by describing God as the "great companion—the fellow sufferer who understands,"[53] for such was the theological conclusion of a philosophical view that saw God as totally involved in the process. In his personal religious beliefs, Whitehead was probably an agnostic; it was from his philosophical perspective that he spoke theistically. Those who knew him suggest that his agnosticism arose as a reaction to the static and dogmatic definitions of God provided to him by preachers in the contemporary world of his early life in England. Also, those dogmatic views were incompatible with the suffering he saw in the world around him, including the tragic death of his son, Eric.[54] His philosophy was an attempt to provide an alternative view to the church from which he was intellectually alienated.

V

There is overall optimism in the Whiteheadian portrayal of God, for God is seen as a fellow sufferer with humanity in this world, as a gracious provider of new possibilities, and as the one who lets nothing be forgotten and pass into oblivion. But theology must also address questions such as sin and evil. Of evil, Whitehead stated, "All simplifications of religious dogma are shipwrecked upon the rock of the problem of evil."[55] If there is to be progress in a universe where there is at least limited free will, then there can be activity that is less than perfect, as opposed to activity that is closer to being perfect. This is evil. Freedom is permitted in the creative process, so that if evil is a possibility, there can be sin that leads to tragedy. But evil is also a stepping stone to good, for overcoming evil stimulates the

---

[51]Whitehead, *Process,* 342.
[52]Ibid.
[53]Ibid., 351; and Bacik, "Whitehead," 218.
[54]Lowe, *Alfred North Whitehead,* 181–200.
[55]Whitehead, *Religion,* 77.

emergence of good. After evil has been chosen, God provides new opportunities to actual entities to overcome the evil of the past. God can use the evil that has been chosen by the entities as part of the potential for future decisions by the entities. Sin is not disobedience against a moral code or law, but rather it is a violation of the loving relationship with God and the self-violation of the inherent human drive to goodness. Because God is part of the process of the universe, God shares in the pain of evil.[56]

Human beings epitomize the highest level of consciousness. Whitehead believes in what some have called a "panpsychism," the belief in an element of spirit or consciousness in all reality. With consciousness we humans are the leading edge of the evolutionary advance. A human being is a "society" of actual entities in a state of constant becoming. A human being is actually nothing; he or she is in process. We are complex aggregates of entities, and the conscious "enjoyment" of each present moment unifies all those entities in us. We fashion ourselves by selecting from past actualities to create a better future—just as any actual entity has freedom in the process of prehension. People are limited by many factors, but they have the freedom to mold and integrate the past into a present event. Groups of people may be determined and predictable, but individuals are free. Although we have freedom to cut off our potential for growth, God's impact on us is "persuasive" with a love to draw us into the future of creativity.[57] Our unity is in our memory of the past, enjoyment of the present moment of becoming, and anticipation of the future. "Becoming" is a "more concrete reality" than that described by "being," for being is an abstraction from concrete facts that we experience. Becoming truly describes what we are—complex entities in process. We are in constant change; we are not the small person we were as a child, or ten years ago, or even an hour ago. A person's memory, like that of God's "consequent body," brings all the experiences together in a meaningful relationship. Furthermore, a human being is always in relationship with the entire created order, including both conscious beings and nonconscious beings and objects.[58]

For Whitehead the human body and mind or soul are both abstractions. Our soul and body are an essential unity, and their existence depends on the particular organization of actual entities for that person at that time. The "soul," or the "mind," is a society, a related series of entities that are subjects, the sequence of the experiences that constitute it. The soul is not separable or immortal in the Platonic sense; it is part of the physical world— found primarily in the human brain. The mind, the body, and the external world are linked by perception in an organic way. Language is responsible for the human mentality; it caused the "soul" of humanity to develop. A

---

[56]Pittenger, *Whitehead,* 26, 48, 51.
[57]Whitehead, *Modes,* 228; and Cobb, *Natural Theology,* 39.
[58]Pittenger, *Whitehead,* 21, 29; and Kraus, *Metaphysics,* 162.

major evolutionary development occurred when the soul or the psyche of people no longer served the body but began to direct the body for its own purposes. This occurred in several significant stages up until two thousand years ago, when more rational and reflective thought began to develop in primitive societies. Language was the process of symbolization through which concepts were rationally ordered, and it caused evolutionary development to move forward significantly.[59] There is no separate immortal soul, but rather the person is remembered by God and preserved in the "consequent nature" of God. This system avoids the duality of body and mind found in early modern philosophical endeavors, for "conceptual feelings" pass into "physical feelings" as the creative advance moves the process of becoming from the "primordial body of God" into the "consequent body of God." This flow renders the dualism of the spirit and the physical obsolete, for both are complementary sides of the process. In this "philosophy of organism" evolutionary theory is taken seriously.[60]

In summary, Whitehead's system stresses individuality and creative interaction between individuals with its discourse about the actual entities. Philosophically, the system endeavors to explain that: (1) Time is real and the temporal flow can be adequately described. (2) Men and women are in constant process; they are not static beings. (3) There is mutuality between all entities; that is, relationships between objects and animate creatures characterize the nature of the world. And (4) all things are unique and are preserved by God. Throughout his writings Whitehead assigns importance to insight or intuition so that philosophical discourse does not become dogmatic. This system envisions value as part of the universe and portrays how permanence and change both coexist, especially in the description of the primordial nature and the consequent nature of God.[61] Whitehead's view of God resonates with modern science and the Bible, especially biblical images that speak of divine love. Finally, Whitehead's thought speaks of God dramatically as an interacting individual in the universe.

---

[59]Johnson, *Whitehead's Theory,* 75–76; Pittenger, *Whitehead,* 20; John Cobb, *The Structure of Christian Existence* (Philadelphia: Westminster Press, 1967), 46–59, and *Natural Theology,* 47–91; Cobb and Griffin, *Process Theology,* 88; and Bacik, "Whitehead," 214.

[60]Whitehead, *Process,* 246; and Johnson, *Whitehead's Theory,* 165–66.

[61]Johnson, *Whitehead's Theory,* ix, 9; and Pittenger, *Whitehead,* 22–24.

3

Setting the Stage
Process Theologians

Whitehead's ideas have been developed by contemporary process philosophers, most notably Charles Hartshorne, who especially addresses theological and philosophical issues. Christian process theologians have been inspired by the writings of both Whitehead and Hartshorne, and they include authors such as Norman Pittenger, Bernard Meland, Daniel Day Williams, Bernard Loomer, Schubert Ogden, John Cobb, Marjorie Suchocki, and Bernard Lee.

Continued discussion has led many theologians to believe that pure philosophical process categories may not translate too well into useful theological idioms for all aspects of the theological task, especially in regard to the portrayal of God and human sin. Nonetheless, process ideas may be modified and combined with traditional theological language to produce a meaningful contemporary theology. Evangelical scholars point out that the view of God provided by process philosophy lacks the power and personal relationship to humanity found in the biblical portrayal of God.[1] Yet some evangelicals see the value in integrating modified process categories with traditional classical Christian thought to produce a stronger, albeit non-traditional, theology.[2] Similarly, Norman Pittenger affirms that process philosophical categories must be subordinated to the beliefs of Christian theology to be useful.[3] It would be helpful to consider the thought of some

---

[1]Essays in Ronald Nash, ed., *Process Theology* (Grand Rapids, Mich.: Baker Books, 1987), 3–376.

[2]Norris Clark, "Christian Theism and Whiteheadian Process Philosophy: Are They Compatible?" in *Process Theology*, ed. Nash, 219–51; and Clark Pinnock, "Between Classical and Process Theism," in *Process Theology*, ed. Nash, 313–27.

[3]Pittenger, *Triunity*, 115–17.

43

leading process theologians, for they touch on issues germane to biblical studies, and we shall refer to these ideas later in our discussion.

II

Charles Hartshorne has addressed the question of the nature of God in several volumes, particularly the discussion of how God relates to the world. He, like Whitehead, is critical of the classic notion of divine omnipotence and other concepts that envision God in abstract fashion. He sees Whitehead's view of God as compatible with the Christian view of God, particularly after Whitehead attempted to eliminate the absolute categories of the Divine contributed by Greek philosophy. Hartshorne adamantly maintains that the God of process is more personal than the God of classical theism or classical philosophy. He criticizes the tendency to describe God as unchangeable, omnipotent, omniscient, and omnipresent, with the further ascription of divine immortality and infallible revelation, as things that originate in the divine nature. The only term of this ilk to which he is sympathetic is the notion of "omnipatience," for it stresses more appropriately the dynamic relationship of God to the world. God is a reality who socially relates to the world, and this pattern of social relationships characterizes the nature of reality for the entire world order.[4]

God is perfect, but only in terms of certain aspects of the divine nature. Herein Hartshorne uses classic concepts drawn from Whitehead. God is perfect in: (1) love, (2) knowledge of past and present (Whitehead's "consequent body of God"), and (3) the providing of "all relevant possibilities" (Whitehead's "primordial body of God"). God is perfect because God may be trusted completely—God will bring the best out of every circumstance no matter how evil. Hartshorne suggests that the best symbol for God is the cross, wherein one may see the triumph of good through divine suffering. God is unbounded love in the creative advance of existence. God is the "self-surpassing surpasser of all," which implies the successive enrichment that God experiences by the creative advance and the endless possibilities God offers for that advance.[5]

The world is a "social process" in which God is the supremely relative and dynamic personal principle. Hartshorne's portrayal of God is more personal than Whitehead's—God is "an individual being."[6] In this world

---

[4]Charles Hartshorne, *Reality as a Social Process* (Glencoe, Ill.: Free Press, 1953), 110–25, 145–62, 196–212, *A Natural Theology for Our Time* (La Salle, Ill.: Open Court, 1967), 1–137, *Creative Synthesis and Philosophic Method* (La Salle, Ill.: Open Court, 1970), 227–44, 275–302, *Whitehead's Philosophy,* 63–110, and *Omnipotence and Other Theological Mistakes* (Albany: SUNY Press, 1984), 27 passim.
[5]Pittenger, *Whitehead,* 12; and Beardslee, *House for Hope,* 70.
[6]Charles Hartshorne, *The Divine Relativity: A Social Conception of God* (New Haven, Conn.: Yale University Press, 1948), 1–158, and *Natural Theology,* 34; and Pittenger, *Whitehead,* 12.

there is a "social harmony," especially in regard to the physical realm and human society, and all things must be seen in a holistic perspective. Everything is composed of individual parts (like "actual entities") working together in unity (as the "actual entities" all "prehend" each other in their environment). There is a relationship between the actual entities, which Hartshorne calls "societal realism." An individual relates to the group by means of a "creative synthesis." Each of us is a social entity within society, and society as a whole is one entity functioning in what should be a harmonious relationship.[7] This philosophical perception of reality can be a strong foundation for the Christian concept of social justice.

Cosmic and worldwide creative advance occurs primarily through the geological and biological process of evolution.[8] Evolution not only proposes a forward creative advance, it does so with the concept of chance in the universe. Hartshorne observes that "evolution is at least one way in which freedom of creatures can be given a basic role in a world view," for evolution permits creatures, even without consciousness, to play an active role in their own self-creation.[9] This scientific vision has a certain majesty and beauty, but it needs to be combined with a theological vision that stresses the divine to be a "cosmic mind as cosmic love."[10] If the creative advance involves chance, there is indeterminancy on the inanimate level and freedom of the will on the human level where consciousness is found. Old classical theism, with its notions of divine will and predetermination, denies human freedom. The overall rejection of chance in the universe denies human freedom, but in the creative advance there is chance, indeterminacy, and freedom, as the entities make their choices. Hartshorne eliminates the concept of "eternal objects" from his system, for they suggest determinism. Furthermore, the biblical text implies that God created all creatures and human beings and took a chance by giving to them free will.[11]

The biblical stories of creation also imply a dynamic and developing relationship between God and the created order. In Genesis 1 God is not portrayed in absolute terms, but rather God responds to the creation that is seen as good. In Genesis 2 God creates Adam and then senses that creation is inadequate, so woman is created. God creates, waits, and responds to creation after each creative act. This epitomizes the way that process thought envisions the creative advance. God-world relations in Genesis were not pictured as instantaneous but as progressive and in a developed time-like succession. Likewise, the covenant relationship between Israel and God in

---

[7]Hartshorne, *Reality*, 17–212, and *Whitehead's Philosophy*, 41–61, 111–24; and Cobb and Griffin, *Process Theology*, 7–158 passim.

[8]Hartshorne, *Omnipotence*, 65–95.

[9]Ibid., 83.

[10]Hartshorne, *Creative Synthesis*, 138, and ibid., 86.

[11]Hartshorne, *Beyond Humanism* (Lincoln: University of Nebraska Press, 1937), 125–64, *Natural Theology*, 29–125, *Creative Synthesis*, 6–13, and *Omnipotence*, 67–71.

the Bible is also a "social transaction" quite understandable in process categories. Hartshorne also uses Whiteheadian categories to speak about human afterlife. Immortality means to be remembered by God (in Whitehead's "consequent body of God"). Thus, your life exists in the mind of God regardless of whether or not your individual consciousness remains.[12]

Critical reflection on the philosophy of Hartshorne has led some to suggest that he was not truly a disciple of Whitehead, as is so often claimed, but that he developed his own thought in a parallel direction with Whitehead before he first encountered the latter's writings in 1925.[13] Significant differences between Whitehead and Hartshorne have been delineated: (1) For Whitehead God is an "actual entity," but for Hartshorne God is a series of divine occasions, or a living person. Thus, Whitehead's God is more infinite than Hartshorne's. (2) Hartshorne eliminates the notion of "eternal objects" from his system; he speaks instead of "universals." Possibilities emerge in the creative advance without an "initial aim," even though natural laws may be divinely imposed. (3) Hartshorne refers to the dipolarity of God as God's "abstract essence" and "concrete state," which Whitehead termed the "primordial" and "consequent" natures of God, and this further enables Hartshorne to speak of God as a living person. (4) In general, Hartshorne is more temporally minded.[14] However, despite these differences all agree that Whitehead and Hartshorne together constitute the twin pillars of process philosophical thought from which later process theologians have taken their inspiration.

III

Norman Pittenger acknowledges his indebtedness to both Whitehead and Pierre Teilhard de Chardin. His chief goal is to provide a dynamic view of God involved in all things, but especially in nature and human history. He stresses how this dynamic view coincides with the biblical view of divine presence in nature and history—God is present in every cause and effect in the world. The divine Spirit is active in all human endeavors, not just religious affairs, so that one can speak of the efforts of non-Christians being inspired by the Holy Spirit. God, or the Spirit of God, is a "lure" to lead people in all things, but in particular, the "lure" of the Spirit leads

---

[12]Hartshorne, *Natural Theology,* 55–58, *Omnipotence,* 32–37, 77.

[13]William Sessions, "Hartshorne's Early Philosophy," in *Two Process Philosophers: Hartshorne's Encounter with Whitehead,* ed. Lewis S. Ford (Tallahassee, Fla.: American Academy of Religion, 1973), 10–34.

[14]Charles Hartshorne and Creighton Peden "Whitehead in Historical Context," in *Whitehead's View of Reality* (New York: Pilgrim Press, 1981), 9, 21–22; Lewis S. Ford, "Hartshorne's Encounter with Whitehead: Introductory Remarks," in *Process Philosophers,* ed. Ford, 2–4, and "Whitehead's Differences from Hartshorne," in *Process Philosophers,* ed. Ford, 58, 75–79; and David Ray Griffin, "Hartshorne's Differences from Whitehead," in *Process Philosophers,* ed. Ford, 35–38.

people to work for the common good of humanity and the world. He defends the concept of panentheism as a particularly good model by which to metaphor God, and he defends its integrity over against traditional theism and simple pantheism.[15]

Pittenger pays special attention to the image of a God who suffers in this process of divine self-involvement. The ultimate manifestation of divine suffering is in Jesus Christ, who is the ultimate manifestation of God. Jesus is the full exemplification of humanity; he provides a principle of "inclusion," for in him the full range of the human experience is affirmed. Jesus provides us with a "Galilean vision" of love (a term taken from Whitehead). God is the "Cosmic Lover" or "Love-in-Act" who leads by persuasion and not coercion, and "persuasion" or love is the basic force in the universe. Pittenger uses almost sexual or sensual language to characterize the depth of God's love, for he feels that love that is described with any less passion is mere sentimentality and not worthy of attribution to God.[16] Among people God is manifest in human love and the creation of authentic human community. Human beings are creatures still evolving biologically and in process spiritually, as God is manifest through them. Evil or inadequacy exists because of this evolutionary process, but God can make goodness emerge out of the evil that has happened. God works toward justice by luring people onward with but a minimal measure of coercion, and God seeks to negatively "prehend" or reject evil. God has power, not in an absolute sense, but in the ability to work through the created order, especially through humans. Evil is sometimes the refusal to engage in the creative advance and movement forward as God wills; it is the refusal to cooperate in the great social process of human community. All that is truly good and beautiful resides in God, and it is preserved in God in the "consequent nature." Herein is also our hope for immortality. We are not given afterlife as a gift; rather, we are drawn up in God after death.[17]

Process thought enables us to view the history of Christianity in a more dynamic fashion. In process terms, one might say that "Christianity is...a series of occasions, each joined to its past and each pressing on toward the future."[18] Process thought leads us to recognize tradition as an organic and

---

[15]Norman Pittenger, *Process Thought and Christian Faith* (New York: Macmillan, 1968), 20–22, *Christology Reconsidered* (London: SCM Press, 1970), 141–42, *The Christian Church as a Social Process* (Philadelphia: Westminster Press, 1971), 34–35, 62–64, *The Holy Spirit* (Philadelphia: Pilgrim Press, 1974), 11–128, *Catholic Faith in a Process Perspective* (Maryknoll, N.Y.: Orbis Books, 1981), 12–48, and *The Pilgrim Church and the Easter People* (Wilmington, Del.: Glazier, 1987), 24–29.

[16]Pittenger, *Process Thought*, 55–74, *Christology Reconsidered*, 22–153, *Christian Church*, 44–75, *Catholic Faith*, 30–31, 97–98, *The Ministry of All Christians* (Wilton, Conn.: Morehouse-Barlow, 1983), 87–88, and *Pilgrim Church*, 27, 41. Cf. Pittenger, *Picturing God* (London: SCM Press, 1982).

[17]Pittenger, *Process Thought*, 31–33, *After Death: Life in God* (New York: Seabury, 1980), 190, *Catholic Faith*, 28, 47, 118, and *Ministry*, 22.

[18]Pittenger, *Reconceptions in Christian Thinking* (New York: Seabury, 1968), 87.

developing set of beliefs and to view the church as a "social process," a reality ever changing and evolving to proclaim more effectively its message of divine love. Process theology is the most significant modern form of discourse about God and the world, but to be truly effective as a form of religious expression, it must be combined with contemporary existentialism, new views of history, and modern understandings of psychology. Above all, process philosophical categories must be subordinate to Christian theological concepts, for this is how philosophical theologians have functioned throughout the Christian tradition.[19]

IV

Schubert Ogden follows in the tradition of Whitehead and Hartshorne, and his writings also reflect a keen awareness of the insights of Martin Heidegger, Albert Camus, and Jean Paul Sartre. He observes that the classical idea of God is not very helpful in the light of contemporary philosophical thought. Process thought is used by him in the task of creating a new personal view of God, and this must be added to the message of the biblical text, which by itself is inadequate for us. Ogden weds the anthropology of Heidegger and Bultmann to the views of God found in the writings of Whitehead and Hartshorne, and he generates a new theism in response to Sartre, Camus, and others who see human freedom only in existential atheism. This theistic freedom is found in the ultimate commitment to Jesus, which brings freedom and responsibility to love others.[20] Like Hartshorne he believes that life becomes meaningful for people because of belief in God. Belief in God also provides us with a basis for affirming secular human existence.

Ogden believes that the language or mythology about God found in the Bible can be "de-mythologized" by process thought so that it relates more directly to human experience. He suggests that Rudolph Bultmann did not go far enough in his program of demythologization, so the task must be completed by another generation of theologians. Ogden's demythologized version of the Christian message proclaims that Jesus represents the human primordial responsibility for responding to divine love. Ogden pays special attention to christology. After reviewing contemporary theology for ideas on how to move beyond traditional christology, he sees the best approach to understanding Jesus as one that involves an existential encounter by the believer with Jesus and results in

---

[19]Pittenger, *Process Thought,* 84–96, *Christian Church,* 76–119, *Triunity,* 115–17, and *Pilgrim Church,* 30–112.

[20]Schubert Ogden, *The Reality of God and Other Essays* (New York: Harper and Row, 1977), 1–230, *On Theology* (San Francisco: Harper and Row, 1986), 45–93, and *Doing Theology Today* (Valley Forge, Pa.: Trinity Press, 1996), 95–108, 187–209.

greater social consciousness and political concern.[21] Like Hartshorne, he takes Whiteheadian ideas in the direction of their social implications.

God's redemptive activity is represented decisively in Jesus and what he did. But Jesus reveals that God redeems all history, and thus the story of his death and resurrection is not God's unique mode of redemption. Jesus' actions are part of a process that involves the entire temporal flow, and God's presence throughout the creative advance is a redeeming process. We need to speak less of divine intervention in the world and more of inherent divine presence. Jesus' role is to awaken our awareness of God's work in the process, an activity that also involves all humans in a co-creative process with God. All history is a story of the divine-human relationship, and God's redemptive activity makes history into a unity.[22]

Ogden speaks of God as being involved in the temporal process, or the complete unfolding of the universe. In particular, God is active in human history or in the social arena, and the mode of this manifestation is evidenced most clearly in human consciousness. If God is present throughout the world order, Christianity cannot lay exclusive claim to religious truth. Even though Jesus' importance in the manifestation of divine love is tremendous, the primordial love of God encompasses all people, and the true religions are those that respond to this love of God. We must see the presence of God in the entire development of religiosity in the human condition and confess that the presence of the Divine goes back to the earliest point of human evolution. But God is present in an even wider dimension. God participates in every single moment and lays the foundation for the greater creative advance, and this is what gives God ultimate wholeness–total interaction with the cosmos and humanity.[23]

V

John Cobb affirms process theology primarily because it denies the existence of a God who causes or permits evil. He also believes that the traditional views of God as omnipotent, omniscient, and separate from the universe run afoul of modern sensitivities for several reasons: Our modern understanding of the vast scope of the universe dwarfs our traditional pious views of a God ruling our planet from above; the experience of evil in this world implies that such a God permits or causes such evil; and the concept of an omnipotent deity places limitations on the full development of our humanity. Cobb redefines Whitehead's notion of God to personalize the

---

[21]Schubert Ogden, *Christ Without Myth* (New York: Harper and Row, 1961), 13–185, *The Point of Christology* (San Francisco: Harper and Row, 1982), 1–168, and *Doing Theology,* 109–22; Cobb and Griffin, *Process Theology,* 179; and Gray, *Modern,* 196.

[22]Ogden, *Christology,* 64–168, and *Doing Theology,* 123–38.

[23]Ogden, *Christ,* 157, *Reality,* 144–87, *Is There Only One True Religion or Are There Many?* (Dallas: SMU Press, 1992), 1–104, and *Doing Theology,* 141–84.

deity more. God must be defined as a "living person," in addition to the portrayal that Whitehead gave, in order to make the doctrine of God more coherent. He speaks of the panentheistic characterization of God's involvement in the world as a better description than either theism or pantheism, for it speaks of God as immediately related to every place and every person in an "all-inclusive fashion" (which theism cannot express adequately) without saying that God is merely the sum of all the parts of the universe (as pantheism might imply).[24]

Cobb appropriates the image of "mutual prehension" between entities and people as a metaphor to speak of how God guides both humanity and creation toward a better future. God "lures" and "persuades" people to move in a moral direction. God is the "one who calls us" into the future and toward a more authentic existence. God brings about a "creative transformation" in the process of world order working with human agents. The ultimate example of "creative transformation" is the presence and activity of Christ in the world through the lives of people. Cobb speaks of the primordial nature of God as "creative love" and the consequent nature of God as "responsive love" that responds to human actions. He identifies God with the "tender elements" in love. Whereas Whitehead thought of God more as a conscious actual entity, Cobb prefers to metaphor God as a living being. The total unity of God's experience provides God with the equivalent of a "soul" or a "society of actual occasions" or even pure "creativity" in itself, which permits us to metaphor God as a living being. Cobb's portrayal of God is closer to the views of classical theism according to some critics, yet he advances some rather creative notions. God is metaphored as having two sides, with the Whiteheadian images of the "primordial nature" and the "consequent nature." The "primordial nature" is the masculine side of God, or the *logos,* and the "consequent nature" is the feminine side of God, or the Spirit.[25]

Cobb speaks in processual categories about the evolution of life and humans, especially the human intellectual advance through archaic religion, primitive religion, and finally high religion. He uses Karl Jaspers' model of the "axial age" (800–200 B.C.E.) and characterizes this era as an age wherein rational thought and reflective consciousness emerged in both India and the Near East, and the origin of Judaism and the primordial roots of Christianity may be located. Such categories have been used in the past, also, and may be very useful in future discussion. He speaks of the

---

[24]John Cobb, *God and the World* (Philadelphia: Westminster Press, 1969), 19–41, 77–81, and *Natural Theology,* 192.

[25]Cobb, *God and the World,* 42–66, 81, and *Natural Theology,* 188; Cobb and Griffin, *Process Theology,* 109, 135; and Cobb and David Tracy, *Talking About God* (New York: Seabury, 1983), 42.

emergence of the psyche as an autonomous agent within the body; this emergence gives rise to civilization, culture, and religious sensitivities.[26]

Cobb develops his process theological ideas in several directions. He crafts a dynamic process christology using philosophical categories and insights from world religions. Jesus Christ is the "creative transformation" of the human condition, and his sayings reveal reality to us, especially the "creative-responsive love of God." When Jesus speaks, it is God speaking. As we receive the message of Jesus, we are more open to God. Cobb also suggests that we can use Whitehead's categories to speak of an afterlife, even if Whitehead did not. He draws on the insights we have concerning world religions and combines them with philosophical categories. In particular, process theology can engage in more fruitful dialogue with Buddhism on the idea of the self. Furthermore, process theology can help us develop ecological sensitivities because of the emphasis on the presence of the Divine in the unfolding world process, which includes nature. Process thought overcomes the unilinear thinking created by older *Heilsgeschichte* biblical theology with its overemphasis on the historical dimension of divine self-involvement in human experience.[27] Cobb crafts an ethic of social justice, and his significant interest is in process thought's connection to political philosophy, for he sees process thought moving between the liberal's emphasis on the individual and the conservative's emphasis on society as a whole. The image of Jesus' ministry and teachings provides us with a "disturbing" imperative designed to call us into social action.[28]

In all of these areas—social, religious, and existential—Cobb sees God as the force that moves us toward personal and social advance; God is the forward thrust behind the evolutionary process. God is the one who "offers to us opportunities to break out of all of our ruts, to see things differently, to imagine what has never yet been dreamed."[29] God is the one who makes things new; God is the ground of all hope.

VI

There are other significant theologians who deserve mention for their discussion of process thought and its relationship to theology and biblical studies. Some of these people, like Schubert Ogden and John Cobb, have been associated with what has been called the "Chicago School" of process theology. The era of significant productivity for these authors was the 1960s

---

[26]Cobb, *Christian Existence*, 24–124.

[27]John Cobb, *Christ in a Pluralistic Age* (Philadelphia: Westminster Press, 1975), 13–264; and Cobb and Griffin, *Process Theology*, 102–4, 123, 136–58.

[28]John Cobb, *Liberal Christianity at the Crossroads* (Philadelphia: Westminster Press, 1973), 34–49, and *Political Theology*, vii–xvii, 1–158; Cobb and Griffin, *Process Theology*, vii–xvii, 1–158; and Cobb and Schroeder, *Process Philosophy*, 3–259.

[29]Cobb and Griffin, *Process Theology*, 157–58.

and 1970s. Other members of the Chicago School include Bernard Loomer and Bernard Meland. Valuable works have been produced by other authors in the field. David Ray Griffin authored a work on Jesus as the revelation of God, *A Process Christology* (1973), and a discourse about the problem of evil, *God, Power, and Evil: A Process Theodicy* (1975). William Beardslee, a New Testament scholar, authored *A House for Hope: A Study in Process and Biblical Thought* (1972), in which he wove together theological themes from process thought, the theology of secularity, and New Testament studies. Marjorie Suchocki crafted a process theology that interprets the salvific actions of Jesus and the traditional sacramental and ecclesiastical teachings of the church in process categories and speaks of God as present in an intimate and loving way in the world. Negative prehensions create evil, which is exclusion and perishing of good, or the imposition of values on other values. Evil exists because the entities are free to reject the divine subjective aim, but ultimately evil permits redemption to occur.[30] Roman Catholic theologians have contributed significantly also. Daniel Day Williams authored *God's Grace and Man's Hope* (1949) and *The Spirit and the Forms of Love* (1968), wherein he attempted to relate process thought not only to foundational theology but also to the history of Christian thought. Bernard Lee wrote *The Becoming of the Church: A Process Theology of the Structure of Christian Experience* (1974), and Robert Mellert authored *What is Process Theology?* (1975). Thus, there have been a number of excellent explications of process theology over the past two generations. From these works and the writings of Whitehead we take inspiration for combining process thought and theological themes of the Hebrew Scriptures.

VII

From this brief overview we might suggest helpful ideas for our consideration of the biblical text. Charles Hartshorne and Schubert Ogden, in particular, stress how process theology emphasizes the social dimension in our theological task. The image of a God totally involved in the human process bespeaks the need to stress the imperative for social involvement in our theology. When we turn to the Hebrew Scriptures, we see comparable themes in the classical prophets and the theology of the Deuteronomic reformers. We also sense, on a closer reading of the text, that similar imperatives for the amelioration of social woes may be cited from the Priestly legislation in Leviticus and wisdom texts in Proverbs. Process theology coincides very well with the way biblical scholars have emphasized social themes taken from the biblical text.

---

[30]Suchocki, *God*, 49–22, and *End of Evil*, 65, 75, 80 passim.

Schubert Ogden's call for a more radical demythologizing of symbolism reinforces what biblical scholars in the Hebrew Scriptures have sensed for years. The Hebrew Bible is full of powerful symbolism and metaphor, some of it obvious, most of it quite subtle, much of which the average reader cannot fathom because of the antiquity of the texts. In many narratives in the Hebrew Bible there is ancient Near Eastern mythological symbolism to be found, which already has undergone a degree of so-called demythologizing by the monotheistic authors as they inherited the traditions of the ancient world and shaped them to their value systems in the exilic and postexilic periods. But the modern interpreter needs consciously to affirm this hermeneutical agenda implied by the biblical text and proclaimed by process theology. We need to translate the biblical imagery more clearly from first-millennium B.C.E. imagery into contemporary language and thought. For example, the lure of fertility religions to encourage people to seek personal power and immortality in vain fashion, so often parodied and critiqued in biblical texts, could be more properly translated into modern understandings as the temptation to misuse modern technology for the same reasons. Such interpretative insights are possible with a process hermeneutic that encourages an authentic transformation of the biblical message into meaningful modern idioms.

Schubert Ogden also tells us how process theology can raise our ecological awareness. In the Hebrew Scriptures there are not as many texts that proclaim concern for nature as can be cited for social issues. But there are texts that can be interpreted with a hermeneutic to provide moral imperatives for ecological sensitivity, especially Genesis 1–3, selected Psalms, and wisdom texts. As Ronald Simkins reminds us, our theological agenda of the past two generations—the *Heilsgeschichte* theology of the "biblical theology movement"—led us to slight these passages.[31] Without discarding the values of *Heilsgeschichte* theology, a process hermeneutic can sensitize us to the ecological implications in the biblical texts.

John Cobb sees the importance of process theology in its portrayal of God as involved in the world wherein God is seen as less tyrannical and more compassionate. A process assumption of God as self-involved in the world will lead biblical exegetes to emphasize more of the texts in the Hebrew Bible that say exactly that. Many texts speak of divine concern for the chosen people in a way that implies that God suffers. Process categories will make us intuitively sensitive to that language when we encounter it in the text, especially in the Psalms and the prophets.

Furthermore, process assumptions will make us more prone to affirm the concept of love in the biblical accounts. Cobb's (as well as others') great process imperative is that the experience of God should lead us to an

---

[31]Ronald Simkins, *Creator and Creation: Nature in the Worldview of Ancient Israel* (Peabody, Mass.: Hendrickson, 1994), passim.

authentic, loving existence. In our interpretation of biblical texts it means that we might emphasize more readily the aspects of divine love and compassion, especially when we encounter the dialectic of judgment and hope. The popular mind reads the Hebrew Bible and focuses on the image of a wrathful God and the judgment of God—even Whitehead did that. In our interpretation and pedagogy we need to emphasize the dimension of divine love, grace, and compassion. Gerald Janzen likewise believes that process thought will deepen our metaphors of love in the exposition of the Hebrew Bible.[32] In particular, the theological explication of the image of covenant with process hermeneutical assumptions may unveil additional ways of emphasizing divine love.

John Cobb's interest in "axial age" development may be useful for biblical theologians, for the emergence of Israel's monotheistic faith falls into this period, especially if the later dates of the Babylonian exile and postexilic era are envisioned as the era for this intellectual crystallization. Elsewhere I have focused on how Israelite monotheism may have emerged in the context of an "axial age" intellectual movement throughout the ancient world.[33] Such perceptions help us to situate the development of biblical beliefs in a more universal context and thus understand them better. We are able to envision the emergence of monotheism as part of the evolutionary process of human development, in which we can say by faith that God is active in the total human experience. We will be less inclined to stress the total uniqueness of biblical faith, but we shall see instead those aspects wherein biblical thought shared assumptions with the ancient world and in what ways biblical faith was part of the evolutionary and revolutionary advance of human thought. This nuanced perception will make us more sensitive readers of the biblical text, which records the teachings of those (r)evolutionary monotheistic thinkers.

In conclusion, it is worth considering the writings of theologians who followed in the footsteps of Alfred North Whitehead. Not only may we use Whitehead's categories for expressing biblical themes anew in our age, but the suggestive ideas of process theologians from the past generation may give us a sense of what direction we might take in our quest for a synthesis of process thought and biblical theology.

---

[32]Janzen, "Process Perspective," 502.
[33]Gnuse, *No Other Gods,* 129–76.

4

The Hebrew Bible and Process Categories

I

The idea of utilizing process philosophical categories to explicate theological themes in the Hebrew Scriptures perhaps would have amused Whitehead. His views concerning the Hebrew Scriptures were rather negative, especially in regard to its view of God and its apparent teaching of *creatio ex nihilo* in the book of Genesis.[1] He even spoke of its view of God as the "ruthless moral ruler" of the universe.[2] Psalm 24 could be deemed a magnificant hymn, but it was based on a "barbaric conception of God."[3] He tended to see the rather negative side of the Hebrew Bible as it was viewed through popular piety and sometimes through systematic Christian theology. He developed his notion of "divine persuasion" in reaction to the Hebrew Bible's view of God as a tyrant.[4] Whitehead's apprehensions about the Hebrew Scriptures may spring more from his misunderstandings of that sacred text than from an awareness of its actual message. For example, Genesis 1 does not really teach *creatio ex nihilo;* rather, this was a later Christian interpretation of that biblical text. Nor did Whitehead really perceive the dynamic ways in which the Hebrew Scriptures express views about the nature of God. His caricature of God as a "ruthless moral ruler" is a common misperception found among people who casually read the text and focus on the judgment oracles of the prophets and the

---

[1]Kraus, *Metaphysics,* 40.
[2]Pittenger, *Whitehead,* 40.
[3]Whitehead, *Religion,* 55.
[4]Ibid., 54–56, and *Process,* 342–43; and William Beardslee and David Lull, "Introduction," *Semeia* 24 (1982): 1.

Deuteronomistic Historians. Like so many readers, he failed to perceive the ontologically prior and underlying emphasis on divine love in the initial election of Israel. Readers often fail to appreciate that the anger of God proceeds from an initial divine concern for Israel, which originated with the gracious election of the people.

Thus, Whitehead shares common misperceptions of the Hebrew Scriptures. Had his understandings been more in tune with that which is taught in our modern college and seminary introductory courses, he might have become very interested in the actual points of contact that his philosophical system really had with the biblical worldview. Perhaps, in part, he might have been aware of some of the potential, for he did mention that within the Hebrew Scriptures there was an evolutionary development of the concept of God.[5] This, of course, lends itself nicely to process categories. Indeed, process theologians since Whitehead's time have spoken of the grand evolutionary development of the image of God in the Hebrew Scriptures and how well it dovetails with process perceptions. The Hebrew Scriptures testify to the development of Yahweh from a tribal deity to the sole universal God of the cosmos.[6] It must be remembered also that process theologians, who are fairly well trained in biblical studies, immediately focus on the biblical understanding of a gracious deity, including views from the Hebrew Scriptures, and weave them together into their process theologies. The biblical view of God has far more in common with process thought than Whitehead would have imagined.

In the past generation a few authors have also speculated on possible connections between process theology and biblical studies.[7] Perhaps the directions provided by critical scholarship concerning the emergence of the Israelite religion and ethos might spark greater interest in this topic. In the past we understood the biblical tradition in old, classical theological categories, but now process theism may enable us to see the biblical text in a new fashion. This new process focus may be a more dynamic lens by which to observe the biblical message, and the resultant theologizing may be far more congruent with the original biblical perceptions of reality.[8]

All theologians use a philosophical worldview as a framework for their discourse, either consciously or unconsciously, and modern biblical theologians are no exception. Biblical theologians must be aware of the philosophical assumptions they use, and such a system must be relevant to modern cultural perceptions while remaining faithful to the experiences of the biblical men and women. Advocates of process thought believe their

---

[5]Pittenger, *Whitehead,* 40, and *Triunity,* 23–25.

[6]Ford, *Lure,* 131.

[7]Ibid., ix–xi, 1–136, and "Biblical Recital," 198–209; Janzen, "Metaphor," 7–44, and "Process Perspective," 480–509.

[8]Janzen, "Process Perspective," 480–509; and Ford, *Lure,* 12.

philosophical system is better suited for that task than any other contemporary philosophical system:

> Process theism is the natural ally of biblical history, for process is history abstractly conceived. Process theism can provide the contemporary conceptuality by which we can appropriate this ancient literature, while the biblical tradition can provide those concrete particularities whereby our lives are given final meaning.[9]

When we speak of introducing process philosophical or theological categories into the discussion of the Hebrew Scriptures or biblical theology in general, we immediately sense the similarity between the two intellectual endeavors. Both stress a developmental process over a period of many years or a progressive revelation. Both accept a dynamic view of the on-going development of tradition. But there are deeper nuances of continuity that deserve a more detailed exposition on our part.

II

Central to the system of process thought is the understanding of "becoming," or how each present moment comes into existence. This is described by Whiteheadians as "concrescence," or the process by which the past moment is taken up by the present moment. As we observed, process thinkers prefer not to think of the present fading into the past; rather, they speak of the present's drawing the past into itself. This is a more positive way of speaking. It may be said that the future is drawing the present into itself constantly, and subsequently, Whiteheadian thinkers prefer to say that the future is a "lure" for the present. When transformed into theology, the metaphor is used to describe God, who lures or persuades the present and all humanity into future possibilities, which may be described as gracious gifts or opportunities.[10] This can become a starting point for discourse about the God of the Hebrew Scriptures, who leads the people into the promised land and into the future with words of judgment and hope.

This process of becoming is central to the entire system of process philosophy. Each present moment is viewed as an "apprehension" of the past moment, each "moment of becoming" remembers the past in a new construct. Each moment in the organic flow of time reinterprets as it uses the past and adds the dimension of the present in a new configuration. This organic notion of change sees the present flowing out of the past and into the future in the ever constant moment of becoming.[11] This can provide

---

[9]Ford, *Lure*, 135.
[10]Whitehead, *Process*, 46–48, 281–90.
[11]Whitehead, *Modern World*, 90–126.

a dynamic philosophical undergirding for the way in which biblical theologians perceive the traditio-historical process behind all the biblical texts. Historical events give rise to an oral tradition, which then goes through a developmental process of oral and written transmission until it finally evolves into our present canonical text. Throughout this entire process images and motifs are added and deleted from the transmitted memory of the people as the stories, poems, hymns, and laws are proclaimed anew in every generation. This continual transformation of the traditions parallels the philosophical description of concrescence.

III

Biblical theologians can use the model of concrescence in several ways. A "concrescent occasion" may be said to be the moment of dynamic presence of the Divine in the human process. God lures the past into the present, and in the social realm this means that God leads the people toward a future that they must follow by faith. This is the image of Abraham's going to Palestine, the image of the children of Israel in the wilderness under Moses, the prophets envisioning a golden age that lies in the future, and many other aspects of the divine-human relationship testified to in the Hebrew Scriptures. Furthermore, process thought reflects on the total interaction of God with the world, and this includes the divine relationship with nature, so that process leads us to a sense of ecological balance as well.[12]

Above all, concrescence is the appropriate philosophical concept by which to characterize the commonly used theological image of salvation history, *Heilsgeschichte,* a favorite theme of biblical theologians. The history of Israel was the arena, according to the Hebrew Scriptures, for the most intense form of divine presence and divine purpose in the world, though it was not the only arena. The Hebrew Scriptures contain theology expressed in historical recital, which focuses not on what God is but on what God does.[13] The use of process thought enables us philosophically to undergird our theological and pedagogical explications about this mode of discourse in the Hebrew Bible. This should influence how we transfer these categories of biblical thought into theological talk about God's presence in our own world.

Process models enable us clearly to see God active in the social and historical arena of our world today in a self-involved fashion, for otherwise we might speak of God's breaking into the historical arena in a way that turns God into a *deus ex machina,* an artificial omnipotent deity who intervenes sporadically in an otherwise thoroughly human time continuum. A literal use of the biblical texts would otherwise tempt people to talk of

---

[12]Ford, *Lure,* ix.
[13]Ibid., 25–27.

God in such an interventionist fashion. Process thought envisions God involved in every occasion and in the entire historical experience of a people such as Israel.[14] In turn, we may speak of the divine presence in our own age in a more complete way, in every aspect of human life, in subtle ways, and not as a God who intervenes only at special dramatic moments. The failure to observe such supposed dramatic moments has led many people in the past few centuries to doubt the existence of God.

There also are other roles for the model of concrescence in the Hebrew Scriptures. God lures the past into the present and therefore is active in the moment of becoming; this additionally implies that God is active in every moment of becoming, not just historical events. God is also present in nature, the cultic sphere, and the human mind, all of which are divine manifestations proclaimed by the biblical literature in the Kethubim, the third part of the Hebrew Canon. These divine manifestations are proclaimed boldly by the Psalms and wisdom literature. Process thought can affirm the message of the total Hebrew canon that God is present in the manifold aspects of human existence.[15] With process categories, biblical theologians may move away from a narrow *Heilsgeschichte* theology that stresses the divine presence in human history too exclusively to a more broad affirmation of divine presence in a wide range of phenomena.

God can be said even to suffer the experiences of violence and pain of the earthly creatures.[16] Biblical theologians now affirm this to be what the total canon of the Hebrew Bible tells us. In the past, Christian theology, with its view of an omnipotent God, made us unconsciously reluctant to attribute to God the experience of suffering. We persistently interpreted the Bible in classical categories and thus missed some of its most important messages to us.[17] With the introduction of process intellectual categories into our biblical theology, our propensity to speak of divine suffering and empathy will be undergirded by cogent intellectual assumptions.

All these diverse concrescent occasions—the presence of God in social events, nature, cultic experience, and the human mind—become a sacred history in a deeper sense. Biblical theology can more readily proclaim that God is active in every event: rainfall, crop growth, exodus, Sinai, conquest, and even migrations of foreign nations such as the Philistines and Syrians (Am. 9:7).[18] Process thought and biblical theology combined may give us a deeper natural theology.

---

[14]Janzen, "Process Perspective," 501.
[15]Fretheim, *Suffering*, 75.
[16]Ibid., 76.
[17]Ford, *Lure*, 12.
[18]Claus Westermann, *Creation*, trans. John Scullion (Philadelphia: Fortress Press, 1974), 1–15; Janzen, "Process Perspective," 500–501; and Hans Schmid, "Creation, Righteousness, and Salvation," in *Creation in the Old Testament*, ed. Bernhard Anderson, IRT 6 (Philadelphia: Fortress Press, 1984), 102–17.

IV

The image of concrescence secondarily may help scholars speak of Israel's religious and intellectual advance. The image corresponds well with the new perception of Israel's social and religious development, as discussed in a previous chapter. In the past, biblical scholars spoke of the contrast between Israelite and ancient Near Eastern beliefs. The contrast was part of the biblical theology movement, which stressed salvation history (*Heilsgeschichte*) as a central theme in the Hebrew Scriptures. Now scholars maintain that Israelite and Jewish values do not radically break with the past values of the ancient Near Eastern world; rather, they "flow" out of them. There is much continuity between Israel and the ancient world, and in those instances where Israelite values appear distinctive, Israelite and Jewish thinkers have really taken over themes and insights that had not been able to surface as primary ways of thinking in other cultures. Israelite thought does not break with the past; it simply develops the trajectories of new and creative ideas that were already germinating in the ancient world.

This new mode of understanding and presenting Israelite beliefs can be supported by the philosophical assumptions of process thought. In the apprehension of an old actual entity the new actual entity takes over some elements positively and negates others. The new actual entity emerges directly out of what preceded it, but it is a reconfiguration of old data in a new form. This model can describe very well what Israelite intelligentsia and theologians did as they developed the ancient Near Eastern thought into their own particular biblical worldview. Elements of the old worldview are not negated; they are appropriated and transformed in the "new moment of becoming," which represents the stages of Israelite and Jewish evolution. For example, ancient Near Eastern notions of incipient monotheism eventually surface in the biblical literature as a full-blown radical monotheism.[19] This is an evolutionary advance that involves a reconfiguration of ideas already present in the ancient world, but the reconfiguration is still a radical leap forward. Thus, one can speak of the emergence of monotheism in Israel and among the Jews as both an evolutionary and a revolutionary process. By using the categories of Whitehead we may speak of this monotheistic emergence with intellectual categories that are congruent with our images. The apprehension of an actual entity into a new entity can be seen as a process that is both evolutionary and revolutionary. With this model one may simultaneously speak of continuity with the past and ideational advance. Hence, a processual way of speaking can describe the relationship of the Israelite worldview with those of the Egyptians and Mesopotamians.

---

[19]Gnuse, *No Other Gods*, 129–273.

In addition to our newer critical understandings of how Israelite thought relates to that of the ancient world, modern biblical scholars also view the internal development of thought in ancient Israel differently. It is the perception of critical scholars that Israelites were consistently polytheistic until the Babylonian exile, and even the great prophets and teachers were probably, at best, practical monotheists who called for exclusive devotion to Yahweh without denying the existence of the other gods. Israelites became monotheistic only in the exile, and perhaps many did not become consistently monotheistic until several centuries after the exile.[20] As a result of this new insight we are more prone to view the emergence of monotheism as a relatively gradual and evolutionary process, and this paradigm coincides well with process theological models. Once again, the process model of development and images of apprehension and concrescence may describe the historical emergence of monotheism in the social and historical experience of the Jews. Each generation of preexilic Israelites and post-exilic Jews with their own social and political experiences added to the ongoing development of monotheistic faith.

We may speak of the emergence of this monotheism as an evolutionary trajectory that is also revolutionary by virtue of its ultimate rejection of the polytheism out of which it grew. That rejection may be described in process terms as a "negative prehension," and it may be contrasted with motifs that Israelites and later Jews took from polytheistic beliefs and used in their new monotheistic faith expressions, which in turn may be called "positive prehensions." Hebrew Bible scholars have spoken of the process of synthesis and differentiation to describe this very phenomenon. Israelites and Jews synthesized ancient thought and attributes of other gods into the personality of Yahweh, but at the same time found it necessary to reject certain ideas.[21] Process thought emerges to give substance to this paradigm used by scholars.

Furthermore, emergent monotheism may be seen as revolutionary also by virtue of the fact that in human history an evolutionary trajectory of thought that comes to fruition in a few centuries occurs in a rather short period of time and may be described aptly as a revolution. A few centuries is short compared with the thousands of years involved in the so-called Neolithic Revolution of farming (9000–4500 B.C.E.) or the human evolutionary experience in general.[22] The history of emergent monotheism could be characterized as concrescence, in which a new moment of becoming (the monotheistic revolution) emerges out of the past moment of becoming (the old religions) in an evolution involving both positive and negative prehensions.

---

[20]Ibid., 62–128.

[21]Mark Smith, *Early History,* passim.

[22]Gnuse, "Contemporary Evolutionary Theory as a New Heuristic Model for the Socio-scientific Method in Biblical Studies," *Zygon* 25 (1990): 405–31.

Combined with our new biblical scholarship, process thought can be very helpful by providing the intellectual foundation for what we now seek to describe. Scholars and biblical theologians now speak of the gradual differentiation of Israel from the ancient Near East and the gradual emergence of monotheism in Israel. Process provides intellectual categories of expression for these notions of evolution and gradual emergence without sacrificing the insight that indeed something new in the human experience, and ultimately revolutionary in the human intellectual advance, was accomplished.

V

This model can be used to describe not only how Israelites and Jews appropriated the values of the ancient Near East, it can describe equally the evolution of biblical traditions out of each other. For example, the laws in the Book of the Covenant in Exodus 21–23 are "apprehended" by the Deuteronomic reform laws in Deuteronomy 12–26. Laws from the first law code are repeated in the second code and expanded to cover a wider range of issues to produce a reform code sensitive to the needs of poor and marginal people, such as slaves, women, children, and highland folk. For example, the slave laws in the older code only permit a male debt slave to be released after six years of slavery and under the condition that the woman he married and the children he fathered while in the service of his master must remain behind in slavery (Ex. 21:2–6). The later reform-oriented laws boldly mandate a universal year of slave release every seven years, which permits both male and female debt slaves to be released with their families, and the law further stipulates that the master shall provision them on release to prevent their relapse into debt slavery (Deut. 15:12–18). The legal tradition of Israel may be seen as an evolving trajectory that changed to meet human need. Furthermore, we may see the spirit of this reforming legal tradition still alive in Christianity to inspire us to social reform in our own age. This dynamic view of evolving law and the spirit of the law begs for a set of intellectual assumptions such as is offered in process thought.

Readers of the biblical text may see this same pattern of the evolution of later texts out of earlier texts on a large scale also. The Deuteronomic reform tradition may have developed out of the earlier epic tradition called the Elohist, as well as the classical prophets of the eighth century B.C.E. (Amos, Hosea, Isaiah, and Micah). The later classical prophetic movement grew out of the earlier prophetic movement (i.e., Jeremiah's dependence on Hosea). The later wisdom tradition of Job and Koheleth developed in reaction to the earlier wisdom tradition in Proverbs (especially the religious optimism of Proverbs 1–9), and the more realistic assumptions of Sirach and the Wisdom of Solomon reacted to the pessimistic message of Job and the despairing world-weariness of Koheleth. In all these instances one is reminded of concrescence, in which there are both positive and negative prehensions in the intellectual and religious evolution.

As we observe this developmental process occurring on different levels in the biblical text, in both individual texts and entire traditions, we sense a pattern of how old ideas are taken into a new religious message repeatedly over the ages. This, in turn, reflects the fact that the Israelites and the Jews continually experienced the emergence of new levels of insight into the divine-human relationship in light of their changing social and historical circumstances. In Whiteheadian thought attention is given to how concrescence occurs in the universal context of all the other concurrent moments of becoming. Expressed in biblical terms, we would say that a new theological articulation draws on the past traditions and is stated in response to the critical challenges of the contemporary social, economic, and historical environment.

"In no other culture or span of time has man's understanding of God's ways progressed so much as in ancient Israel."[23] Any introductory study of the Bible impresses students with the insight that the biblical traditions reflect an intellectual and religious odyssey of the ancient Israelites and Jews. When these various traditions are isolated and studied, students hopefully gain deeper understanding into the nature of how biblical peoples evolved in their perceptions of God and the world. At each stage in their religious journey, the biblical traditions drew on the teachings of the past, reconfigured them, and produced a powerful new message appropriate for the psychological and religious needs of that age.

The value of traditio-historical critical study of the Bible is that it has focused our attention on this process more than anything else.[24] Process thought, in addition, can remind us that our modern worldview is congruent in many ways with the images and the thought of the evolving biblical tradition. Consequently, the model of concrescence, or apprehension, may be useful for understanding not only God's action in the human arena but also the way in which Israelites and Jews evolved intellectually and the manner by which sacred texts were generated.

VI

There are many aspects of the teachings in the Hebrew Bible that may be explicated by process theology. This brief overview was done in order for the reader to see the organic relationship between the diverse issues connected to study of the Hebrew Scriptures and process thought. Although many aspects of the foregoing discussion could be elaborated in greater detail, certain themes merit special consideration.

---

[23]Ford, *Lure,* 131.
[24]Gnuse, "Tradition History," in *Dictionary of Biblical Interpretation,* ed. John Hayes, 2 vols. (Nashville: Abingdon Press, 1999), 2:583–88.

The biblical view of God merits discussion as a central issue, because it is part of the historic agenda of process thinkers. A special topic within this discussion, deserving a separate chapter, is the perception that God may be described as suffering with the chosen people and the creation as a whole. Because God is confessed as creator of the world, the topic of creation needs attention, especially the views of creation by combat and the image of continuing creation.

Central themes within the biblical text worthy of process analysis include covenant imagery, the prophetic phenomenon, and the legal traditions. Covenant language, or the more general image of election, permeates the Hebrew Scriptures and above all gives testimony to a dynamic relationship between God and people, which highlights the nature of divine love. The prophets were the intellectual spearhead for the emergence of distinctive views of God, especially monotheism, and the corresponding human response to the divine election. Therefore, the phenomena connected to the prophetic movement deserve our attention. Finally, though Christians read the Hebrew Scriptures and do not perceive the laws as binding on them, they nonetheless have been motivated by the spirit of the legal tradition, especially as much of it surfaced in a new psychological form in the teachings of Jesus. Of course, laws in the Hebrew Bible are still important and relevant in their expressed form for Jews, who constitute the earlier covenanted tradition within the Judeo-Christian religion.

Also worthy of consideration are theological paradigms used by biblical scholars in their teaching and theologizing of the Hebrew Scriptures. Hence, we shall attend to the theological model of *Heilsgeschichte,* both in its classical form and in the more contemporary mode by which it can be revitalized. Finally, the theological understanding of inspiration and the greater canonical process may receive attention, for all these scholarly paradigms may be enriched by use of process thought or the awareness that contemporary philosophical insights can give us a more profound way of expressing our biblical paradigms. It is to be hoped the reader may sense that biblical studies can be furthered either by a conscious use of process theology or at least by the recognition that the modern way of viewing the world is congruent with theological concepts in the Hebrew Scriptures as well as ways of presenting them to the modern world.

5

Process Thought and the God of the Hebrew Scriptures

I

Whitehead's philosophical system had tremendous implications for theological discourse about the doctrine of God. He realized this and clearly addressed the question of how God might be envisioned in process categories. The greatest implication was that God shared in the experience of the world, so that God developed or changed with the world process. Most importantly, God was responsive to the decisions and actions made by humanity. Whitehead viewed God as empathetic to the human creature even to the point of suffering pain with humanity.

In the Whiteheadian scheme God performs two functions. The "primordial body of God" provides options for the process and for the "actual entities" to choose. In personal terms God offers choices to people to select from in their free will. The "consequent body of God" remembers all that has happened, thus preserving things of value. In personal terms God graciously remembers human accomplishments and personal identities (thus offering a form of immortality for finite creatures). Process theology develops these assumptions and spends much energy discussing the nature of God in relationship to this world and people. Process theologians critique classical theology with its Greek philosophical heritage for an "immutabilist" view of God and attack the concept of omnipotence as the source of many theological problems. This rendering of God turns the deity into an impersonal principle and contributes to the Christian soul searching over the origin of evil, for an omnipotent and immutable God becomes the actual source of evil, especially if Christian theology likewise dwells on the will of God, which translates into a strong concept of predestination. Process theologians enter the discussion with their view of a deity involved in the process, who is then not the author and source of predestined evil.

Whitehead observed the Hebrew Scriptures with disgust in terms of their view of God:

> But the Jews, looking around, saw always an Oriental despot, and so, looking over the world at large, thought there must be a despot over all, and the consequence was they conceived one of the most immoral Gods ever imagined. The total absence of humour from the Bible is one of the singular things in all literature.[1]

His views, of course, were wrong. There are many different views of God in the Bible, tender views, including that of mother. There is also a fair degree of humor. Process theologians who follow in the footsteps of Whitehead know this better than did he. The contemporary process theologian looks at the language of the Hebrew Scriptures and sees God portrayed as a deity who has entered into the personal life of a particular people, called Israel. This God, called Yahweh, is portrayed with human emotion–a God who can delight in creation (Ps. 104 and Prov. 8), who can repent of having made humanity or having chosen Israel, who can experience a change of mind when it comes to punishing Israel, and who can provide a prophetic utterance and then countermand that divine decree in response to human supplication. To the process theologian, these biblical texts testify to a deity described in the writings of Whitehead.

II

Particular aspects of process philosophy may be used in helpful fashion to elucidate biblical theology. A central theme in process theism is the "lure of God," the persuasive power of God to draw the present into the future. This theological idiom replaces the notion of divine will acting out of pure omnipotence with the more dynamic image of a God involved in the life of the world. The concept of a divine "lure" or "persuasion" may be used to interpret many biblical themes and passages.[2] For example, one could speak of the divine lure that elicits worship of the deity as an appropriate response.[3] This deity lures, or entices, the world and believers to move into the future in harmony with the divine will and to make morally right decisions. In the ongoing creative process God "persuades" the forces

---

[1]Lucien Price, *Dialogues of Alfred North Whitehead* (London: Reinhardt, 1954), 195. Of the New Testament view of God, Whitehead said in these dialogues, "What kind of deity is it that would be capable of creating angels and men to sing his praises day and night to all eternity? It is, of course, the figure of an Oriental despot, with his inane and barbaric vanity. Such a conception is an insult to God," 273.

[2]Beardslee, *House for Hope,* 89; and Ford, *Lure,* 19.

[3]Janzen, "Process Perspective," 504.

in the world, and people especially, to engage in a productive form of creation, or co-creation, with God.[4] God is not a cosmic watchmaker, but a gardener in the vineyard who nurtures growth in human creatures.[5]

The biblical traditions may be called on to attest to "divine persuasion" or the "divine lure" in a way that more sensitively uses biblical metaphors than old classical theological discussions of divine omnipotence. Rather than saying that God has willed events to transpire in predestined fashion, we might speak of how God offers predetermined options from which people freely choose. The options might be characterized as predetermined, because they are selected by God over other options that might have been offered. History is open as God seeks to draw people forth to correct decisions and perhaps even to a higher level of "new perfection." Human freedom and corresponding responsibility is affirmed; the future is not absolutely predestined by God and therefore is not capable of being predicted by divination.[6] The emphasis here is then on the freedom of the human will, but the divine will is not eliminated. God offers choices and "persuades" humans to select wisely, but ultimately the decision, wise or foolish, results from the human choice.

Such a paradigm suits the narrative accounts in the biblical text. The man and the woman in the garden in Genesis 3 freely choose to eat the fruit of the tree, and then for their second decision they choose not to take responsibility for their actions. The man blames the woman, who then blames the snake, and ultimately they both blame God. Yes, there are two sins, not one! First, they choose to eat the fruit in direct violation of the divine command, then they fail to take responsiblity for their actions and thereby deny the freedom with which they acted in the first place. The man and the woman freely choose, but once their decision is made, they are trapped by the results of their decisions—expulsion from the garden and alienation from God. Hence, they freely choose between options that have fixed results. This reflects the intellectual paradigm of a freedom of choice between two or more predetermined options, and it accords well with the philosophical image of the primordial body of God providing choices.

Once the man and the woman were expelled from the garden, God was still gracious. God taught them to make clothing and gave them actual names, Adam and Eve (prior to this they were simply "the man and the woman"). Finally, they were allowed to have the greatest blessing of all, children. God did not desert them, but graciously continued a relationship

---

[4]Cobb and Griffin, *Process Theology,* 48; and Day Ray Griffin, "A Naturalistic Trinity," in *Trinity in Process,* ed. Joseph Bracken and Marjorie Suchocki (New York: Continuum, 1997), 26.

[5]Ford, *Lure,* 21.

[6]Ibid., 27, 123.

with them that included future moral choices to be made. Even out of the evil of their rebellion God brought good things to pass, and the promise is made that somehow in the future God will redeem the fallen nature of these two people.[7] From the Hebrew Bible's perspective, that chance came with Moses and the Law; from the Christian perspective, that chance came with Jesus.

The primordial body of God continually offers new choices to the actual entities, or to people, if you wish, who must make freely chosen decisions. Even if the wrong choice is made, the primordial body of God offers new options that include the possibility of rectifying the errors of previously made decisions. These new choices are determined by the past decisions that have been made, yet at the same time the gracious deity offers choices that can atone for past mistakes and rectify the errors if the moral agent wills to make the correct and moral decision.

This process metaphor of the lure of God bespeaks the image of a gracious God, who offers new chances and possibilities to human creatures, as well as the hope of redemption and restoration, even if past decisions were wrong. The possibility of a new beginning with the choice of new predetermined options from the primordial body of God is the chief sign of forgiveness and restoration of the divine-human relationship.

III

The lure of God, or the persuasive aspect of the divine nature, can have two sides—judgment and hope. In the Hebrew Scriptures there is much rhetoric that reflects these two sides of the divine message. Both the threat of judgment and the promise of hope or salvation were used by oral spokespersons and authors of written literature to encourage the people. Judgment imagery elicited the response of repentance and obedience to the Law or Torah. Hope and salvation imagery provided hope to repentant or despairing people by saying that Yahweh still loved them and would be with them to guide them to a better future. Both appeals are lures of God that focus the attention of the people on the future and seek to elicit a moral response or a hopeful attitude. In process thought these two appeals are the mode by which the primordial body of God influences the decision-making process of sentient beings as they move into the subsequent "moments of becoming." Words of judgment are actually enriched by words of hope, for both together attempt to lure the people into the future.[8]

Prophets proclaimed oracles of judgment and oracles of hope or salvation. Preexilic prophets proclaimed oracles of judgment predominately

---

[7]Pittenger, *Catholic Faith,* 47.
[8]Ford, "Biblical Recital," 199, and "The Divine Curse Understood in Terms of Persuasion," *Semeia* 24 (1982): 81–87.

in order to warn the people to avoid worshiping other gods and oppressing the poor. Oracles of salvation predominated in the exilic and postexilic prophets, for to those people the most meaningful message was the promise for a restoration to the land and the hope of a brighter future. In covenant imagery judgment and hope resonate behind the metaphors of conditional and unconditional covenants.[9] The Deuteronomistic Historians and the prophets (especially Amos, Hosea, Micah, Zephaniah, Jeremiah, and Ezekiel) spoke of how the sin of the people might break the covenant made with Yahweh and lead to loss of divine election and the land. Priestly editors and other prophets (Isaiah for the most part, the later Jeremiah, the later Ezekiel, Second Isaiah, and most of the postexilic prophets) spoke of how Yahweh would be faithful to the people forever and never break the covenant. The former group implied that the covenant was conditional on human response; the latter group implied that it was unconditional and guaranteed by the grace of Yahweh.

The language of conditional and unconditional covenant, like the language of judgment and hope oracles, is the language of persuasion. When Amos tells the Israelites that they will be totally destroyed, this is rhetoric. If he really believed their destruction was inevitable, he would not have bothered to speak. His rhetorical language seeks to elicit a response; it is the language of persuasion. Gerald Janzen prefers to speak of the judgment oracles of the prophets as examples of divine "patience persuasion."[10] Too often Christians view judgment oracles as evidence of a wrathful God, whereas process theology leads us to stress their positive persuasive force. Judgment oracles are messages from God through a prophet to lead the people forward to positive behavior; they are not predetermined intentions emanating from the divine realm.

Likewise, the radical vision of hope promised by Second Isaiah in Isaiah 40–55 did not come true literally. His, too, was rhetorical language of persuasion designed to give hope to exiles and to encourage some to return to Palestine. The language of the prophets is the language of divine persuasion, which draws forth an appropriate human response, moral behavior, or a new set of attitudes. This language of divine persuasion in process categories is the lure of God for humanity. It is in the language of judgment and hope that the Hebrew Scriptures most evidently parallel philosophical metaphors in process thought.

Eventually, the language of judgment and hope oracles, the imagery of conditional and unconditional covenants, would be inherited by Christians and evolve into its rhetoric of law and gospel. Here, too, Christians articulate a rhetorical message designed to alter the behavior or

[9]Delbert Hillers, *Covenant: The History of a Biblical Idea* (Baltimore: Johns Hopkins University Press, 1969), 1–188.

[10]Janzen, "Process Perspective," 502–3.

the attitudes and self-perceptions of Christian believers. We, like the ancient Israelites, seek to obtain a response of repentance or the recognition of forgiveness that flows from the Divine.

IV

The lure of God can be characterized in the Hebrew Scriptures from another perspective. God lures individuals and the people of Israel as a whole into the future. In the process by which God calls a person to be a follower, patriarch, or prophet, the divine commission is a lure to which a person must respond. Once response has occurred, the person is in a divine-human relationship in which the word of God comes again and again to that person to obey, follow, fight a battle, or give an oracle. We could say that the person is an actual entity moving forward in the ever-present moment of becoming as he or she responds to the primordial body of God. In personal terms, the chosen representative of God is said to respond to the divine call.

The best images of being persuaded or lured by God are in those narratives wherein a person or a people are called to journey forth to the promised land. In these instances the promise of the land is a great reward that awaits people when they react to the lure placed before them. Abraham is called by God to leave behind his home in the city, his family, and presumably even some of his wealth and go forth to a land he has never seen in the far west. The Jewish and Christian traditions have looked on Abraham's actions as a great paradigm of faith, a leap of faith to a foreign land in a hoped-for but not foreseeable future. In process terms this is a grand response to a true lure of God into an uncertain future.

The purpose of the Abraham traditions of Genesis in their final written form may have been to inspire Jews in Babylonian exile to courageously undertake the return trip home to Palestine after 539 B.C.E., when such permission was given to them by their Persian overlords. If so, countless Jews were called upon to emulate the courage of Abraham and undertake the same trek from Ur to Palestine. We observe that Abraham leaves Ur of the Chaldees, which is the name the city would have had during the Babylonian exile. In addition, Abraham passes through the city of Haran in north Mesopotamia, which was a significant shrine for Chaldean Babylonians during the exilic era. It appears that the stories have been crafted by exilic editors to inspire Jews of that era to follow in the footsteps of Abraham. Not only is Abraham's call an example of the persuasive lure of God, but even the story itself became the lure of God for a later generation of Jews.

Other narratives of divine lure are those of the children of Israel wandering in the wilderness with Moses, which are recounted in Exodus and Numbers. Here, too, the future is promised to the people in an enticing way. To arrive at the promised land they must obey the will of God, keep the Torah, and follow Moses. The image of the journey to the promised land, the land "flowing with milk and honey," underlies other stories both within the Hebrew Bible and in later Jewish traditions. God lures the people onward with the hope of a fertile land, and the land itself becomes a lure persuading the Israelite band to move forward. But there is a condition to the lure toward the land, and that is the necessity of obedience. Repeatedly the Israelites fail. They worship the golden calf (Ex. 32–33), rebel against the authority of Moses, murmur countless times, and hesitate to enter the land because of the fearsome inhabitants who reside therein. Thus, they are condemned to wander aimlessly in the desert for forty years. The lure, or the persuasion of God for the land, was a lure to obedience. If they had obeyed, the journey would have been quicker.

Commentators also suspect that the stories of the wilderness wanderings were told in their present fashion as a warning to later generations, bespeaking the need for obedience to God. They told later generations that their ancestors were not perfect. Their ancestors sinned, as did they, and were in need of forgiveness, as were they. Again, the stories serve as a lure to the self-awareness of human finitude, for the way in which you regard your ancestors is the way in which you regard yourself. Think of them as perfect, and you will arrogantly view yourself in like manner; view them as finite, and you accept your own finitude. If they were led by divine grace, then you must be led by divine grace also. These stories of wilderness wanderings called on later generations to admit their human frailty, repent, and rely on the grace of God.

These accounts in their final written form were designed to speak to Jews in Babylonian exile and the postexilic period. Those later Jews saw that as their ancestors wandered in the wilderness seeking the promised land, so also they languished in diaspora, scattered all over the world, seeking to return to Jerusalem. As their ancestors were graciously guided in the wilderness by Yahweh, so also Yahweh would be with them in their diaspora. Yet again the stories were a lure to a later generation to encourage them to trust in a God who is forever with the exiles in the wilderness, be it the wastelands of Sinai, Babylon, or the greater world of today.

In sum, there are accounts in the Hebrew Scriptures that speak to exiles seeking the promised land. That symbol of the promised land functions literarily and existentially as a lure that calls people forward. Even more than that, the stories actually are a lure to personal and religious insight. The stories call on people of later generations to see the presence of the Divine in their midst, wherever they are—in the exile of Egypt, the Sinai wilderness, or Babylon. As their God is with them, new options, hopes, and possibilities are offered to them. This is the language of process theology, the image of a gracious deity who forever offers to the people the possibilities that provide new hope for an uncharted future.

V

Sometimes the people do not heed the call or follow the will of Yahweh. They rebel and wish to return to the wilderness rather than go into the promised land. People are free, and they are free to rebel. In the moment of becoming, an actual entity chooses which path to take, and it does not always choose the lure or persuasion of God. Once a wrong decision has been made, the primordial body of God provides more options, and new decisions are placed before the people. But when this happens, God is hurt and angry. Classical theology could not come to grips adequately with language in the Hebrew Bible about God's disappointment or anger with decisions made by the Israelites. But in process thought God is intimately involved in the world and its development, so that God actually changes in response to human decisions. God can be sorrowful or angry and can even experience pain in response to the decisions of people.

Biblical texts speak of the pathos of God and even the occasional divine repentance of the decision to destroy Israel after the people have rebelled. The rhetoric of the divine will, which comes through the prophetic demand for people to follow God, contains the image of a God angered or agonized by the human refusal to obey the Law. Before Moses in Exodus 32–34, Yahweh repented of saving Israel from Egypt and expressed the desire to destroy the people. Such imagery is discordant with the language of omnipotence, omniscience, and omnipresence, but it flows more smoothly with process assumptions of divine self-involvement.

In biblical imagery God is not predetermined, nor has human history been foreordained; rather, Israel's free response changes not only their destiny but the very nature of God. God is absolute only in regard to divine love for people, which remains forever and is foundational to all other actions, even wrath. God becomes angry with people only because first God loved them so very much. God is absolute in regard to love, but in terms of the various aspects of the relationship with humanity, God changes in response to human decisions. By being related to humanity in the flow of time, God does not know the future; rather, God and humanity together work out events. This becomes the fabric of the salvation history that is recorded in the Pentateuchal texts. Applying to God the language of past, present, and future actions and feelings is meaningful only if God changes in that relationship with creation and humanity.[11]

Israel rebels against God and for a time appears to thwart the divine will in the biblical narratives. Yet process theology has no difficulty absorbing these ancient narrative images. Though the divine will might be opposed temporarily by human freedom, eventually the divine will may lure or

---

[11]Fretheim, *Suffering,* 35, 41, 47.

lead the creation in desired directions. To say these things in the light of the recorded narratives of Israel's experiences truly emphasizes the gracious nature of God. God gives the people of Israel the power to relate to the Divine and interact with the Divine.[12]

VI

There are times when it appears to the reader that the biblical images may be rather strong, perhaps suggesting more than just a divine lure. God may be portrayed as king, judge, savior, and sometimes divine warrior, and each of these metaphors is a truly powerful image of divine persuasion in the understanding of that age. Such images are rather absolute and may appear more coercive than persuasive to us. But we must balance the coercive and the persuasive imagery.[13] A wide range of images for God is found in the Hebrew Scriptures, and we must bring them all together in a unified focus to obtain the correct perspective on how God is metaphored. Certainly, images such as the divine husband, father, and even mother, which we find in the oracles of Hosea, impress us as appropriately persuasive, because they have the nuance of compassion as well as authority. These must be combined with the more absolute terms to gain a total picture of how the Divine is personified. Frequently, all these diverse images were metaphored by the same prophets, thus indicating the depth of their personification of God. All the images must be combined in a characterization of God as persuasion or lure.

In addition, we must recall that biblical people lived in the first millennium B.C.E., a rough-hewn, primitive, and authoritarian age in which metaphors of king, ruler, and divine warrior spoke to their consciousness in vivid fashion. The biblical authors, and the prophets in particular, sought to evoke strong imagery in the minds of their listeners. So we must be ready to recognize that much of the language is rhetorical, and it is appropriate for the understandings of that audience. What impresses post-Enlightenment Westerners as strong language may have been more appropriate for ancient Palestinians as an image of divine persuasion.

One way to break through our perception of God as harsh ruler in the Hebrew Bible is to look closely at texts wherein God the ruler is metaphored as responsive to human requests. Too often we ignore these passages in our theological portrayal of God. For example, when Yahweh became so angry with the Israelites for constructing the golden calf that he wished to destroy them, Moses dramatically interceded with Yahweh to save the people (Ex. 32:7–14; 33:12–17). If the image of an angry deity is a coercive image, then

---

[12]Ford, *Lure,* 59–60; and Fretheim, *Suffering,* 37.
[13]Ford, *Lure,* 30–31.

in the very same story we have the counter image of a human being changing the mind of God. Commentators sensitive to process thought point out that these passages testify to a God who not only attempts to persuade the people but is also willing to be "persuaded by the people or a single human being."[14] Coats says of this text that God is revealed as a powerful king who offers sufficient freedom to the people that they might coerce God.[15] Fretheim observes that herein we have textual testimony that speaks of the respect God has for human insight as an important ingredient in shaping the future.[16]

Another account wherein Yahweh involves a human being in the decision-making process is the dialogue with Abraham in Genesis 18:17–33 over the fate of Sodom and the other cities of the plain. Herein Yahweh states that the divine purpose will not be hidden from Abraham (v. 17), and in fact, the ensuing dialogue with Abraham implies that the human being may change the mind of the deity somehow. While the other two messengers go on to Sodom, Yahweh remains to talk with Abraham (v. 22), which is a significant gesture. Yahweh "drew Abraham into that sphere of decision making power within which Sodom's fate would be decided."[17] Abraham even haggles with Yahweh over the number of righteous in the city that may merit the city's continued existence (vv. 23–32). Furthermore, the divine decision will not be finalized until after the deity has visited the city (v. 22). There is a conditionality here in the divine intention to destroy the cities that depends on the involvement of Abraham. In the past we read this passage in light of God's omnipotence and assumed that the divine will was determined and that Abraham was allowed to make these petitions simply to demonstrate his faith. But that misconstrues the text's emphasis on the divine-human bartering, and the biblical author must have intended this dialogue in verses 23–32 to be there for a reason. That metaphor of bartering implies divine responsiveness to human petition. Of this and other related passages, Fretheim boldly states, "Metaphoric language must have some reasonable relationship to reality; such language says something about God."[18] We have ignored the message of this passage–that God responds to petition and involves people in the decisions that shape the course of human events. "God holds back on a final decision, not because God is indecisive, but because God wants the decision to be shared."[19] Even when God considers the destruction of people–a most authoritarian

---

[14]Ibid., 128; Fretheim, *Suffering,* 50; and George Coats, "The King's Loyal Opposition: Obedience and Authority in Exodus 32–34," in *Canon and Authority,* ed. George Coats and Burke Long (Philadelphia: Fortress Press, 1977), 91–109.

[15]Coats, "Loyal Opposition," 106.

[16]Fretheim, *Suffering,* 51.

[17]Janzen, "Metaphor," 19. Cf. Ford, *Lure,* 128.

[18]Fretheim, *Suffering,* 54.

[19]Ibid., 56.

image–there is still room for a human intercessor to be involved in the decision.

This is where Whitehead went astray with his caricature of the Hebrew Scriptures. He read this imagery in a flat fashion and failed to take into account that it was orally proclaimed in a grand kerygmatic fashion by the spokespersons of God and that it addressed a rustic people in a difficult and harsh age. The language sounds harsh only because that is how it was best communicated. One should add that many modern readers share this mistaken reading with Whitehead. Too often people read the imagery of the Hebrew Bible literally and conclude that therein a God of wrath and judgment is proclaimed. They fail to read the biblical text in its historical and literary context. The judgment imagery serves as a literary foil for the more important imagery of hope and divine love.

VII

When the biblical narratives are read in a slow and critical fashion, readers begin to sense that in subtle fashion the elusiveness of God is emphasized. Although many accounts portray God's revelation in direct and dramatic fashion, overall the distance and hidden nature of God may be proclaimed even more by these texts. God is direct yet elusive. Richard Elliott Friedman observes how the entire book of Genesis reflects on the progressive retreat of God from humanity. In Genesis 2–11, God walks with and speaks to people most directly. For the patriarchs in Genesis 12–38, God appears in the form of a human messenger at times, in dreams and heavenly voices, and sometimes the text merely refers to a theophany with no external phenomena. Then in the Joseph novella of Genesis 39–50 God retreats to a great distance and is spoken of by the narrative figures with no allusions to theophany. Even the dreams are symbolic visions rather than auditory messages, and they come more often to pagans.[20] I suspect that this is not so much a history of revelation as it may be a literary and theological structuring device by the final exilic or postexilic editor of Genesis, because the Joseph novella may well be a postexilic creation. That final author may be reflecting on the perceived distance of God for postexilic Jews, who envisioned God as present in the ancient times but not in their own age.

Elsewhere when dramatic theophanies occur, we need to appreciate more the infrequent nature of the theophany and the distance of God in the theophanic experience. When Yahweh appears to Moses, it is at special times and in special places. The theophanies occur on isolated mountains in the wilderness, and Moses alone goes up to the mountain, leaving others

---

[20]Richard Elliott Friedman, *The Disappearance of God* (Boston: Little, Brown, 1995), 7–140.

behind. The vast majority of people did not experience God. So distanced were they that at one point they built a golden calf, believing Moses to be dead (Ex. 32–33). The text stresses the unique relationship that Moses has with God, for to him God speaks directly, although not to others (Num. 12:6–8). The singularity of Moses as recipient of divine revelation implies a distant and hidden God for the people of Israel as a whole. Even with Moses there is a sense of the distance of God. At one point Moses has to be hidden from the glory of God and to be limited in his view of God, lest he be destroyed (Ex. 33:20–23). In those foundational traditions, which speak of revelation at Sinai to the great mediator Moses, God is distant and elusive.

This theme continues in the later literature. To certain individuals God comes only through the medium of dreams (Balaam, Samuel, Nathan, and Solomon), further implying divine elusiveness. Before Samuel receives the dream theophany at Shiloh, the text says that the "word of the LORD was rare in those days" (1 Sam. 3:1). This situates the theophany to Samuel in context: God appears to the boy in an age when God is distant for the people of Israel, including the high priest, Eli, and his sons. Elijah retreats to the wilderness of the mount of Horeb, presumably the same as Sinai. Only here will God appear. Yet when the divine theophany does occur, it is not the dramatic nature theophany associated with the previous experiences of Moses. Rather, the divine theophany comes in a still, small voice. Perhaps this is an etiological account for how the prophetic word came to the later classical prophets—not in dramatic form, as in an ecstatic experience, but in the internal and psychological awareness of the Divine. Friedman sees this as further testimony to the divine retreat from human experience.[21]

Finally, with the classical prophets there is no real description given for the reception of the prophetic word. The texts quite tersely say that the "word of the Lord came to" a particular prophet. Dramatic theophanic imagery is usually not provided (except for Ezekiel's vision of the "glory of God" in the chariot theophany of Ezek. 1–3). The most that can be said of dramatic theophanic imagery is that occasionally some prophets have a vivid set of dreams or visions, such as Zechariah (Zech. 1–8). God is neither seen nor described, for God is elusive.

This theme has been exposited in detail in a biblical theology produced by Samuel Terrien, *The Elusive Presence.* Terrien focuses on this theme of a distant and elusive God in much of the Hebrew Bible. He, of course, also carries the theme brilliantly into the exposition of the New Testament. Terrien perceives an aspect of the theophanies of the Hebrew Bible that too seldom receives attention—that the underlying assumption behind the theophanies is the transcendence and elusive nature of God.[22]

---

[21]Ibid., passim.

[22]Samuel Terrien, *The Elusive Presence: Toward a New Biblical Theology* (New York: Harper and Row, 1978), 63–477.

VIII

This elusiveness of the deity is emphasized by circumlocutions used to describe the divine activity in the world. Circumlocutions are expressions used to denote God without actually saying or implying directly that it was God who did something. These expressions may refer to an aspect of the divine nature or speak of some symbolic extension of the deity. Thus, to speak of the "hand of God" or the "face of God" or the "arm of the Lord" is really a respectful way of saying that God appeared or did something. The expressions bespeak a symbolic extension of the deity metaphored in anthropomorphic fashion, so that God can be described as acting without being portrayed crassly. The process theologian points out that such human anthropomorphic terminology is a way of envisioning God as active in the human process with terminology comprehensible to the human mind. They are processual metaphors. The process theologian would say that circumlocutions enable believers to speak of diverse activities unified in one divine being, for each of the circumlocutions stresses a particular facet of the divine nature.[23]

Other terminology may be isolated, some of which took on a venerable aura as a special way of speaking about God. The "angel of God" or the "angel of the Lord" is an expression that really refers to God in narrative texts usually attributed to the old Elohist epic source. In Deuteronomy and the Deuteronomistic History, the expression the "name of the Lord" was a circumspect way of describing Yahweh's presence, especially in the temple, when the authors did not wish to say that Yahweh became localized. Thus, the transcendent God of the universe could become graciously present for people in the temple, but biblical theologians respectfully spoke of that presence as the "name of the Lord." Ezekiel and the Priestly editors metaphorically spoke of the "glory of God" or the "glory of the Lord" as residing among the exiles in Babylon (Ezekiel) or in the restored temple (Ezekiel) or descending to the Tent of Meeting to encounter Moses (Priestly editors).

The most significant metaphors in this regard are the postexilic images of Wisdom as an extension of God. This dramatic personification could even take on feminine form, since the word for "wisdom" in Hebrew is feminine. Wisdom could be described as a female consort deity of Yahweh, as in Proverbs 8. For monotheistic postexilic Jews the image may have been taken from polytheistic contexts, such as the Isis cult in Egypt, but the metaphor of Wisdom remained a dramatic extension of the persona of Yahweh. (Perhaps it was the final stage in debunking the old preexilic consort

---

[23]John O'Donnell, *Trinity and Temporality: The Christian Doctrine of God in the Light of Process Theology and the Theology of Hope* (New York: Oxford, 1983), 29–31. He suggests that these circumlocutions imply that the Hebraic concept of God is monotheistic but not monistic, 29.

of Yahweh, Asherah, by metamorphizing her into an abstract principle that was an extension for God.) This circumlocution evolved eventually into personified Torah for later Jews and become part of the imagery associated with Jesus as the divine Logos, as in John 1.

As a process theologian surveys this language of divine elusiveness and circumspect circumlocutions, he or she senses that this is an attempt to speak of a gracious deity who deigns to enter into the human process. The very human words, including hand, face, arm, angel, name, glory, and even wisdom, are terms that describe the realia of this world. The process theologian affirms that this is how the Divine works–through the everyday things of this world, the temporal process. The reluctance to speak of God directly reflects the feeling of the biblical people that God was elusive and transcendent. The process theologian responds that when the Divine enters into the human process, this is the feeling that one perceives. God is not *deus ex machina* who can be clearly seen; God is perceived only by faith.

The biblical use of physical metaphors to describe the presence of God in theophanic form indicates two aspects of revelation. The theophanies indicate that God is not identical with the world in pantheistic fashion; God is separate from the world into which revelation has come. But for God to be perceived and understood by people, the deity must assume creaturely forms. The apparent bluntness in describing these physical forms may be a symbolic way of declaring that the transcendent God deigns to take simple human form so that people may apprehend the Divine. This is the central theme of process thought. The Hebrew Bible's images of divine self-revelation are metaphors for a God who has become part of the process of the cosmos. Without such self-involvement by the Divine, people would have no concept that there was a God. In fact, there would be no force to enliven and move the universe, for God is the source of the processual advance (Whitehead's "primordial nature" of God).

The process theologian further senses in these blunt biblical metaphors of divine self-revelation that "God's appearance in human form reveals vulnerability."[24] By taking on such an earthy appearance, God becomes enfleshed in our cosmic process. Christians see this most dramatically in the incarnation of Jesus. This enfleshment by God entails a serious commitment to people and a dependence on their response, for when God takes human form and talks to someone such as Abraham, God risks being rejected, as Israel so often rejected God. A negative response to the will of God, to the word of God spoken by a prophet, or to an anthropomorphized vision of God is a significant insult. God becomes vulnerable to human rejection in these direct and dramatic theophanies. God can be hurt.

---

[24]Fretheim, *Suffering*, 106.

There is a further implication with these direct self-manifestations of God. When God becomes involved and runs the risk of rejection, it implies that the future is radically open to the human decision-making process. God becomes enfleshed in the universe and thus does not know the future. The future is open-ended, and its development is contingent on human decisions. How then shall we speak of an "all-knowing" God who deigns not to predetermine the universe and therefore not really to know the future? Process thought can provide the language. God knows the future in terms of "possibilities" that may occur, and these possibilities for human decision are provided by God directly (Whitehead's "eternal objects")–they are in the primordial body of God. When the human decisions are made, then God knows the events as actualities and no longer as possibilities. This is the movement from the primordial body of God to the consequent body of God. Therefore, we can speak of God's knowledge being limited once God has entered into the process of this world. "God knows everything there is to be known," but not that which does not exist, for it is not yet known.[25] The future exists as possibilities and the past exists as actualities, and, properly speaking, only the past may be known.

If we speak like this, we confess that God cannot act in isolation from the world after having entered into it, and this is part of the divine decision to become incarnate in the world process. Thus, God entered into a relationship with the world and undertook "kenosis," the emptying of divine power and characteristics. Christians have attributed this process to Jesus for centuries. Now we confess that the Hebrew Scriptures testify that kenosis has been the process by which God always has related to the world.

If we, as modern theologians, step back and say how the presence of the Divine is felt, we probably would say that the Divine is experienced through human consciousness. We sense that the biblical tradition uses metaphors not only to respect the transcendence of God but also to give expression to the impossibility of adequately defining the divine presence felt by religious intermediaries. Although the biblical text would not say that God is manifest in human consciousness, many theophanic manifestations imply it. When a person in the biblical narratives has a vision or experience of the Divine, it is felt by him or her and not by those around. Prophets in the books of Kings experience a "word" from the Lord when other prophets are with them, but the others do not experience it. Paul's theophany on the road to Damascus was experienced by him, and the text says that the others did not see anything, but heard the voice (Acts 9:7). In general, the prophets speak of the word of the Lord coming to them, as though it were an internal voice or feeling. Elijah at Horeb in 1 Kings 19:13 heard the still, small voice, and this stood in contrast with dramatic theophanies of the past. Prophets and seers (Amos, Zechariah,

---

[25]Ibid., 58.

Daniel, and others) had visions that appear to be individual, psychological phenomena. Perhaps this might be the symbolic meaning of Moses' presence on the mountain by himself while the Israelites waited in the valley below. To the modern reader this testifies to a God manifest in subtle fashion in the human mind rather than the external world, even though such external phenomena may be described in the biblical text for rhetorical purposes. Yet again there is continuity between biblical imagery and process thought that sees God as active through the dynamic processes of our world. The most significant form by which actual entities move through successive moments of becoming is in the consciousness of the highest sentient beings, people. It is appropriate that the divine that enters into the process of the universe would do so manifestly through the medium of human consciousness.

IX

In the testimony of the Hebrew Scriptures God was a lure to Israel and the Jews, leading them toward a monotheistic faith and high ethical values. This emergent monotheism came to fruition in the Babylonian exile and the postexilic era. New perspectives provided by scholars now stress the gradual emergence and later appearance of monotheism and its corresponding worldview, and this certainly should tempt theologians to consider the image of God's luring the ancient Israelites and Jews toward a deeper intellectual and religious development. Throughout the vicissitudes of monarchy and exile the vocal prophetic minority prevailed, and monotheistic faith arose due to the persistent "enticement" of God in the lives of these people. God slowly brought an unfolding of the intellectual implications of monotheism.

We might acknowledge that this monotheistic development is still unfolding in the Judeo-Christian tradition today. We are still part of the monotheistic transformation that is occurring in human history. Perhaps we are still unfolding the implications of monotheism and the imperatives for social reform that go with it. If this enticement by God still occurs for us today, the challenge for us is whether we choose to heed this divine enticement. If so, we can speak of an ongoing salvation history, which is an intellectual and social-political development that encompasses the entire biblical tradition and the history of the Christian faith. We are still in the dynamic process of that tradition. God is still a lure for us.

In conclusion, possibilities of discourse and theologizing that combine process thought and biblical themes can be most fertile in the consideration of the doctrine of God. Process theology directs us to certain aspects in the biblical traditions for specific metaphors. The most important metaphor is the lure, or persuasion, of God. Making such a connection will lead us to emphasize much more the gracious nature of God and move away from imagery that characterizes God in stern, judgmental, or even coercive terms. Process thought leads us to see God's direction of Israel, as well as the proclaimed messages of religious intermediaries, in the context of a gracious choice provided to the people. Process theology leads us to emphasize the presence of the Divine in the human process and to be more sensitive to metaphors stressing the elusiveness of God and the circumlocutions that testify to the respect biblical authors had for the distance of God. These metaphors confess a divine being who is graciously active in the life of a people but remains subtle and elusive.

6

Suffering of God in the Hebrew Bible

I

All simplifications of religious dogma are shipwrecked upon the rock of the problem of evil.

Alfred North Whitehead[1]

I affirm that God does suffer as he participates in the ongoing life of the society of beings. His sharing in the world's suffering is the supreme instance of knowing, accepting, and transforming in love the suffering which arises in the world.

Daniel Day Williams[2]

These two quotes, one by a philosopher, the other by a theologian, epitomize the views of process thinkers as they address the philosophical and religious problem of evil. Whitehead's statement articulates well the process criticism of traditional Christian theology. Process thinkers believe that classical theology must posit an omnipotent deity who is responsible in some way for the existence of evil, either as predestined by the active will of God or permitted according to the so-called permissive will of God. John O'Donnell, a process thinker, boldly states, "Classical philosophical theism's apathetic God could only intensify the question" of why there is

---

[1] Whitehead, *Religion,* 77.
[2] Daniel Day Williams, "Suffering and Being in Empirical Theology," in *The Future of Empirical Theology,* ed. Robert Evans (Philadelphia: Westminster Press, 1971), 191–92.

suffering.[3] Process thinkers try to avoid this conclusion by attacking the underlying philosophical assumptions of classical theology in its unconscious characterization of God. In their perception God is not separate from the world and omnipotent in the abstract sense. Rather, as the second quote by Daniel Day Williams declares, God is intimately involved in the process of the world and human life, sharing with humans the pain they experience. God is part of the process, not an absolute and abstract philosophical principle of omnipotence. O'Donnell again observes that we need a new concept of God to "point in the direction of a God who participates in the suffering of his creation."[4] Such a new concept can be found in a very old source, the Bible.

The biblical tradition portrays God as personally and emotionally involved in the human dimension more clearly than traditional Christian systematic theology has been capable of doing for the past two thousand years. Process theologians have noted on several occasions how the biblical testimony speaks of God as active in the world to overcome evil and to create new things. God redeems and creates not only with divine power, or "persuasion," if you use process language, but also with divine suffering.[5] God also may be described as suffering in the struggle with humanity by which God seeks to produce religious advance. One would think of the Hebrew prophets in this regard, who sought to call the people forward toward monotheism and the practice of social justice in their society.[6] However, the ultimate symbol of divine suffering is the portrayal of the death of Jesus, whom Christians confess as God.

Instead of speaking of the suffering of God in the death of Jesus, traditional theology has chosen instead to emphasize that this sacrificial death of Jesus is the means by which God forgives human sin and restores the divine-human relationship. To be sure, this is the language of Paul, who speaks of the death and resurrection of Jesus as an act of redemption, sacrifice for sin, reconciliation, and victory over death, which then causes God to declare people righteous (justification). Paul emphasizes the importance of both the death and resurrection of Jesus, but in the piety of Western Christendom, both Roman Catholic and Protestant, an emphasis on penitential piety connected to the death of Jesus especially has been the hallmark of religiosity from the sixteenth to the mid-twentieth century. Theologians and preachers highlighted the forgiveness of sins won by the death of Jesus mediated through the proclaimed word and the sacraments (two or seven, depending on your tradition).

---

[3]O'Donnell, *Trinity and Temporality*, 23.
[4]Ibid., 23.
[5]Beardslee, *House for Hope,* 89; Cobb and Griffin, *Process Theology,* 48; Griffin, "A Naturalistic Trinity," 26; and Ford, "Contingent Trinitarianism," 59.
[6]Beardslee, *House for Hope,* 89.

The death of Jesus was suffered not by God the Father, but by Jesus as God alone. The death of Jesus bore the transferred guilt of millions of people throughout history, and those sins were placed there by God the Father, who then declared people forgiven or justified and redeemed by Jesus' atoning death. The classical expressions were articulated best by Anselm of Canterbury, Martin Luther, and John Calvin, all of whom especially emphasized the courtroom language of justification, for this spoke most clearly to their medieval and early modern audiences. This strong language from the courtroom preserved the majesty of God the Father, emphasized the seriousness of human sin, and above all, called forth a tremendous religious response to Jesus' death on the part of Christians, including sometimes very emotional confessions of sin and conversions. Any attempt to speak of God the Father suffering in the person of Jesus was dismissed as an idea bordering on the heresy of "Patripassionism," the heresy that harms the doctrine of the Trinity by attributing the sufferings of the second person of the Trinity to the first person of the Trinity. Unfortunately, it was overlooked that there might be a significant difference between saying that God suffers and saying that God the Father suffers, so for fear of saying the latter the Christian tradition refused to admit the possibility of the former.

II

In the history of the church theological concerns with Trinitarian articulations prevented theologians from formulating a powerful symbol of God's self-identification with the human condition. Any attempt to move in that direction was fraught with the danger of receiving the label of heresy. Such is the price that traditional, systematic theology sometimes forces us to pay. It was indeed a valuable message to proclaim to guilty people that they were forgiven and, even more importantly, accepted by God despite their human frailties. But an image of divine self-identification with human suffering might have spoken more meaningfully to countless Christians in the past two thousand years whose lives contained so much suffering, from those medieval Christians haunted by the specter of the Black Plagues to people of all ages whose lives were devastated or terminated by the horrors of war. Instead, too many Christians have wrestled with the notion of God as the final judge or ultimate ordainer of such things as the Black Plagues and other afflictions of the human condition. The image of a stern but fair God who transferred, or who had to transfer, the punishment of human sin to Jesus for the sake of divine justice is an image congruent with the view that many people had of God after their own personal experiences with war, natural disaster, and pestilence. Anselm's portrayal in his work *Cur Deus Homo* of a sacrificial victim who had to be God in order to atone for the magnitude of human sin resonates with this image of a just yet almost horrific deity. God the Father was virtually using God the Son as a scapegoat, if one wishes to view this theologem in a negative light.[7]

As the initial quotes indicate, process philosophers and theologians have reacted negatively to these traditional portrayals of God and proposed instead their image of a God in processual relationship to the world. Twentieth-century theologians also have begun to question some of the deductions traditionally made from the Trinitarian formulations of the ancient church. Pollard observed that in the interrelationship of the Trinity, the attributes of Jesus as the Son of God are shared in some degree by the Trinity or God. If the Son suffers, this suffering should be a characteristic of God, otherwise we have docetism—a denial of the incarnation of God in Jesus.[8]

Similar suggestions by other systematic and historical theologians have given process theologians grist for their arguments that indeed God ought to be described as suffering. J. K. Mozley evaluated the debate concerning the impassibility of God, whether it is correct to speak of God's experiencing human emotion in a theological and formal sense.[9] Subsequently, T. E. Pollard, B. R. Brasnett, and K. J. Woolcombe, all in the Reformed tradition, developed his ideas and suggested that we ought to speak of God as experiencing human emotions, even feeling pain and suffering.[10] Chief among their arguments were the testimonies of Hebrew prophets who dramatically spoke of Yahweh as experiencing the pain of the chosen people. From a different direction, Kazoh Kitamori spoke of the suffering of God by drawing on not only biblical passages but also the theology of Martin Luther.[11] His work was directed to a Christian audience in Japan, so he wove into the exposition an Asian Christian perception of suffering. In conclusion, theological discussion has paved the way for a processual expression of the suffering of God.

As of late, biblical theologians also have addressed more seriously the question of divine identification with human experience. Such authors seek to redress the imbalance of theological discourse that stresses the absolute aspects of the Divine. Christians, for example, are willing to attribute suffering to Jesus, whom they confess as God, but they are fearful of saying that Jesus suffered according to his divine nature, lest they fall into the heresy of patripassionism. But now biblical theologians and some preachers are more willing to speak in those categories of divine suffering and divine

---

[7]René Girard, *The Scapegoat,* trans. Yvonne Freccero (Baltimore: Johns Hopkins University Press, 1986), passim.

[8]Pollard, "Impassibility," 361–62.

[9]J. K. Mozley, *The Impassibility of God* (Cambridge, U.K.: Cambridge University Press, 1926), passim.

[10]Pollard, "Impassibility," 353–64; B. R. Brasnett, *The Suffering of the Impassible God* (Richmond, Va.: John Knox Press, 1965), passim; and K. J. Woolcombe, "The Pain of God," *SJT* 20 (1967): 129–48.

[11]Kazoh Kitamori, *Theology of the Pain of God* (London: SCM Press, 1966), passim.

identification with the human condition. The continental theologian Jürgen Moltmann boldly declares that Christians henceforth ought to attribute suffering to the Trinity as a whole, not just to Jesus as the second person of the Trinity.[12] This would certainly be affirmed by biblical theologians of the Hebrew Bible who discuss and reflect on numerous texts that speak of God in general experiencing a form of suffering.[13] Even a conservative Protestant theologian such as Donald Bloesch acknowledges that traditional theology has failed in this regard, and that modern process theology does coincide more closely with the images of the biblical text and provides a more adequate proclamation of the suffering of God in pastoral theological categories.[14] Imagery taken from the Hebrew Bible can help develop such concepts in Jewish and Christian theology.

III

Biblical theologians in the past have addressed the theological issue of divine suffering and its portrayal in the Hebrew Scriptures. A number of years ago two significant studies were undertaken by Henry Wheeler Robinson, who spoke of a transcendent God who graciously entered into the physical reality in order to create the world, redeem people, and suffer in this process of self-involvement with humanity.[15] The God of the Hebrew Scriptures was dynamic, not static, and this implied the Divine's experience of human suffering.[16] Another British author in that same era, Harold Knight, devoted a significant section of his work on the prophets to the suffering God imagery.[17] Another contemporary, Josef Scharbert, wrote a volume about pain in the Hebrew Bible.[18] Also, significant articles were authored by several scholars. Sheldon Blank observed that prophets, especially Hosea, Jeremiah, and Second Isaiah, give utterance to divine pain in oracles wherein they appear to be expressing their own pain.[19] Lester Kuyper observed that talk about divine repentance in the Hebrew Scriptures is really confession about the importance of human response

---

[12]Jürgen Moltmann, *The Crucified God* (New York: Harper and Row, 1968), 200–290.

[13]Claus Westermann, "The Role of Lament in the Theology of the Old Testament," trans. Richard Soulen, *Int* 29 (1974): 37–38, and *Elements of Old Testament Theology,* trans. Douglas Stott (Atlanta: John Knox Press, 1982), 174; Sibley Towner, *How God Deals with Evil* (Philadelphia: Westminster Press, 1976), 15–156; and Fretheim, *Suffering,* 1–166.

[14]Donald Bloesch, "Process Theology and Reformed Theology," in *Process Theology,* ed. Nash, 51–53.

[15]Henry Wheeler Robinson, *Suffering Human and Divine* (New York: Macmillan, 1939), 139–62, and *The Cross in the Old Testament* (London: SCM Press, 1955), passim.

[16]Robinson, *Suffering,* 150–53.

[17]Harold Knight, *The Hebrew Prophets* (London: Lutterworth, 1947), passim.

[18]Josef Scharbert, *Der Schmerz im Alten Testament* (Bonn: Peter Hanstein, 1955), passim.

[19]Sheldon Blank, "Doest Thou Well to Be Angry?" *HUCA* 26 (1955): 29–41; the title comes from the conclusion of the book of Jonah wherein God expresses sorrow over the thought of destroying Nineveh.

and obedience in the divine-human relationship and even more importantly a strong statement about the nature of divine love.[20] More recently, Erhard Gerstenberger devoted a brief but significant section in his book *Suffering* to this topic.[21] But several works deserve particular attention.

Terence Fretheim addresses the issue most effectively in his work on divine suffering. Like process theologians, Fretheim observes that in the biblical worldview God wills to become involved in the world, and this implies divine self-limitation and acceptance of human limitations. The Bible offers metaphors concerning God's acceptance of pain, but we have ignored them in the crafting of biblical theologies and in the greater task of generating systematic or foundational theologies. Fretheim observes that now a "metaphor shift seems in order," as we need to cultivate the "recognition of those metaphors which have been neglected."[22] In the Hebrew Scriptures God accepts the finitude of being involved in a temporal process of a particular people. We need to integrate those concepts in our biblical theologies and in the greater theology of the Judeo-Christian tradition.

Fretheim describes five modes of discourse in the Hebrew Bible concerning divine suffering: (1) God experiences pain when the chosen people sin and rebel against God, as testified to in the prophets. (2) God identifies with those who suffer and mourn, as especially testified to in the Psalms. (3) God bears patiently the slow moral response of people, as the prophets declare. (4) God may suffer vicariously for people. And (5) God suffers symbolically in the metaphors spoken by the prophets and in their own personal rejection by the people.[23] God is revealed as "one who is deeply wounded by the broken relationship" with humanity. By these experiences of pain God has willed to become vulnerable to humanity and has entered most fully into the process of time and the world by becoming part of the life and the experiences of ancient Israelites. Ultimately, Christians see this divine pathos and vulnerability to be most evident in the death of Jesus in the New Testament.[24]

Fretheim's categories resonate with insights expressed by the modern Jewish theologian Abraham Heschel and his work on the prophets. Heschel sought to organize his discussion of the prophets around the theme of divine pathos, and one can sense that his work is also a deep personal response to the Jewish Holocaust of the mid-twentieth century.[25] His thought inspired

---

[20]Kuyper, "Suffering," 257–77.
[21]Erhard Gerstenberger and Wolfgang Schrage, *Suffering,* trans. John Steely (Nashville: Abingdon Press, 1980), 98–102.
[22]Fretheim, *Suffering,* 13.
[23]Ibid., 107–66.
[24]Ibid., 106, 123, 165.
[25]Abraham Heschel, *The Prophets,* 2 vols. (New York: Harper and Row, 1962), 2:1–268. Cf. Moltmann, *God,* 270–78, who integrates Heschel's discussion of the pathos of God into his theology of a suffering God.

a number of authors, including Fretheim. Heschel believed that the heart of prophetic consciousness was the awareness of God's pathos, or the pain experienced by God because of the chosen people.[26] He affirmed, "God does not stand outside the range of human suffering and sorrow. He is personally involved in, even stirred by, the conduct and fate of man…Whatever man does affects not only his own life, but also the life of God insofar as it is the life of God."[27] Heschel reacted strongly against any theology, Jewish or Christian, that spoke abstractly of God as absolute and "wholly other," and he maintained that both Jewish and Christian belief systems were unfortunately influenced by too much Greek philosophy, with its antipathy to human emotion.[28] For him the biblical text dramatically spoke of a deity with passion and pathos, that is, the ability to suffer with creation. This powerful divine pathos was the result of God's covenanted relationship with Israel and the later Jews. He could say, "To the biblical mind the conception of God as detached and unemotional is totally alien…God looks at the world and is affected by what happens in it; man is the object of His care and judgment."[29] Heschel's ideas resonate rather excellently with process theology's modes of discourse.

IV

A consideration of some of the biblical texts that these scholars have meditated on is worthy of our attention. In diverse ways God is said to suffer in the Hebrew Scriptures, but too often we have simply overlooked these passages or accepted them as metaphors not worthy of serious use in the theological endeavor. Historians of Christian thought have pointed out how traditionally commentators read these dynamic passages, which spoke of God's sorrow at Israel's disobedience and God's repentance of the intention to destroy Israel, and they dismissed them as mere metaphors. Such passages were seen to be simple anthropomorphisms typical of that age, or metaphors that were best interpreted symbolically. Instead, those commentators turned their attention to other texts that spoke of the abstract and transcendent characteristics of God. Contemporary historians of Christian thought suggest that traditional commentators imposed their philosophical assumptions, gleaned from the Greek philosophical tradition, on these texts in the Hebrew Bible.[30] The classic example of an interpreter who worked with such Greek philosophical presuppositions was Augustine, who wove biblical theology together with well-developed Neoplatonic

---

[26]Heschel, *Prophets,* 2:2–103.

[27]Ibid., 4, 6.

[28]Ibid., 27–47.

[29]Ibid., 37, 263.

[30]Robinson, *Suffering,* 139–62; Pollard, "Impassibility," 353–64; Kuyper, "Suffering," 257–77; and Ford, *Lure,* 131.

thought as mediated through Plotinus. But Tertullian, Clement of Alexandria, and Origen also dismissed passages in the Bible about divine emotions as symbolic metaphors not worthy of serious theological use in defining the nature of God. Later commentators, including even Martin Luther and John Calvin, who were deeply immersed in the biblical text, nevertheless formulated their hermeneutical approaches to biblical passages that spoke about God with their inherited classical philosophical assumptions.[31] Yet the presence of these images of divine suffering and repentance in the biblical text is significant. Perhaps we were led by the dictates of our classical theism to ignore them, but now process theological assumptions demand that they receive attention by theologians and preachers in the proclamation of our beliefs concerning God and divine action in the world.

Several texts show God's sorrow at the mere creation or salvation of humanity because they have acted so reprehensibly. This implies a degree of divine doubt and dissatisfaction with previously undertaken divine actions. Such divine self-recrimination certainly is a strong metaphor for a God who enters into the process, especially the process of creation and co-creation with humanity. It almost implies that God doubts divine omnipotence, for apparently mistakes can be made by God. God also can experience remorse concerning previous divine actions in a particular present moment. This implies that God has entered into the temporal flow, for in a future moment God can metaphorically question a previous moment. Such is the case only if there is tremendous freedom in the process and God and humans interact. The result is that there can be for a time apparent failure in the divinely willed plan for humanity. Such texts would include Genesis 6:5–7:

> The LORD saw that the wickedness of humankind was great in the earth, and that every inclination of the thoughts of their hearts was only evil continually. And the LORD was sorry that he had made humankind on the earth, and it grieved him to his heart. So the LORD said, "I will blot out from the earth the human beings I have created–people together with animals and creeping things and birds of the air, for I am sorry that I have made them."

This is a powerful passage. God is said to be both sorry and "grieved" to the heart. The entire creative process is doubted by God, who now seeks to destroy all that was made, animals and people. This is not a little mistake that God now ponders; it is the entire creation that is deemed a failure. This is a high moment of self-doubt by God, and it must entail a

---

[31]Robinson, *Suffering,* 139, 144, passim; Pollard, "Impassibility," 353–64, who discusses the views of Tertullian, Clement of Alexandria, and Origen; and Kuyper, "Suffering," 259, 262–67, who discusses the views of Philo, Augustine, Calvin, Francis Turretin, and Stephen Charnocke.

tremendous sense of divine pain. As Gerald Janzen aptly stated about this text, "the indignant pain which it gives leads God to a change of mind concerning the viability of such a world."[32] Yet we have ignored this passage in our theology. Process thought calls us to remember and use this text.

Within the prophetic corpus God is said to suffer remorse because the Israelites have rebelled and sinned against the divine will. In Isaiah 63:10 God again is said to be "grieved" by the sins of the people before the exile, so much so that God became their "enemy." In Jeremiah 3:19–20, "God suffers the effects of the broken relationship at multiple levels of intimacy."[33] The prophet speaks dramatically for God when he says:

> I thought
> how I would set you among my children,
> and give you a pleasant land,
> the most beautiful heritage of all the nations.
> And I thought you would call me, My Father,
> and would not turn from following me.
> Instead, as a faithless wife leaves her husband,
> so you have been faithless to me, O house of Israel,
> says the LORD.

Jeremiah portrays God as a heartbroken husband deserted by his wife, a powerful message by which to metaphor God. Jeremiah is dependent on Hosea in his early oracles, for Hosea, too, uses familial metaphors to portray God's emotional distress over the sin of the people.

Divine pathos is manifest in Hosea 11:1–4, where God is metaphored as a heartbroken mother:

> When Israel was a child, I loved him,
> and out of Egypt I called my son.
> The more I called them,
> the more they went from me;
> they kept sacrificing to the Baals,
> and offering incense to idols.
> Yet it was I who taught Ephraim to walk,
> I took them up in my arms;
> but they did not know that I healed them.
> I led them with cords of human kindness,
> with bands of love.
> I was to them like those
> who lift infants to their cheeks.
> I bent down to them and fed them.

---

[32]Janzen, "Metaphor," 19.
[33]Fretheim, *Suffering*, 116.

The imagery here is incredibly emotional, but we have not given it the attention it deserves. Seldom, if ever, do people on the popular level acknowledge the very feminine portrayal of God as mother in this text. God tenderly loves the child, calls to the child, teaches the toddler to walk, lifts the infant to her cheeks, and feeds the infant (the image of nursing perhaps), all of which are the mother's responsibility. Nor is the tremendous pathos recognized here; the mother mourns the loss of her child. Process thought may open our eyes to observe and preach the obvious meanings found in this text. This passage most poignantly implies the potential for humanity to affect the divine being emotionally.[34]

The image of the broken-hearted parent may be found elsewhere in the prophets. In Isaiah 1:2–3 God speaks:

> Hear, O heavens, and listen, O earth;
> for the LORD has spoken:
> I reared children and brought them up,
> but they have rebelled against me.
> The ox knows its owner,
> and the donkey its master's crib;
> but Israel does not know,
> my people do not understand.

In Jeremiah 31:20 God, as a broken-hearted parent, proclaims:

> Is Ephraim my dear son?
> Is he the child I delight in?
> As often as I speak against him,
> I still remember him.
> Therefore I am deeply moved for him;
> I will surely have mercy on him,
> says the LORD.

The most passionate divine parental lament comes in Jeremiah 4:19–22:

> My anguish, my anguish! I writhe in pain!
> Oh, the walls of my heart!
> My heart is beating wildly;
> I cannot keep silent;
> for I hear the sound of the trumpet,
> the alarm of war.
> Disaster overtakes disaster,
> the whole land is laid waste.
> Suddenly my tents are destroyed,
> my curtains in a moment.

---

[34]Janzen, "Metaphor," 7–44; and Collins, "Process Hermeneutic," 109.

> How long must I see the standard,
> and hear the sound of the trumpet?
> "For my people are foolish,
> they do not know me;
> they are stupid children,
> they have no understanding.
> They are skilled in doing evil,
> but do not know how to do good."

At first the reader suspects that it is Jeremiah who is speaking autobiographically. But when the speaker says "they do not know me," we sense that it is God speaking through the prophet, for such a reference can refer only to the knowledge of God. Then the power of the first verse strikes us, for we realize that it is God who writhes in pain over the people. "God suffers with his people? Indeed! According to the Old Testament perspective it could not be otherwise."[35]

In other metaphors the prophets speak of God as being pained at Israel's sin in the same way that a spouse feels pain when deserted by a marriage partner. The prophet Hosea developed this metaphor the most, portraying Yahweh's relationship to Israel as the same as his broken relationship to Gomer, who likewise was unfaithful. But the image is found in other prophets too. Jeremiah 2:2–3 speaks of Yahweh's fond memories of a once faithful Israel:

> I remember the devotion of your youth,
> your love as a bride,
> how you followed me in the wilderness,
> in a land not sown.
> Israel was holy to the LORD,
> the first fruits of his harvest.

Jeremiah 3:1 repeats the same theme:

> If a man divorces his wife
> and she goes from him
> and becomes another man's wife,
> will he return to her?
> Would not such a land be greatly polluted?
> You have played the whore with many lovers;
> and would you return to me?
> says the LORD.

When Yahweh is portrayed as the jilted husband, it obviously projects a passionate anger and pain onto the divine persona. As Gerstenberger observes, the Hebrew Bible readily portrays "God's mind by the analogy

---

[35]Gerstenberger and Schrage, *Suffering,* 102.

of human emotions," and he sees this as "far from the calm, the superiority, and the eternity of the Greek belief in God."[36]

God "is deeply wounded by the broken relationship" caused by human sin.[37] How people respond to the will of God shapes the future that they and God have together, and according to these metaphors God is affected deeply by their failures. Sinful human response affects and hurts God, and that provides a strong moral imperative to humans to act morally and obediently. Their response is important to the ongoing relationship they have with God.

Another way in which the prophets metaphor the pain of God is the image of divine suffering with the people, especially with the pain experienced by the prophets themselves. When God speaks through a prophet, God becomes bound up together with that prophet, as is evidenced in many of the oracles wherein the autobiographical words of a specific prophet begin to mingle with the words of God. At that moment in the oral proclamation, "God and the prophet become as one in order to communicate to Israel—God is absorbed into the very life of the prophet." As Yahweh speaks through the prophets of the first millennium B.C.E., each individual "prophet becomes a veritable embodiment of God" and each prophet is "a more extended appearance of the Word of God in human form."[38] This is a form of incarnation that, for Christians, anticipates the even more dramatic incarnation of God in Jesus.

In the laments of Jeremiah we may observe this in most dramatic form. At times it seems that the prophet is speaking, and then there are strong hints that it is the divine voice of God speaking. Such a text is found in Jeremiah 8:18–21:

> My joy is gone, grief is upon me,
> my heart is sick.
> Hark, the cry of my poor people
> from far and wide in the land:
> "Is the LORD not in Zion?
> Is her King not in her?"
> ("Why have they provoked me to anger with their images,
> with their foreign idols?")
> "The harvest is past, the summer is ended,
> and we are not saved."
> For the hurt of my poor people I am hurt,
> I mourn, and dismay has taken hold of me.

---

[36]Ibid., 99.

[37]Fretheim, *Suffering*, 123. Fretheim likewise provides substantial commentary on these passages in Isaiah, Jeremiah, and Hosea, 111, 116, 123.

[38]Ibid., 150–51, 153.

The reader initially might suspect that Jeremiah is speaking auto-biographically until the last half of verse 19 is read. Here clearly Yahweh is speaking, for only Yahweh could be provoked by the images of idols. Thus, the references to grief, heartsickness, mourning, dismay, and pain are feelings experienced by God. The prophet portrays before the people the very anguish of God, and his laments are "reflective of God's own mourning."[39] In a similar way the pain experienced by the Suffering Servant in Isaiah 53 is also profoundly the experience of God's pain reflected through the life of the prophet.

In the prophetic corpus we find the most powerful and moving images of a suffering deity. For in these texts we hear the message of spokespersons who had a dynamic relationship with Yahweh and became a living embodiment of Yahweh's word and will for the people. As a consequence, they also reflect the divine pathos experienced by Yahweh in the covenantal relationship. In the past we have been led by our classical theology to ignore these passages, but process theology calls on us to let them live in our theology and pastoral praxis with a new vibrancy.

V

In process theology God is seen as being involved in the world and its development. This self-involvement includes the acceptance of finitude and pain by the Divine. God must suffer if the divine involvement with the world is total.[40] Traditional Christian theology has no way to speak of God's suffering, or it has at least ignored those images in its discourse, whereas the notion would be implicit in a process theological system. Biblical theology and process thought together express more completely a portrayal of the divine nature, especially in regard to the question of suffering and theodicy, than theological models in the classical tradition. They capture a key concept in the Christian faith, the notion of divine incarnation. In this regard, an alliance of biblical and process thought may produce a more meaningful form of discourse to undergird practical theology, especially for the pastoral practice in church and synagogue.

---

[39]Ibid., 158, 161–62.
[40]Ford, *Lure*, 92.

7

Creation
God and the World Process

I

Whitehead believed that the Hebrews made a mistake concerning their view of God as creator. He rejected the notion of *creatio ex nihilo,* which he thought was taught by the Hebrew Bible.[1] Seven weeks before his death in 1947 he gave this response:

> It was a mistake, as the Hebrews tried, to conceive of God as creating the world from the outside, at one go. An all-foreseeing Creator, who could have made the world as we find it now—what could we think of such a being? Foreseeing everything and yet putting into it all sorts of imperfections to redeem which it was necessary to send his only son into the world to suffer torture and hideous death; outrageous ideas…God is in the world, or nowhere, creating continually in us and around us. This creative principle is everywhere, in animate and so-called inanimate matter, in the ether, water, earth, human hearts. But this creation is a continuing process, and "the process is itself the actuality." In so far as man partakes of this creative process does he partake of the divine, of God…His true destiny as co-creator in the universe is his dignity and grandeur.[2]

---

[1]Pittenger, *Whitehead,* ix–x; and Kraus, *Metaphysics,* 40.
[2]Price, *Dialogues,* 366.

Ironically, Whitehead's retort more correctly describes the teachings of Genesis 1 and the Hebrew Scriptures than his rather ill-informed critique. It is most appropriate to take the categories of Whitehead and use them to explicate the Hebrew Bible's understandings of creation. Both the Hebrew Scriptures and process theology envision the created world as a dynamic process that brings "novel order and ordered novelty into being out of the settled past."[3] Biblical theologians may use process philosophical categories to highlight more clearly the dynamic creation imagery in the Bible, and thus we shall distance ourselves from the static categories of *creatio ex nihilo* that have been placed on the Bible courtesy of Greek philosophy.

II

God is portrayed as creator in diverse ways throughout the Hebrew Scriptures. Yahweh is extolled in the Psalms as the creator and sustainer of the world, especially in the Hymns of Praise. Although the prophets spend most of their energy speaking of the covenant between God and Israel, the Torah, and the demand to keep religious faithfulness to Yahweh and justice in society, there are images of God as the creator. Prophetic allusions, such as the doxologies in Amos, allusions in Jeremiah, and several significant discourses in Second Isaiah, envision Yahweh as creator of the world in addition to being the redeemer of the Israelites in the exodus and throughout their history. Wisdom thought is concerned with the created order, justice in the world, and the way in which God sustains the natural and social structures in which people live.

Wisdom literature, in particular, contains several texts that characterize God as creator of the world, most notably the hymnic elements in Proverbs 8, which are a creative rearticulation of Genesis 1. The passage refers to the creation of the world by Yahweh, as it also extols personified and feminine Wisdom, who was with Yahweh as a creative assistant during that process (Prov. 8:22–31).

The creation accounts in Genesis 1–2 expend special effort to speak of the creative endeavor of Yahweh in a dramatic hymn that lauds the total power of God in creating the world. These texts are formulated to distinguish monotheistic Israelite belief from polytheistic Babylonian beliefs, so that Jews in exile might comprehend the distinctive importance of their faith. The passage especially parodies Babylonian creation accounts such as the *Enuma Elish* and the *Atrahasis Epic,* and additionally it may contain imagery taken from Egyptian myths. In sum, the biblical passage is Israel's response

---

[3]John Cobb, "The Relativization of the Trinity," in *Trinity in Process,* ed. Bracken and Suchocki, 10, who says the modern theory of the "big bang" may epitomize the image of God's creative working in the process of our temporal flow.

to the ancient world that their God, not the other deities, has created the world. Allusions to creation abound in the Hebrew Bible.

Although New Testament texts do not speak readily of the creation of the world, nonetheless, there are valuable images. The primary focus of New Testament texts is on the new creation that will come at the end of time. Paul speaks of how the creation groans in travail in anticipation of the second coming of Jesus in Romans 8:18–22. Throughout the New Testament there are allusions to the new created order, the new heavens and earth, which will arise at the end of time—especially in Revelation 21–22. However, references to the original creation of the world were not really developed by the authors of the New Testament.

In general, biblical images of creation can be another category of thought worthy of consideration by a process theologian. Traditional Christian models of classical theology viewed creation with the affirmation that God was so powerful that the world was created out of nothing (*creatio ex nihilo*). However, biblical scholars are quick to point out that this thrust does not really reflect literally what the biblical text says, nor does it capture the dynamic spirit found therein. Genesis 1 describes Yahweh as creating the formless mass that was present at the beginning of the creative process, thus implying that perhaps there was "something" rather than "nothing" at the beginning. Many allusions in the prophets, wisdom literature, and the Psalms testify to Yahweh's power in the creation, as though there is a hint of the combat imagery so often found elsewhere in ancient Near Eastern mythology.

Two examples will suffice. In Psalm 74 the Jewish congregation calls on God to act in time of national calamity. To this end they appeal to the powerful acts of God from the ancient times. They proclaim:

> You divided the sea by your might;
> you broke the heads of the dragons in the waters.
> You crushed the heads of Leviathan;
> you gave him as food for the creatures of the wilderness.
> You cut openings for springs and torrents;
> you dried up ever-flowing streams. (Ps. 74:13–15)

In Isaiah 51, and in other texts, the exilic prophet Second Isaiah merges the imagery of God as creator of the world with the image of Yahweh's delivering the Israelites at the sea crossing. He uses the ancient combat image of creation, for it portrays Yahweh's cutting the primordial waters of chaos in half at the beginning of time, just as Babylonian narratives described Marduk's defeat of the goddess Tiamat. The motif of Yahweh's cutting water in half is definitely reminiscent of Yahweh's parting the sea for the Israelites to cross during the exodus. Thus, the prophet can merge the images of creation of the world and salvation in the exodus to cast a new image: Yahweh will save the people again by cutting a path in the wilderness for them to return home from Babylon. In Isaiah 51 we read one of several hymnic statements that weave creation and exodus together with a hope for return from exile, but in so doing it draws heavily upon creation by combat images:

> Awake, awake, put on strength,
> O arm of the LORD!
> Awake, as in days of old,
> the generations of long ago!
> Was it not you who cut Rahab in pieces,
> who pierced the dragon?
> Was it not you who dried up the sea,
> the waters of the great deep;
> who made the depths of the sea a way
> for the redeemed to cross over?
> So the ransomed of the LORD shall return,
> and come to Zion with singing;
> everlasting joy shall be upon their heads;
> they shall obtain joy and gladness,
> and sorrow and sighing shall flee away. (51:9–11)

Echos of this combat with the chaotic waters at creation can be found even in texts from a later period. The hymn to God as creator and feminine Wisdom, the assistant creator, in Proverbs 8 still has the allusion to the combative waters:

> when he established the fountains of the deep,
> when he assigned to the sea its limit,
> so that the waters might not trangress his command,
> when he marked out the foundations of the earth. (8:28b–29)

In all these texts names such as Rahab, Leviathan, and the dragon are images of the chaotic waters that existed at the beginning of creation. The portrayal of God defeating these waters was a motif found in much of the ancient world's creation mythology. Genesis 1 reduces the waters to being a passive recipient of the divine command that separates them, and the text phrases it this way to emphasize the total power of God. But this leads us to see the creative process less dynamically and more as a creation out of nothing. That is why it is important to give equal attention to other texts that describe creation in more bombastic fashion, so that we might avoid describing the creative process in static terms.

III

The Bible also stresses the notion of the continuing creative actions of God, which sustain the world and defend creation against evil and chaos.

Traditional theologies have encapsulated these biblical notions very nicely, and rather systematically, under the category of "divine preservation." The most important texts that can be said to refer to divine preservation are not captured in spirit too well by classical Christian theology, however; for the Bible also speaks of creation by combat and the divine suppression of chaotic forces, which more or less embarrass traditional theological systems, and subsequently the images are ignored or dismissed.

Herein, process thought again may offer a significant contribution to biblical theology, for in process thought creation is defined in a dynamic and evolutionary fashion. Creation is not a singular act at the beginning of some supposed temporal trajectory, but a throbbing and unfinished process that is being pulled forward energetically by divine interaction with the world. Creation "is not simply the recombination of the old, but depends upon novel structuring possibilities hitherto unrealized in the temporal world."[4] Such imagery bespeaks the overall evolutionary process by which modern people understand our world, for in evolution the life forms on this planet are constantly in flux and continually engaging new mutations in the generation of new variant life forms. God and the creation work together in the creative advance.[5] This continual creative activity of God may be seen by the eye of faith to be the entire evolutionary process. God "lures the evolutionary process to an ever-richer complexity productive of increasing freedom"; that is, God leads the evolutionary process toward higher sentience, or people.[6] Even though the biblical authors were totally unaware of the evolutionary process as we envision it, the biblical tradition uses language that is congruent with contemporary evolutionary thought. The biblical tradition portrays the universe not as eternal and self-perpetuating, but as contingent on the creative and active power of God.[7] This may be seen more clearly by a reflection on the biblical texts of creation.

IV

In Genesis 1 God is portrayed as creating the world in a dramatic and cosmic perspective in a hymnic narrative generated by Jewish priests during or soon after the Babylonian exile. Literally, the text speaks of God's ordering the chaotic form of raw material into an ordered cosmos. The text does not really say that God created the material of the world out of nonexistence, but rather that order and purpose were given to the chaotic, "formless" mass that was there. The way in which the priests portrayed the

---

[4]Ford, *Lure,* 21.

[5]Fretheim, *Suffering,* 74.

[6]Ford, *Lure,* 63.

[7]Bernhard Anderson, "Introduction: Mythopoeic and Theological Dimensions of Biblical Creation Faith," in *Creation in the Old Testament,* ed. Bernhard Anderson (Philadelphia: Fortress Press, 1984), 15.

creative power of God is similar to Whitehead's understanding of creation as a creative, ongoing process.[8]

Traditionally, Christian theologians have looked at this passage and moved immediately into discourse about *creatio ex nihilo,* in addition to theologizing about the majesty and transcendence of God. This mode of discourse was inspired by the influence of Greek philosophy, which had made itself felt in late Jewish thought already before Christian church fathers imbibed of Platonic philosophy. All of this was, of course, good theology for that age. Today process thought approaches the creation narrative, sees the term *creatio ex nihilo,* and hears imagery of total divine control with a nuanced allusion to the predestination of the world and human experience.[9] Process thought finds this stark and absolute imagery unacceptable in the face of other biblical images about God.

In process categories God is not a static, omnipotent being who generates the universe out of nothing by sheer incomprehensible power. God engages in creative activity and responds to the world in an interactive process. Hence, the statement that God found the creative act of each specific day to be good is highly important, for it means that at each stage of the creative endeavor God stopped and took account of what was unfolding.[10] Perhaps the text even speaks of divine pleasure exhibited at the end of each individual creative act. If we focus on this language in Genesis 1, we may see the cosmic creation as a dynamic, evolutionary process.

Historically, classical theism spoke of a "continuing creation" that flowed from the divine actions of those first symbolic seven days. Such a concept strove to describe the activity of God in preserving world order. Process thought can connect the concept of "continuing creation" even more readily to the theological image of initial creation in Genesis 1, for process thought sees the first seven days as a dynamic process in which God takes close personal interest in evaluating each stage of creation after its completion. If that first set of creative acts is an organic process, then one more readily perceives that there is a "continuing creation." The first seven days are not to be viewed as an absolute set of once-and-for-all-time accomplished acts, but rather as the symbolic beginning of a creative trajectory that still continues with divine presence in our world today. Such a perception brings our theological perspective on reality closer to the worldview generated by contemporary science, especially the evolutionary theory with its dynamic, organic, and ever-changing view of nature.

Similar views of creation may be obtained from Genesis 2. Here the biblical text in subtle fashion implies that humanity in the form of "The Adam" (who is sexually undifferentiated at this stage) co-creates the world

---

[8]Ford, *Lure,* 83.
[9]Griffin, "Naturalistic Trinity," 23–24.
[10]Hartshorne, *Omnipotence,* 77.

with God. God provides the animals, and "The Adam" names them. Although scholars have disagreed concerning the significance of this act, and whether "The Adam's" action truly constitutes a significant creative endeavor on his part, all admit that the deity has provided an important task that involves sharing the work of creation. Genesis 2 continues with the creation of the woman, who is taken from the man, and this creative act by God subsequently gives the man a masculine identity. Hence, male and female arise together. For the process theologian, what is truly significant is that God creates "The Adam" and then seeks to find a suitable helper, which is an admission that the creature is not yet perfect.[11] In fact, God experiments with the creation of various animals to find a suitable partner. If God experiments in creation, this countermands the view of God endorsed by classical theists, who speak of the omnipotent and omniscient deity. Genesis 2 describes a deity personally concerned with the feelings of his newly created human, and a deity who appears anxious to find a solution to the problem of loneliness, no matter how much experimentation is required. This is not the view of God embraced by a classical theist, but it is the God of a process theologian. The God of process theology enters into creation in a caring fashion and works within the parameters of the creation, experimenting with animals until finally the creation of woman (and concomitant sex) is unveiled. This story, *in nuce,* anticipates the rest of the Bible, wherein God enters into a dynamic and sometimes painful relationship (from God's side, too) with people.

V

Throughout the early chapters of Genesis the reader observes evidence of a dynamic relationship between God and people in terms of lordship over the cosmos. In Genesis 1 the man and the woman are in the "image" and "likeness" of God, terms reserved in the ancient Near East for kings who represent the gods in their function of rulership. Furthermore, the man and the woman are commissioned to "rule," *radah,* another word attributed only to kings. Their rule extends over creation, so that they become like God in their function on the earth. From a process perspective this is an indication that God deigns to enter into a process of co-rule and interaction with the newly created humans, truly a sign of divine compassion. Thus, the man and the woman co-rule creation according to Genesis 1, and the man helps to name the animals in Genesis 2 in what appears to be an act of co-creation. The vision of God and humanity together creating and sustaining world order accords well with the process portrayal of divine interaction in the temporal process. In process categories the

---

[11]Ibid.

"image of God ultimately is the divine immanence in the human and temporal process.[12]

Although people are created by God, they are given the ability to exercise their freedom to the extent that God gives authority over to them. The royal imagery associated with the man and the woman, and especially the imperative to rule over creation, implies that God has given great authority to humanity in the governance of the world.[13] From this time onward the administration of world order will be a cooperative endeavor between God and people.

The creative efforts of God have their analogies in the created order. As God creates the world, so also the world and humanity together continue a process of creation in a parallel or subordinate fashion. In Genesis 1 God creates the cosmos, but as this occurs, the cosmos is commanded to continue the creation process now that it has been set in motion in the primordial age.[14] In Genesis 1:11 the earth is commanded to bring forth vegetation, and the plants subsequently are commanded to continue the activity of propagation: "Let the earth put forth vegetation: plants yielding seed, and fruit trees of every kind on the earth that bear fruit with the seed in it." In Genesis 1:24 the earth is commissioned to bring forth animals: "Let the earth bring forth living creatures of every kind: cattle and creeping things and wild animals of the earth of every kind." Although we have not interpreted the passages in this way, the biblical text probably implies an almost personified view of the earth's power to co-create with God in the primordial age. In the other texts this imagery recurs. In Psalm 104:14 the poet declares that God makes the grass and plants grow, and Haggai 1:10–11 more dynamically speaks of how the earth itself brings forth vegetation.[15] The passage in Haggai seems to justify an interpretation of Genesis 1 that views the earth in a personified fashion as co-creator. In general, the continuance of growth and reproduction in the plant and animal realm would indicate to ancient and modern people that the earth indeed does engage in co-creation. God speaks to every level of the created order and persuades it to bring forth the best that it can, and this divine imperative or persuasive lure continues throughout all time.[16] We would say from a process perspective that God is in the growth process that throbs in the living world around us. This would be an organismic way of articulating the concept of "continuing creation" or "preservation."

[12]Janzen, "Process Perspective," 499–500, and "Metaphor," 17; Gale Yee, "The Theology of Creation in Proverbs 8:22–31," in *Creation in the Biblical Traditions,* ed. Richard Clifford and John Collins, CBQMS 24 (Washington, D.C.: CBA, 1992), 85–96. See also Michael Kolarik, "Creation and Salvation in the Book of Wisdom," in *Creation in the Biblical Traditions,* ed. Clifford and Collins, 107.
[13]Ford, "Biblical Recital," 201.
[14]Fretheim, *Suffering,* 73.
[15]Ibid.
[16]Ford, "Biblical Recital," 204.

One could combine this imagery with our contemporary understanding of biological evolution. God works together with creation as it has evolved toward increased complexity over billions of years. The evolutionary advance does not occur by chance, but it is the result of a transcendent power "luring" various forms of life toward increased complexity and richer possibilities of order. What appears to us as indeterminacy in the biological realm really results from a certain form of freedom in responding to the divine lure. The eye of faith sees a co-creative process in what "God proposes and the world disposes."[17] Lewis Ford can vividly say:

> God is not the cosmic watchmaker, but the husbandman in the vineyard of the world, fostering and nurturing its continuous evolutionary growth throughout the ages; he is the companion and friend who inspires us to achieve the very best that is within us. God creates by persuading the world to create itself.[18]

This analogy extends also to the human realm. In Genesis 1:28 the imperative is given to the humans to "be fruitful and multiply," which is an obvious allusion to sexual reproduction. This is an imperative given to rational beings who engage in acts of sexual reproduction consciously. At this level of sentience one could say that the beings are more seriously engaging in a co-creative act with God than are the plants and animals. Such a perception corresponds to Whitehead's assumptions about the conscious and creative level of participation in the world process by those actual entities who have a higher level of sentience.

The co-creative process shared by God and the world is intensified at the level of human beings; it is "a decisive sharing of creative powers with the human."[19] The command is repeated for Noah and his sons in Genesis 9:1, 7, clearly indicating that this is a command given to all people. We are all commanded to engage in the co-creative process, not only in biological reproduction, but also in our other creative endeavors. One of the Hebrew verb forms used in the creation accounts is *'asah,* a term that elsewhere is used in the biblical tradition to describe actions of people who make things. The use of this verb to describe divine activity by analogy may give blessing to the works of people by implying that they, like God, create things in the world process. At this level of human consciousness and free will the divine lure moves from the biological sphere to the cultural sphere, and the force of the divine lure or divine persuasion is manifest in religious and moral beliefs and aspirations.[20] Thus, we, like the entire cosmos, are drawn forward by the divine lure and yet are free to choose among the options offered to us.

---

[17]Ibid., 203.
[18]Ibid., 202.
[19]Fretheim, *Suffering,* 74.
[20]Ford, "Biblical Recital," 203.

In process thought we confess that all the creative acts of people have the presence of the Divine in them, and in every instance the Divine works with human free will and intentionality to co-create in the world process. Fretheim aptly describes this process:

> Both God and the creation are involved in every such ongoing creative act, though God always relates to this order in ways that are appropriate to its nature...Both God and the human are effectively involved in the process, and God's involvement is appropriate to the nature of the human and is not all-determinative.[21]

Crucial to this statement by Fretheim is the observation about the appropriate level of divine involvement. God is involved to the degree to which the creative partner can cooperate consciously. This again dovetails with Whitehead's observations about the level of consciousness in the actual entities that determines their level of creative cooperation. It equally implies for the satisfaction of the theist that there is a transcendent aspect of God that is outside the universe and not involved in the process of this world order (and obviously beyond human comprehension and our ability to theologize upon–*deus absconditus*).

Hence, we can speak of the biblical text's giving testimony to a wide range of co-creative activity that brings God together with the world and humanity. A process theologian might speak of a cosmic process of "self creation of the creature out of its past" under the "inspiration of God's directing aim."[22] The world, both nature and conscious human beings, creates the cosmos under the guidance of the divine lure. This testifies to a God who primarily works through nature and history rather than breaking into it and perhaps even defying the laws of nature. It implies that the level of divine involvement may differ according to the degree of cooperation that comes from the created order. There is a divine power present in the process, but it does not preempt human free will or the world's capacity to take its own direction (such as in evolution). God lures the world to generate newness and to bring forth a "creative advance of the world toward more complex forms of order, whether in nature or the human community."[23] Fretheim can say, "God is present at every occasion and has a hand in every event, working along with other causes, rather than through

---

[21]Fretheim, *Suffering*, 74.

[22]Ford, "Contingent Trinitarianism," 57.

[23]Marjorie Suchocki, "Spirit in and through the World," in *Trinity in Process,* ed. Bracken and Suchocki, 175.

interferences or interventions. Thus God's influence is effective to some degree in every event, though it is more significant in some events."[24]

VI

There are other significant perceptions of creation that may be derived from the early chapters in Genesis and other texts in the Bible. The biblical text sees the harmony of the relationship between people and the world, and people and the animal realm, more clearly than do we today. By way of negative evidence we may point to the curses placed on the man and the woman in Genesis 3:14–19. These curses include not only alienation between God and people and also between the man and the woman created by the pain of childbirth, but also the alienation between people and the animal realm (symbolized by conflict with the serpent) and the ground (symbolized by the sweat involved with agricultural labor). From the perspective of the Hebrew Scriptures these alienations were overcome by obedience to the Torah, and from the Christian perspective these alienations, in part, are to be overcome by the new age established with Jesus' resurrection. But the bottom line is that alienation between people and both the animal realm and the ground were seen to be very important curses that had to be overcome. In their primal relationship in the garden, the man and the women lived in harmony with the planted earth (symbolized by the fruit trees of which they could eat) and the animal realm (symbolized by dialogue with the serpent). The biblical text throughout sees the people of God living in close relationship with the earth. In Deuteronomy 27–28 the blessings and curses that come on the people affect most directly the fertility of land. In judgment oracles of the prophets one of the greatest punishments to be visited on the people is infertility of the land, and the greatest threat of judgment is exile from the land. Israelites were agriculturalists, living in small villages, close to the life of the earth and the animal realm. They, more than we, understood this bond.

Process theology combined with our interpretation of the Bible may help us recover the biblical feeling for the connection between people and the natural order. Process thought views people as having an organic unity with each other, being part of a corporate humanity.[25] As such, the biblical rhetoric about the solidarity of people and their need to take responsibility for each other and the world around them is strengthened accordingly in our retelling of the narratives. In process thought, people and the natural order, including animals, are seen as a holistic unity, all part of the creative advance, all containing the power of the immanent Divine within them.

[24]Fretheim, *Suffering,* 75.
[25]Janzen, "Process Perspective," 498–501.

Process thought reflects on the interaction of God with the world and has a sense of ecological balance. In our biblical and systematic theologies we should develop a sense that God engages in dialogue with both people and nature.[26] In our modern world it would be good for us to sense that God has chosen a sacred people, but that the presence of a immanent and self-involved God is found in not only human beings but also the natural order. We would live with greater respect for our world. If, indeed, we are moving toward ecological disaster, the use of process categories in our religious discourse, including biblical theology, may be a necessary task in our pedagogy and theology.[27]

VII

Creation ought to be seen as a dynamic and ongoing process wherein God enters into the temporal dimension to create continually a world order. The biblical text provides imagery of the dynamic nature of this divine participation in creation. Drawing on imagery deeply rooted in the ancient Near East, the biblical traditions also speak of God's engaging in combat with certain forces in the universe in order to maintain cosmic stability and a worldly environment suitable for created humanity. The imagery of creation by combat and the continuing process of maintaining created order by combat were images that the author of Genesis 1, in particular, wished to mute with the portrayal of creation by divine word in six days. Nevertheless, the biblical text uses such imagery elsewhere in poetic fashion to extol the majesty and power of God. The process theologian has no difficulty accepting these metaphors as ways of describing God's creative activity. In process thought the image of a God who creates the world out of chaos implies that God works within natural parameters, within the forces of the universe. This betokens a God who has become part of the process, and it is preferable to the image of *creatio ex nihilo,* which implies total dictatorial control and predestination, ideas abhorred by process theologians.[28]

Two scholars, Jon Levenson and Ronald Simkins, provide excellent exegetical analyses of the biblical concept of creation that capture the dynamics of these passages in the biblical tradition. By their interpretation, God did not create things out of nothing so as to generate an ordered but static universe; rather, God established order over the forces of chaos and evil. For these actions the creation must continually praise the creator, and that is probably why most of these allusions are located in the poetry of the Psalms and the language of the priest turned prophet, Second Isaiah. This

---

[26]Ibid., 502; and Ford, *Lure,* ix, 21.
[27]Suchocki, "Spirit," 177.
[28]Griffin, "Naturalistic Trinity," 23–24.

order must be maintained by divine action, a continuing struggle between God and the forces of chaos and evil. God's promise to keep cosmic order is foundational to the covenant relationship, according to Simkins and Levenson, and this is a theme that the vast majority of biblical commentators have sidestepped in the past with their emphasis on sacred history and covenant.[29] Levenson observes:

> The concern of the creation theology is not creatio ex nihilo, but the establishment of a benevolent and life sustaining order, founded upon the demonstrated authority of the God who is triumphant over all rivals...YHWH's mastery is often fragile, in continual need of reactivation and reassertion, and at times, as in the laments, painfully distant from ordinary experience, a memory and a hope rather than a current reality.[30]

Levenson's work, in particular, emphasizes the role of the divine in maintaining an ongoing struggle with the forces of evil and chaos. His strong emphasis on the importance of conflict imagery and the control of chaos in the biblical portrayal of God resonates well with process thought. Whereas classical theology might be offended at the idea of a God involved in conflict, process theism sees it as a significant mode in describing God's involvement with the world. This becomes the corollary to a sacred history process model. Just as God may be seen to be involved in the history of the world, luring people into the future, so also the biblical concept of creation views God as self-involved in the natural order, fighting continually to prevent the forces of chaos from destroying the chosen people of old and today. Process models permit this powerful and ancient biblical language, the image of conflict in the natural order, once more to emerge in a modern theological expression.

Process theologians often speak of how God suffers in the struggle against evil, or the struggle to lure humanity to do good and thus avoid inflicting evil or pain on fellow human beings or the world itself.[31] In general, they react against the classical theistic view of God in favor of a process view precisely because the former view posits a God who either causes evil or permits it to happen. Cobb and Griffin refer to this as the view of God as a "controlling power."[32] Process theologians speak of a God who suffers with humanity or engages in a struggle to remove pain from the world. In part because the actual entities, including people, have the freedom to refuse the divine lure, evil will happen. To say that evil exists because free

---

[29]Levenson, *Creation*, 3–50; and Simkins, *Creator and Creation*, 82–120.

[30]Levenson, *Creation*, 47.

[31]Beardslee, *House for Hope*, 89; Griffin, "Naturalistic Trinity," 26; and Ford, "Contingent Trinitarianism," 59.

[32]Cobb and Griffin, *Process Theology*, 9.

will exists is a frequent answer given to the question of suffering, especially by Jewish intellectuals. But process thought undergirds that response philosophically by speaking of the will of God as a lure to the entities who may choose freely to ignore it. Schubert Ogden maintains that the existence of freedom causes pain and evil in the world, but that the very existence of value does likewise. If something can be sensed as good, then something else correspondingly may be termed evil. Pain exists because there is sentient feeling and, ultimately, consciousness in the universe. Sin exists because there is the freedom in conscious beings to corrupt the divine lure of love.[33] This language of Ogden reminds us of the deeper images of Genesis 3. Once placed in the garden with their free will, the man and the woman have the potential to corrupt what God intended. It is the price to be paid for consciousness, intelligence, and free will. Once the creature has chosen evil, God, the origin of the divine lure to love, must suffer indeed.

Especially with the language of creation, categories of process thought bring together the distant language of the biblical age and a modern philosophical system. But the biblical portrayal of creation may profit more from process models than some of the theologoumena discussed, for biblical notions of conflict between God and the created order were lost completely by classical theism, swallowed up or ignored by the perception of the *creatio ex nihilo* concept in our theology and confirmation manuals. Process thought can preserve the imagery and the language of the Bible and render it intellectually acceptable for modern theologians.

---

[33]Cobb, *God and the World*, 96.

8

Covenant
God Enters into Relationship with Humanity

I

The concept of covenant has been extremely important to biblical theologians for years, especially those in the field of Hebrew Scriptures. In the 1930s Walther Eichrodt formulated his magisterial *Theology of the Old Testament*[1] around the central notion of covenant, and his tripartite division of the discussion of the theological themes in the Hebrew Scriptures was reminiscent of the threefold division used by Christian theologians (Father, Son, and Holy Spirit) in traditional systematic theologies. Eichrodt's concept was praised and critiqued by various biblical scholars, but it clearly remained a seminal work in the field.[2] It was placed in contrast with Gerhard von Rad's *Old Testament Theology,* which provided a more historical and developmental analysis of the Hebrew Bible, a traditio-historical study of the Hebrew canon.[3] Later scholars used the concept of covenant in other ways. Delbert Hillers traced it as a leitmotif throughout the Hebrew Scriptures and the New Testament.[4] Other scholars, biblical theologians, and textbook authors used the notion as an organizing theme or a significant aspect of biblical theology.

[1]Walther Eichrodt, *Theology of the Old Testament,* trans. J. A. Baker, 2 vols., OTL (Philadelphia: Westminster Press, 1961, 1967), passim.
[2]D. G. Spriggs, *Two Old Testament Theologies,* SBT 2d ser. 30 (London: SCM Press, 1974), 11–33.
[3]Gerhard von Rad, *Old Testament Theology,* trans. D. M. G. Stalker, 2 vols. (New York: Harper and Row, 1962, 1965), passim.
[4]Hillers, *Covenant,* 1–188.

Covenant as understood by the biblical theologians, especially Eichrodt, stressed the election of Israel, or any people of God, by the grace of Yahweh. Election established a relationship in which Yahweh would protect and direct of the destiny of the people; in return, the people would be exclusively faithful to Yahweh and obey the Torah. This obedience would keep the relationship healthy and lead to the blessing of the people in their national destiny and everyday life, including land fertility. The covenant could be described in conditional terms, especially with an appeal to the Sinai legislation and the efforts of Moses, in such a way as to elicit the response of repentance for past failures and a renewed attempt at obedience by the people. Such imagery is found in the Deuteronomistic History and prophets like Hosea, Micah, Jeremiah, and Ezekiel. Or again, the covenant could be described in unconditional terms to emphasize the total grace of Yahweh, who would forgive the people and forever keep them under divine protection, restoring them from calamity or exile. Such imagery often included appeals to the covenant made with David or Abraham.[5] Leading biblical traditions in which this language is found include the Priestly tradition, with its numerous covenants with Adam (Gen. 1), Noah (Gen. 9), Abraham (Gen. 17), perhaps Jacob (Gen. 35), and Moses, all of which were editorial additions to the archaic epic tradition. Prophetic spokespersons were chiefly Isaiah, Second Isaiah, and postexilic prophets, but one also could include the later hope oracles of Jeremiah and Ezekiel. Thus, there appeared to be two modes of speaking about covenant, one calling for repentance and obedience, the other proclaiming forgiveness and restoration. Each mode was dependent on the circumstances to which the biblical authors spoke. Hillers traced the development of these two covenant concepts through the Bible, showing how the unconditional covenant became foundational for early Christians. Hence, the concept of covenant has been extremely important in Hebrew Bible studies and biblical theology for several generations.

Critical scholars investigated the historical and cultural origin of the notion of covenant prior to its adaptation by the biblical authors. In the 1950s George Mendenhall sought to demonstrate the close relationship of biblical notions of covenant with the covenant formularies of the second millennium B.C.E. Hittite treaties,[6] and independently, Klaus Baltzer came to the same conclusions.[7] This, of course, suggested that the historical Moses might have used such language and imagery in formulating the earliest

---

[5]Ronald Clements, *Abraham and David,* SBT 2d ser. 5 (London: SCM Press, 1967), 9–88.

[6]George Mendenhall, "Ancient Oriental and Biblical Law," *BA* 17 (1954): 26–46, and "Covenant Forms in Israelite Tradition," *BA* 17 (1954): 50–76; and Mendenhall and Gary Herion, "Covenant," *ABD* 1:1179–1202.

[7]Klaus Baltzer, *The Covenant Formulary,* trans. David Green (Philadelphia: Fortress Press, 1971), 1–93.

laws and teachings in Israel. Later investigations implied a much later origin for the introduction of the idea of covenant into Israel by noting that the truly close parallels between biblical formulations and those of the ancient Near East lie with the Assyrian treaties of the eighth and seventh centuries B.C.E.[8] The implication of this later dating was that the original formulation of the oldest laws would not have had covenant imagery, but that this imagery was introduced into the biblical text by Deuteronomistic authors. They would have been responsible for editing material in Exodus and for the creation of the entire book of Deuteronomy, where the covenant imagery is to be found.

This later date seemed to demean the importance of the covenant concept in the opinion of some, since it implied that the notion was not present in the foundational biblical texts and the primordial experience of Israel in the presettlement and early settlement days. But that is probably an inappropriate conclusion. Our biblical text in its present form, which is canonical for Jews and Christians, has the imagery of covenant as a significant unifying theological theme. Whether it was early or late in Israel's historical experience does not alter its importance in our present biblical text, from which we do our theology.

This critical scholarly study of ancient Near Eastern covenant formularies provides us with a sharper focus on the theological nuances in the biblical text. Ancient Near Eastern covenants were political treaties between nations often imposed with military might by a strong nation or group of people on a weaker group; usually Hittites and Assyrians imposed them on their conquered or coerced vassals. Scholars referred to such treaties as suzerainty treaties, and they spoke of the suzerain-vassal relationship between the superior nation and the conquered people. Such treaties often included some historical reference to past events between the two nations, the stipulations laid on the vassal, the swearing of an oath of obedience to the treaty, an appeal to everyone's gods, curses and blessings that would follow on the breaking or the keeping of the treaty obligations, and then miscellaneous references to guidelines for public reading and deposit of treaty copies. Biblical scholars saw connections with the conditional model of covenant found in the biblical text. They observed great form-critical similarity between the ancient Near Eastern covenant formularies and the written text of Exodus 19–24 and the entire book of Deuteronomy. In particular, there were historical prologue (Ex. 20:1; Deut. 1–11), stipulations (the Ten Commandments of Ex. 20 and the Deuteronomic laws of Deut. 12–26), blessings and curses (Ex. 20:5–6; Deut. 27–28), and other parallels.

---

[8]Dennis McCarthy, *Treaty and Covenant,* AnBib 21 (Rome: PBI, 1963), 27–152; Lothar Perlitt, *Bundestheologie im Alten Testament,* WMANT 36 (Neukirchen-Vluyn: Neukirchener, 1963), passim; and Ernest Nicholson, *Exodus and Sinai in History and Tradition* (Richmond, Va.: John Knox Press, 1973), 33–52.

The implication was that the biblical authors used this language to impress on their audience the seriousness of their relationship with Yahweh. They had made a treaty with Yahweh, which implied their obedience to the Torah, and they needed to keep these laws, lest they be punished and lose their land. Such ancient Near Eastern imagery put teeth in the appeal of the Deuteronomic reformers and the prophets for people to worship only Yahweh and to keep the laws. Also, a vivid contrast was established. Instead of the foreign powers, especially tyrannical Assyria, Yahweh was to be seen by the Israelites as the only true lord in the cosmos. The Deuteronomic Reformers and the prophets were attempting to move the people toward monotheism in the late seventh century B.C.E., and this is when much of that covenant imagery emerged in biblical texts. In much the same way, early Christians declared that Jesus Christ alone was *kurios,* or Lord of the cosmos. "Lord" in Latin, of course, meant Caesar. Hence, Christians defied the authority of Caesar in Rome, and particularly his claim to divinity, when they said that Jesus alone was Lord, and for that they often had to die in the arena. The ancient Israelites began this pattern of faith affirmation of absolute trust in God in the face of the oppressive authorities of the age with their proclamation that Yahweh alone was ruler of the universe. Yahweh alone had true power over the destiny of Israel, not the Assyrians or the later Babylonians, and especially not the gods of those nations whose universal rule was legitimated supposedly by the imperial conquests of their respective peoples. The covenant image, especially the conditional model, emerged when Israelites as a people were moving in a monotheistic direction, in the late seventh century B.C.E. and during the Babylonian exile, when the motif would make the most sense.

II

Much ink has been spilled by biblical theologians on exegetical, historical, and theological questions connected to the study of covenant. Yet one aspect has been touched on only lightly by critical scholars, and that is the relationship of covenant and contemporary process theology. There are obvious connections, most significantly the fact that covenant implies a dynamic and evolving relationship between God and people throughout a historical process. Charles Hartshorne spoke of how the notion of covenant between God and Israel should be best described as a "social transaction."[9] Covenant language is close to the hearts of process thinkers, because they seek to describe the world as a social process, and the relationship of all things in the world, especially those that have consciousness, is described in terms of social relationships.[10] The covenant

---

[9]Hartshorne, *Omnipotence,* 77.
[10]Pittenger, *Pilgrim Church,* 30–45.

between God and Israel symbolizes the "reciprocal character of effective creative activity: divine initiative and creaturely response."[11] Robert Doud speaks of the biblical covenant not as a "static, once and for all, covenant," but as "a developing reality, always being restruck in a new event, which intended to be faithful to the past and creative of the future." The power of the covenant was in its "steady offer of divine love" and testimony to a God who leads people through the challenges of historical experience.[12]

The imagery of covenant bespeaks a dynamic relationship between God and the people of Israel, especially with the predominant set of covenant images, those of the conditional covenant. In this model there are several implied movements of divine and human will on the part of the participants that are interrelated or contingent on each other. How God acts will determine how people act, and how people respond will determine how God acts. Such imagery appears crude and anthropomorphic to the classical theist, but to the process theologian the images testify to a gracious deity who enters into a contractual relationship with mortals.

Biblical theologians have not spoken of the specific dynamics of each of these theoretic responses of God and humanity. Often biblical theologians assumed that such a way of speaking was simply the language of that age. They considered other aspects of the text and indeed found meaningful insights for understanding the thought of ancient Israel. But it might be of value to investigate the movements of human and divine will or response in the covenant relationship to see how they resonate with modern process theology.

The first movement is one of divine will and a form of incarnation, for God consents to enter into a relationship with people. The language of process sees this entrance of God into human relationships as paradigmatic of the universal divine presence in time and nature.[13] Given the strong international treaty imagery taken from ancient Near Eastern sources by the biblical authors, we may speak of God's entering into something that can be characterized as an ancient contractual relationship. It "involves the mutuality of shared power" between God and people.[14]

To speak of the covenantal election of Israel by God as a contractual relationship makes this divine activity sound more human and even political. That is what the biblical authors intended. They wished to concretize the divine-human relationship symbolized by election and covenant talk as something human and perceptible in social and political categories. We

---

[11]Ford, "Biblical Recital," 205.
[12]Robert Doud, "The Biblical Heart and Process Anthropology," 17, an unpublished paper graciously shared with this author.
[13]Ford, *Lure,* 126.
[14]Janzen, "Metaphor," 23.

must heed their intent and likewise envision the covenant in concrete human terms. God deigns to enter into contract with the people—God "inks" a document and becomes "bound" to people.

God exercises divine freedom in entering into this relationship with humanity. But once God has "freely made such promises, thereafter God's freedom is truly limited by those promises...God's freedom is now most supremely a freedom *for* the world, not a freedom *from* the world."[15] As Fretheim's words imply, the very notion of covenant demands that we rethink our perception of divine omnipotence. As God has been revealed to Israel in its historical existence, God has become limited by promises made to that people. Traditional theology would be uncomfortable with saying it thus, but process theology has no problem confessing that God enters into relationships with people in an incarnational process and is not omnipotent, but gracious. To maintain omnipotence in a relationship with people requires that God be a tyrant who manipulates every human action. Fretheim observes, "For the sake of the relationship, God gives up the exercise of some power. This will in turn qualify any talk about divine control or divine sovereignty. Total control of the other in a relationship is no relationship of integrity."[16]

As God offers the covenant relationship to people, it is an example of divine persuasion or divine lure. Exodus 19:3–6 appears to be the first covenant wherein God offers this relationship to a corporate people rather than an individual in the narrative sequence of the Pentateuch (not necessarily the oldest covenant tradition, however). It is an offer of a covenant relationship, not a "unilateral imposition of a treaty."[17] If read from a process perspective, Exodus 19:3–6 portrays God offering a "deal" to the people to which they may respond if they feel the "terms" are good:

> Then Moses went up to God; the LORD called to him from the mountain, saying, "Thus you shall say to the house of Jacob, and tell the Israelites: You have seen what I did to the Egyptians, and how I bore you on eagles' wings and brought you to myself. Now therefore, if you obey my voice and keep my covenant, you shall be my treasured possession out of all the peoples. Indeed, the whole earth is mine, but you shall be for me a priestly kingdom and a holy nation. These are the words that you shall speak to the Israelites."

The Lord first reminds the people what has been graciously done for them by divine power, so that the human response should be one of thankfulness. Then the people are told of the special status they will receive,

---

[15]Fretheim, *Suffering,* 36.
[16]Ibid., 37.
[17]Janzen, "Metaphor," 23.

and the hint is given that land will be available—especially if the Lord owns all the land in the world. This sounds like a strong "sales pitch" to the people by God.

The second movement is the theoretic response of the people to accept the covenant offer. The classical prophets from the eighth century B.C.E. onward and the Deuteronomistic Historians of the seventh century B.C.E. sought to provide theological and metaphorical images to their contemporaries wherein they envisioned this great contractual process occurring in the primordial time of Moses at the foot of Sinai. This lent legitimacy to the divine-human relationship by ascribing antiquity to it. In actuality, the language of international treaties and a contractual relationship in the divine election of Israel was generated by the Deuteronomic Reform movement in the seventh century B.C.E. The prophetic and the Deuteronomic reformers really were calling upon their own generation to respond to the message of Yahweh and accept the covenant relationship. Acceptance, above all, implied exclusive devotion to Yahweh and the maintenance of a just and fair society, as delineated by the laws in the reform code of Deuteronomy 12–26.

The third movement would be a theoretic response of the people or the king, described by the prophetic and Deuteronomic rhetoric under the rubrics of, "If you obey…!" For if they obeyed the law as circumscribed by the covenant obligations, then they would be blessed by God. The language could also be uttered by a prophet speaking to an individual ruler. Jeremiah proclaimed that the king had freedom of choice to obey the stipulations of the covenant, and that accordingly God would respond to either decision. In Jeremiah 22:4–5 we read,

> For if you will indeed obey this word, then through the gates of
> this house shall enter kings who sit on the throne of David, riding
> in chariots and on horses, they, and their servants, and their people.
> But if you will not heed these words, I swear by myself, says the
> LORD, that this house shall become a desolation.

In this passage, Yahweh dramatically becomes self-committed by an oath to respond to the decision of the king. These two short verses in Jeremiah are writ large in the blessings and curses spoken by the people in Deuteronomy 27–28.

Symbolically, Deuteronomy, as a sermon, calls on the audience in Jerusalem around 620 B.C.E. to envision themselves standing at Sinai and accepting this covenant and its laws. In Deuteronomy 27–28 the people are to envision their ancestors of 1200 B.C.E. and themselves in 620 B.C.E. calling down on themselves blessings for keeping the laws and curses for breaking the laws. Presumably, the goal of the theologians was to enable the people to see themselves being blessed for their obedience to the laws. The blessings found in Deuteronomy 28 pertain to matters of state and fertility of the land. If we obey the law, say the people of both ages, Yahweh will defend us from national enemies and grant fertility to the land.

Now a second obligation has been placed theoretically on God. In the contractual relationship God now promises to bless people for their obedience. These blessings are not the abstract spiritual blessings that so often we Christians call for, but rather they are concrete phenomena of political independence and good crop yield. Both these things were difficult to come by in the tenuous and sometimes violent conditions of the ancient Near East. People lived in a subsistence economy wherein the natural elements could push people into starvation ever so quickly, and the political scene was one of extreme violence and grave liability for small nations like Judah and Israel. To obligate Yahweh to provide national protection and adequate food for people with such rhetoric in the seventh century B.C.E. was a bold move by the Deuteronomic reformers or, perhaps we might say, a great leap of faith.

From a process thinker's point of view it must be stressed that Yahweh is described as entering into a concrete processual relationship with a people that involved significant commitment from the divine side. One can clearly see whether Yahweh has kept the divine side of the obligation in these texts. We shall not engage in the discussion of how postexilic Jews had to deal with the perceived failure of some of these promises of God for a righteous and faithful people, especially as expressed in the book of Job, wherein Job symbolizes the suffering postexilic Jews. Rather, we observe how the language of the text commits Yahweh to a binding dynamic relationship in which the Divine must respond to human behavior, whether it be good or bad. The divine actions are not predetermined, and Israel's response will contribute "to the shaping not only of its own future, but to the future of God."[18]

The fourth theoretic movement in the covenant relationship is another potential action of Yahweh. If Israelites are unfaithful, they must be punished, and these punishments are spelled out in Deuteronomy 27. As with the blessings, they are symbolic and cover a host of potential woes that could befall a people, most of which refer to political-national issues and fertility of the land. Like the blessings, they are stereotyped, and some of them may have been drawn from the curses listed in the Assyrian treaties of the previous two centuries. The imagery of the curses, like the blessings, demands an intense personal interaction with the human realm on the part of God.

But there is an additional factor with the curses that is not true for the blessings. Curses brought on the people by sinfulness require Yahweh to reject the divine graciousness that led to the initiation of the covenant relationship. God must punish the people and deny the graciousness that

---

[18]Fretheim, *Suffering*, 47.

we claim is the foundational characteristic of that divine nature. This has to be painful for God, or at least for the theological image of God that is projected by biblical authors. In effect, human action leads to divine self-denial. God must curse the chosen people and undercut the goal of the divine plan. The imagery attached to divine punishment portrays Yahweh of Israel and the God of all time as enmeshed in the human process more dramatically than most other imagery (except for the death of God on the cross). It is an image that we can come to grips with only with process theology.

Fifth, there is the movement of repentance. This is a human response designed to elicit a response from God. Throughout the oracles from the prophets of the preexilic era one hears the plea to repent, to turn (*shuv*) from sin and follow Yahweh. The Hebrew word for repentance evokes the image of turning around and walking in another direction. It is a physical image, and it carries with it the overtones of necessary actions that must follow contrition for sin. In Hebrew, repentance implies that one must do more than feel sorry; appropriate actions must follow. Christians too often equate repentance with sorrow. (Perhaps it is the sorrow of being caught more than the sorrow for what one has done.) The equation is made worse because the New Testament word for repentance is *metanoia,* which means "change of mind." Perchance the nuance of this word has allowed too many Christians to emphasize the sorrow at one's sin without intention to make amends. At any rate, one of the values for retaining the Hebrew Scriptures in the Christian canon is the need to combine the Hebrew word with the Greek in order to produce the fuller meaning of repentance.

For the Deuteronomistic Historians the concept of repentance was extremely important. In their literary presentation of Israel's epic traditions they sometimes created an artificial sequence of history that stressed the need to repent. This is most evident in editorial comments in the book of Judges. Herein biblical historians prefaced the memories and folkloristic accounts of each judge with the statement that the land had peace, but the people sinned by worshiping other gods, and then Yahweh sent a foreign oppressor to punish them. Only after they repented did Yahweh raise up a deliverer to drive out the foreign oppressor. Hence, the historical narratives have been shaped to produce a pattern of grace–sin–punishment–repentance–deliverance.

The important thing to notice is that deliverance or salvation was contingent on human repentance. Once the Deuteronomistic Historians establish this pattern with their heavy-handed editorial comments early in their history, it becomes easier to elicit the image with later narratives. Thus, in 1 Samuel 1–7 the same pattern appears in traditions that have been artificially merged by the Deuteronomistic Historians. The historians bring together the Samuel Idyll of 1 Samuel 1–3 with part of the Ark Narrative in 1 Samuel 4–6 and create a juxtaposition of both of these literary pieces with the beginning of the Deuteronomistic Historians' negative commentary on kingship (found in 1 Sam. 7:1–8:22; 10:17–27; 12:1–25). The resultant picture shows a state of grace with Samuel and Eli at Shiloh (1 Sam. 1), the sins of Eli's sons (1 Sam. 2–3), the loss of the ark (1 Sam. 4–6), the repentance of the people (1 Sam. 7), and Samuel's military victory (1 Sam. 7). The artificial nature of the sequence is evidenced by the fact that Eli's sons are portrayed positively in 1 Samuel 4, but negatively in 1 Samuel 2–3, and Samuel is portrayed with military skills only in 1 Samuel 7. The Deuteronomistic Historians created these tensions to generate the important sequence of grace–sin–punishment–repentance–deliverance. The pattern recurs in subtle fashion throughout the narratives.

Repentance is the prerequisite to deliverance, salvation, or forgiveness. This pattern diverges from the pattern of grace–sin–punishment–forgiveness observed by commentators in the Primeval History of Genesis 2–11. So this pattern is not ubiquitous in the Hebrew Scriptures; it is characteristic of Deuteronomistic historiography. The implication is that people need to repent before they can be saved. In the minds of preexilic Deuteronomic Reformers this meant that Israelites had to repent of previous sins, stop worshiping other gods, maintain justice in their society, and thus keep the covenant obligations. In the later edition of the Deuteronomistic History, which may have emerged during the Babylonian exile,[19] the implication is that repentance in exile may lead to restoration. Of course, when restoration came after 539 B.C.E., the Deuteronomistic History was authenticated as an authoritative text in the minds of the Jews.

From the perspective of process theology repentance is also important. It is a key human endeavor that restores the divine-human relationship previously sundered by sin. In itself, this strongly affirms human freedom in the Hebrew Scriptures by implying that people can initiate action to restore their relationship to God. Granted, we in the Protestant tradition have spoken frequently about the magisterial grace of God, which brings us to God without our free will (such as Luther's *Bondage of the Will*), and some of us have spoken dramatically of predestination. But we must put aside our Christian assumptions and read the Hebrew Scriptures to see what they say. The Hebrew Scriptures lay heavy emphasis on free will and the necessity for people to take responsibility for their actions. Included in this is the need for human beings to repent before God, so as to initiate the reestablishment of the covenant relationship.

From the perspective of process theology the importance of human repentance is that it testifies to the dynamic nature of the divine-human relationship. God has willed to enter into this relationship and can be

---

[19]Frank Cross, *Canaanite Myth and Hebrew Epic* (Cambridge, Mass.: Harvard University Press, 1973), 274–89; and Richard Nelson, *The Double Redaction of the Deuteronomistic History* (Sheffield, U.K.: JSOT, 1983), 13–128.

affected by human response, by repentance. This is the third time in the theoretical movements of the covenant relationship that we may speak of the response of God to human actions and emotions. Human obedience theoretically leads a gracious God to bless people. Human sin tragically leads a gracious God to temporarily deny that grace and punish people. Finally, human repentance leads a gracious God to restore the divine-human relationship. When people change their minds, then God's mind changes to permit restoration of the relationship.[20] In every instance a human activity leads to a possible divine response.

The process theologian observes this not as a limitation on the sovereign power of God, but as the total graciousness of a deity who has entered into a relationship with humanity. When God enters into the process, God becomes contingent. Contingency in the covenant relationship means that God responds to humanity, to their obedience, sinful rebellion, or repentance. The Christian analogue to this divine entrance into the human condition of a legal, contractual, covenant relationship is the incarnation of God in the person of Jesus Christ.

The final movement in the covenantal relationship is divine forgiveness. It is a response of Yahweh to Israel's confession of sin, an action contingent on a human plea for mercy. The contingency of this action is part of the divine graciousness, for the mere existence of a mechanism by which God promises to be gracious is an act of graciousness in itself. But the actual forgiveness is yet a further act of grace on the part of God. For the Deuteronomistic Historians the final deliverance or act of salvation was the dramatic conclusion in their pattern of history and the most evident manifestation of Yahweh in the human arena. In Babylonian exile the implication that such restoration could occur is what gave many Jews the hope to continue in their faith. Hope oracles of Ezekiel and Second Isaiah gave continued expression to these beliefs, and they too may have provided Jews with the necessary hope to maintain their Jewish identity.

Biblical authors spoke of "divine repentance" also. God could be said to repent of the evil that had been done to the people and subsequently forgive and restore them. This image of divine repentance, or the changing mind of God that is powerful, testifies to the intense way Yahweh related to Israel, or how God relates to a people of any age. It declares that God has entered into an intimate relationship with humanity that may be described with a very human emotion. An emotion that implies change in the human mind, even vacillation, reflects human finitude and uncertainty. Yet when applied to Yahweh, it testifies to the relationship that the deity has with the creature. When people repent of their sin and God repents of the intended

---

[20]Bernard Lee, "An 'Other' Trinity," in *Trinity in Process*, ed. Bracken and Suchocki, 205.

punishment, the forthcoming forgiveness frees God from the painful need to deliver that judgment.[21]

Yahweh may repent in a negative or a positive sense. In Genesis 6:6 Yahweh repented that humanity had been created because of the evil they committed. This repentance led to the judgment of the universal flood in the days of Noah. In 1 Samuel 15:35 God repented of having chosen Saul as king. In contrast, the repentance of Yahweh in 2 Kings 20 extended Hezekiah's life, a rather generous response. Either way, to describe Yahweh as repenting was the biblical authors' way of speaking of the intense self-involvement of God with the created order.[22]

Biblical theologians have been wont to refer to such imagery as anthropomorphism and attribute it to a primitive type of thinking in the ancient world. Divine repentance occurs frequently in the Pentateuchal source called the Yahwist. But our contemporary understanding of the tenth- or sixth-century B.C.E. Yahwist tradition (depending on which scholarly opinions you heed) mitigates that caricature, for the Yahwist wrote at a time when ancient Near Eastern thought was sophisticated enough to transcend such so-called crude anthropomorphisms. Clearly, the Yahwist, as well as other biblical traditions that use similar language, chose to craft anthropomorphic and anthropopathic imagery for literary and theological reasons. The Yahwist most likely used such intense and personal language of Yahweh to stress the personal and gracious dimension in the divine nature. If this assessment of the Yahwist's theological style is correct, then we are kin to the Yahwist. In process theology we wish to rediscover the dynamic language of the Bible, though it be from an intellectually distant era, to once more stress the graciousness of God.

From a theological perspective the final dramatic act of salvation or deliverance in the covenant relationship is that which manifests the nature of God in the divine-human relationship most clearly. It is the single act that gives power to the whole covenantal relationship, for it implies that this relationship endures into the future despite threats that once were given. This final act of forgiveness legitimates the other form of covenantal discourse that speaks unconditionally of a eternal covenant, one in which Yahweh will be faithful to people perpetually. From the process theologian's perspective, it is the symbol of God's victory in the interaction with humanity. Divine purpose has prevailed in the contractual relationship called covenant. God has deigned to enter into a relationship with people and has willed to be gracious. Although threatened with human rebellion, the covenant has survived, and the ultimate characteristic of the divine self, love or grace, has been made manifest. From the beginning of the process God lures people into the relationship, hopefully seeking obedience.

---

[21]Raitt, *Theology,* 217.
[22]Ford, "Contigent Trinitarianism," 56.

Even sin and rebellion will not break the process by which God continues to covenant with people, for forgiveness and restoration reestablish the covenant and the continued divine lure.

III

Covenant imagery offers a resource to speak meaningfully with process categories. Implied divine and human responses in the covenant relationship testify to a God deeply self-involved in a relationship with humanity. God moves people forward into a more meaningful relationship with the Divine and each other by a clarion call to obedience to the Law. Process theologians speak of how God offers continual decisions for people to move forward freely toward God. If they choose wrongly, that is, if they choose to sin by being self-destructive or by turning away from the Divine, then a gracious God offers yet another choice or lure into the future. This model of covenant, as we have presented, reflects that process of luring by God. God offers people the chance of obedience, which leads to well-being and a relationship with the Divine. Even when they turn away, the possibility of repentance and divine forgiveness permits the continuation of the lure toward obedience and consequent well-being.

9

Prophecy
Spokespersons for the Divine Process

I

> Two strains seem to run through Hebrew thought; one,
> mild, gentle, gracious, sympathetic, and full of insight:
> Isaiah, Amos, Jesus; the other, harsh, vengeful,
> humourless, treacherous: the very characteristics of the
> oriental despot. Both are in Paul, but the second comes
> out strongly.
>
> *Alfred North Whitehead* [1]

This quote of Whitehead, more than any other of his, indicates his lack of awareness of critical study on the biblical text–especially the portrayal of Amos as gentle and gracious, and his portrayal of Paul. The prophets contain words of judgment and hope often placed in dialectic tension with each other, and to stereotype them so blithely, as Whitehead does, misses this point completely. Had Whitehead a better working knowledge of critical scholarship on the prophets, he would have appreciated the tremendous potential for reconciling his thought with prophetic theology.

The phenomenon of prophecy is extremely significant in the study of the Hebrew Scriptures, and equally important is the reflection on the message of the prophets in the greater exposition of the overall theology of the biblical text. The prophets have been considered to be the most important spokespersons for the classic beliefs expressed in the Hebrew Scriptures, and in particular, they are often credited with bringing

---

[1]Price, *Dialogues*, 137–38.

monotheism and concepts of social justice to the masses in Israel. Their proclamations may have been the most powerful force to cause the emergence of the classic expression of Jewish faith in the Hebrew Bible. If process thought can be used significantly in the explication of the Hebrew Scriptures, it should be able to provide thought-provoking new perspectives by which to view Israel's prophetic tradition.

II

Prophets felt called by God in a powerful and intimate fashion, and they spoke of how they experienced God overwhelmingly. They proclaimed themselves spokespersons for God, and sometimes they described how they stood before Yahweh's throne or in the council of Yahweh. Isaiah, in particular, proclaims that he was drawn up into the throne room of Yahweh during his prophetic call experience in Isaiah 6. Such deep encounters with Yahweh coincide with the ways in which process theology speaks of God. Process thought sees God intimately involved in human experience and naturally assumes that a religious spokesperson, such as a prophet, could speak earnestly of a divine-human encounter. Process thought would not regard such experiences as unusual or even supernatural; rather, they would be the natural form of divine presence in the universe. Process thought accepts the belief that God is present in an intimate way for humanity and especially for those special *homines religiosi* who quest for the mystical experience, and that this manifestation would occur through the medium of human consciousness. Process theology observes the reports of prophetic experiences with Yahweh and views them as classic examples of the Divine experienced by the sensitive and reflective human spirit searching within for the power of the transcendent.

Process thought would view the religious experiences of the prophets as similar to those of other mystics within the Judeo-Christian tradition as well as individuals outside the tradition. Revelation to the prophets would not be considered *sui generis,* as if it were some form of special revelation. Rather, prophets would be seen as having experienced the natural, mystical religious experience available to all sensitive *religiosi* found elsewhere in the world. This conclusion would proceed from the process theologian's assumption concerning the divine presence in the world, a presence immanent and available to all people. So special revelation would be excluded in the consideration of prophetic inspiration.

Similar evaluations have been made of the prophets by previous scholars in the field of biblical studies, most notably Johannes Lindblom, who compared the prophets to medieval mystics in the Christian tradition and to the Siberian shamans.[2] Hence, in the debate concerning the question

---

[2]Johannes Lindblom, *Prophecy in Israel* (Philadelphia: Fortress Press, 1962), 1–104, 299–311.

of continuity or discontinuity between the Hebrew prophets and other religious intermediaries, process thought would be inclined to stress continuity. Scholars influenced by *Heilsgeschichte* theology of a former generation would be inclined to distinguish the experiences and messages of the prophets, especially the classical prophets, from prophetic experiences of contemporaries in the ancient Near East. But recent biblical scholarship is more inclined to observe the continuity of prophetic phenomena in Israel and the ancient world, and process theology reinforces that tendency.

Process thought diverges from the traditional portrayal of the prophetic religious experience in some ways, however. Whereas traditional understandings speak of the divine self-revelation of God that breaks into our universe to manifest the will of God to the chosen prophets, process theology speaks of the already present power of the Divine in the human mind that the prophetic personage is able to discover. Panentheistic process thought asserts that the originating locus of the Divine experienced by the prophets is already in the world; it is not a force that breaks in from the outside. To this end a process thinker would refer to all those passages in the prophetic corpus that speak of encountering the presence of Yahweh in an internal way, springing from the human consciousness, rather than an outside revelatory phenomenon. The process interpreter would seize on the passage wherein Elijah experiences the "still, small voice" on Mount Horeb (1 Kings 19) in contrast to the traditional nature theophanies of the past such as Moses experienced (Ex. 19–24). The process interpreter has a good argument, because it may be that the tradition of Elijah's experience became a classic oral tradition for the prophets to understand and explain their own reception of the "Word of Yahweh" as an inner voice, or a divine disclosure of Yahweh in their consciousness.

III

In the public proclamations of their experiences of the will and word of Yahweh prophets sometimes described their own personal prophetic calls. We see in the prophetic call experiences of prophets such as Isaiah (Isa. 6:1–13), Jeremiah (Jer. 1:4–10), and Ezekiel (Ezek. 1:1–3:15), as well as dramatic personages such as Moses (Ex. 3:1–4:17) and Gideon (Judg. 6:11–24), a fairly well stereotyped formula by which the prophets or heroic personages recall their initial encounter and commission by Yahweh. This formulaic presentation became standard among the prophets, because it seemed to be the best way by which to legitimate themselves before the people. Scholars cannot determine exactly when this formulaic structure fell into place and became part of the standard prophetic vocabulary. There is, however, consensus on the format of the formula.

There is within all these call narratives: (1) a reference to the theophany of God; (2) the commission from God telling the human being that he will be a prophet; (3) a statement by the person of his unworthiness to be a prophet, often involving some reference to a problem with speaking, which is called the prophetic denial; (4) a divine response overturning the reservations or denial by the prophet; and (5) a sign from God affirming the call of the prophet.[3] Perhaps the most important component of the entire format, at least for the prophet when speaking to the audience, is the prophetic denial. For herein the prophet declares that he does not wish to be a prophet, nor does he desire to speak the particular message that he brings, which so often is one of judgment. By saying that it was the inexorable will of Yahweh that forced him to become a prophet and proclaim the often distasteful message, the prophet sought to convince his audience of two things. Initially, they should not blame him for a judgment message, because it really came from Yahweh. In addition, he tried to establish his credibility as a true prophet, for if he did not wish to be a prophet, then the reason he spoke was due to the compulsion of Yahweh.

Obviously, this formulaic prophetic call narrative was a literary fiction, at least in part, for most prophets. Perhaps some experienced such a psychological prophetic call experience because they so intensely believed that this is what should happen, that their mystical religious experience was subsequently interpreted by them in this mode of discourse. Either way, the actual public use of the prophetic call narrative format, however many prophets may have used it in real life, was an attempt to elevate their own credibility and to avoid a negative crowd reaction to a judgment oracle. This implies that they had experienced a mystical encounter that they had to put into their own words. They used the call narrative format for rhetorical reasons.

As the process theologian looks at this language in the biblical text, he or she recognizes it as stereotypical language spoken for particular reasons. On the other hand, he or she realizes that it is the language of the text and should be respected as such. As sacred text it has religious significance and it speaks of the Divine meaningfully. For the process theologian a prophetic call narrative looks more like a lure from God than a demand, even though the prophets seem to portray it in that latter light. But we must recognize that the purpose of the literary form is to convince the audience that the prophet only reluctantly has assumed the prophetic mission. The literary form still speaks of a God who is willing to talk to human beings and tempt them into being prophets, and that sounds more like a divine lure than a threat.

---

[3]Georg Fohrer, "Die Gattung der Berichte über symbolische Handlungen der Propheten," *ZAW* 54 (1952): 101–20; Norman Habel, "The Form and Significance of the Call Narratives," *ZAW* 77 (1965): 297–323; and Klaus Baltzer, "Considerations Regarding the Office and Calling of the Prophet," *HTR* 61 (1968): 567–81.

As the prophetic call narratives speak to us, they testify to an intensely personal experience of God. God is not only felt by the prophet in theophany, which is most likely an experience of the human mind, but this deity engages in dynamic dialogue with the human recipient of the revelation. The human person, male or female, may challenge God. Most significantly, this challenge, this prophetic denial, this human "talk-back" to God is recorded in the sacred text. To that human challenge God responds, and the response is on two levels. Yahweh responds directly to the denial and overturns it with an oral message. For example, to Jeremiah Yahweh says simply, "Do not say, 'I am only a youth,' for to all to whom I send you you shall go, and whatever I command you you shall speak" (Jer. 1:7, author's translation). In addition to this oral response Yahweh gives a sign to the prophet. Isaiah's mouth is touched with a coal, Jeremiah's mouth is touched by the finger of God, Ezekiel has to eat a scroll, and Moses receives several signs (a leprous hand, a stick that turns into a snake, and the promise of a return of the slaves to the mountain).

For the process theologian this bespeaks a God active in the process, a God who can be experienced intimately by a human being. It also testifies to a God who works in a relationship with a prophet by dialoguing in a debate. Finally, the image of God as a lure is very strong in all these passages. To be sure, the prophet portrays the call by Yahweh as something to which one cannot say no. But the prophet did say no for a time, and God was willing to argue with the person, as it were, thus functioning on a very human level.

Perhaps, indeed, a prophet might have been able to say no. In their call narratives the prophets emphasize to the audiences that Yahweh overwhelmed them and sent them forth. But a prophet could say no the first time, and perhaps a prophet could continue to say no. In that case, Yahweh would have to continue to lure the prophet into the mission. Jonah certainly seemed to say no to the call to Nineveh, not only by running off to sea and by having the sailors throw him into the sea, but also by giving a most harsh and cryptic judgment message in Nineveh. God lured Jonah several times, and Jonah refused to take the divine bait, or lure, in those instances. It seems that Yahweh's willingness to debate with a prophet not only once, but on several occasions, is more a testimony to the graciousness of Yahweh than to an inexorable will.

In his study of the prophet Balaam in the book of Numbers George Coats made a cogent argument for a process perspective on the nature of the divine "compulsion" that led Balaam ultimately to bless the Israelites.[4] Contrary to the initial impression, says Coats, Balaam was not driven mechanically by God. Balaam inquired of God several times as to whether

---

[4]Coats, "The Way of Obedience: Traditio-Historical and Hermeneutical Reflections on the Balaam Story," *Semeia* 24 (1982): 53–79.

he should undertake Barak's mission. Each time Balaam was free at the occasion of ritual to decide for obedience to Yahweh or disobedience. Balaam had to seek his own way by inquiring of God at each step of the process.[5] In these texts God seeks response by persuasion, not coercion.

If this be the case, then the process theologian has a good point to make. God wills to enter into dialogue with prophets, and that is a God in process with the world. Furthermore, the process theologians would tell other interpreters of these texts that perhaps they need to readjust their focus on the story line. Rather than stressing the inexorable will of Yahweh in calling prophets, we should rather speak of the willingness of Yahweh to debate with prophets. We should speak not so much of how Yahweh overwhelmed a prophet's arguments, but sense that Yahweh was willing to come back several times with repeated arguments to lure a prophet into assuming the mission. If we add the story of Jonah to the other prophetic call narratives, we might get the impression that Yahweh would not necessarily destroy or punish the prophet were he or she to challenge Yahweh a second time. We have simply assumed that on the basis of the stereotyped formulas of the prophetic call narratives in which the prophets do respond after one challenge and one divine response. The story of Jonah should make us think twice, for it suggests that God would continue to lure the prophet into the mission. This makes the prophetic call appear less of a threat and more of a persuasion or a lure.

IV

As critical scholars evaluate prophetic identity, they stress how the prophets function primarily as proclaimers of public oral messages. Prophets were spokespersons for Yahweh on social and religious issues in ancient Israel. Modern folk tend to superficially use the term *prophet* and mean thereby someone who envisions and predicts the future. Biblical scholars are quick to point out that although the prophets sometimes appeared to function in a visionary mode, their primary role seems to have been that of public preachers speaking to their own generation in order to elicit a moral response. Scholars sometimes like to state that the classical prophets were "forthtellers," not "foretellers." Even though that may be a bit over-generalized, it is a necessary statement to make to a modern audience in order to stress the important social and religious messages that the prophets conveyed to their generation. Process theologians who refer to the prophets often emphasize that the prophets spoke not words of prediction but rather words of divine intent, which implied that the anticipated action need not necessarily transpire.[6]

---

[5]Ibid., 73–74.
[6]Ford, *Lure,* 24, 133.

When we listen to the language of the prophetic oracles, we observe how they projected themselves as public spokespersons of God. They used language taken from the ancient world, especially from the diplomatic discourse of the contemporary Assyrian Empire in the eighth century B.C.E. A prophet would begin an oracle with language taken from diplomatic formulas of messengers who went from royal court to royal court conveying important political information. When the prophet began an oracle with the expression "Thus says the Lord," or "Thus says Yahweh," he used messenger formulas that diplomatic envoys had used for more than a thousand years. Similarly, the expression in the passive mood, "Thus it is said of the Lord," which terminates occasional prophetic oracles, also came from those diplomatic messenger formulas.

In addition, Assyrian messengers often spoke their messages outside the city walls to an entire populace rather than speaking directly and more privately in the court of the king, as had been the custom for many years. They did this to terrify the public with threats of Assyrian conquest and terrorism. Classical prophets may have borrowed this technique of speaking to public crowds in order to cast themselves as formal messengers of Yahweh, delivering oracles from the divine realm. This made their audiences more inclined to take the messages seriously, and it also provided diplomatic immunity for the prophet by suggesting that the words were not those of the prophet but of God. In this way the prophet subtly implied that the crowd ought not kill the messenger because of the message; it came from God, not the prophet.

A process theologian looks favorably on all this imagery. The prophet envisions himself or herself as the present manifestation of Yahweh before the people. In part, this is a necessary theatrical move by the prophet to gain the attention of the audience for the sake of the message. Nonetheless, the process theologian would say that we should take this language seriously as a valuable theological metaphor, for herein we have a symbol of the incarnation of God in the human world and in every human being. For a brief moment, in the symbolic delivery of that oracle, the prophet is God speaking a message of either judgment or hope to the people. This is congruent with the process theologian's view of God as manifest in the human process. We should envision this prophetic proclamation not as one in which God comes from another realm to be revealed through the words of the prophet, who was temporarily seized. Rather, God is already in the human consciousness of the prophet. The prophet, as a sensitive religious personage, is able to become the spokesperson for that divine will in dramatic form, but that divine presence was already inherent in the consciousness of that prophet.

In our biblical introductions we often speak of the characteristics of the classical prophets. We speak of them as called by God, poets, public speakers, and messengers for Yahweh. The process theologian intuitively sees these as theologoumena by which to speak of the dramatic and powerful divine presence in our world through the religious sensitivities of a prophet.

V

As mentioned previously, it is commonplace for people to equate the word *prophet* with a predictor of the future, even though this was not the primary function of the biblical prophets. Yet the prophets did speak of the future conditionally. They predicted not an ironclad future that was inevitably predestined to transpire, as though they were divinators. Rather, they spoke of a future that might come if the people did not repent. They most frequently spoke of a future that would come as a result of decisions made by people in their own free will in the present time to which the prophet spoke. Thus, it is better to say not that the prophets predicted the future, but rather that they anticipated it. They anticipated what might be the results of the decisions made by their contemporaries as Yahweh responded to human decisions in the future.

This way of speaking characterizes the relationship of Yahweh to the people in a more interpersonal and dynamic fashion. In effect, Yahweh responds to the decisions of the people in an organic fashion quite comparable to the way in which process theologians speak of the interaction of God with the world. Classical theism, with its view of an omnipotent deity clearly separate from the universe, would be unconsciously inclined to view the preordained will of God as being spoken by the prophet in a mode that appears like prediction. Process theology enables us to perceive the nuance in the biblical text more effectively. Prophets did not so much predict the future as they anticipated the possible future that might result as God responded to humanity.

In our contemporary textbooks and pedagogy, critical biblical scholars and theologians prefer not to speak of prophets as seers or predictors of the impending events who actually gazed into the future, as though they were divinators using crystal balls to predict the unalterable will of God. Although that might have been the common understanding of many people in the ancient Near East, the classical prophets had begun to depart gradually from that mode of perceiving reality. Prophets anticipated the future in the light of their people's relationship with Yahweh and their understanding of the divine will. They were more like our modern preachers, social critics, political analysts, and even environmentalists, who warn what might happen to people in the light of their present behavior. Prophets gave conditional warning of what might transpire in terms of judgment for unrepentant people who continued to go against the will of Yahweh, or they announced forgiveness, hope, and salvation for a responsive or oppressed people.

When the prophets uttered those oracles, which later became the mainstay of messianic hopes and the oft-quoted passages of Christians who saw them fulfilled in Jesus Christ, the prophets were not gazing into the future. They did not see the little baby in the straw in Bethlehem. Rather, they anticipated that Yahweh, who was faithful, would in some way dramatically deliver the chosen people in a new and unexpected manner in the future. They were anticipating a future hope for people; they were projecting into the future age their own personal, prophetic experience of the living God. They sensed that the ultimate attributes of God were faithfulness, grace, and mercy; that forgiveness and hope would prevail over judgment; and that ultimately God would bring a glorious future for the Israelites. The prophets could not see this, but they expected it, hoped for it, and gave expression to it with powerful symbols.

Christians believe that Jesus somehow fulfilled these symbols, sometimes in most ironic fashion. Basically, prophecy is not prediction, but anticipation. Into this understanding of the prophetic vision, process categories may give biblical theologians richer understandings by which to describe the prophetic trajectories from the original oracular expressions to the final Christ event. Process thought describes Jesus as the fulfillment of the prophecies of the Hebrew Scriptures, because he is the culmination of an evolving trajectory.[7] A traditional static view of Jesus' fulfillment of the prophetic expectations naturally sees the phenomenon as one of prediction and fulfillment, but process thought, with its sense of an evolving process, envisions the fulfillment differently. Jesus is the culmination of a dynamic process, and each stage of the process can be viewed as having value in itself.

The ancient prophets spoke a meaningful word of prophetic discourse to their own age. But as those prophetic words were dynamically apprehended in the human advance, the prophetic words could speak a newly reconfigured message to each subsequent generation. Ultimately, the prophetic words were apprehended by the Christians who gave them an ultimate reconfiguration connected to the Christ event. The prophetic anticipations of Jesus can be envisioned thus with process thought in a way that does justice to our modern critical, scholarly understandings as well as the traditional christological interpretations of the church.

VI

Process thought concurs with contemporary critical biblical scholarship that posits that prophecy is not merely prediction, despite the appearance of announcements concerning future events. Process thought suggests that when a prophet speaks, divine intent has been declared in the human arena, and that divine intent will remain until it has been brought to some form of fruition or fulfillment. The process theological metaphor of divine

---

[7]Cobb, *Pluralistic Age,* 98–99.

persuasion or lure comes to mind when speaking of such prophetic proclamations or the promise-fulfillment motif. The prophetic oracle may be viewed as a form of divine persuasion by which God lures the believing community of Israel, or even modern Christians, into the future toward the fulfillment of the anticipated vision of hope.[8] The final fulfillment of any prophetic vision is dependent on the continued presence of God in the process, who first spoke to the community of faith. God cannot be separated from the word given through a prophet; "God is absorbed into the very life of the prophet."[9] God is believed by the later Christian community of faith as having worked through the messages of the prophets and the subsequent course of history to bring about the fulfillment of promised words once given in vague and veiled fashion. There is a dynamic process that involves the divine and the human dimensions in interaction from the first proclamation of a prophetic anticipation to its final fulfillment, or faith-envisioned fulfillment.[10] For Christians the ultimate trajectory is the totality of all the hopes, expectations, and anticipations that were dynamically and ironically drawn together by ancient Christians as they spoke of Jesus.

Process thought permits us to envision the prophetic tradition in three-dimensional fashion. Biblical scholars tend to view the trajectories of promise and fulfillment from the viewpoint of the prophet in an ancient social-historical context. But process thought combined with critical knowledge makes us retreat and view prophetic trajectories from a fuller theological perspective. The trajectory from prophetic expectation to Jesus Christ for Christians may be seen as an organic continuum, and the focus is on the lure of God, the divine persuasion, which continually works through the human condition to draw the prophetic anticipation to final fulfillment.

There is another way to exemplify this mode of characterizing prophetic oracles. Even within the prophetic corpus there is evidence that the prophets anticipated a conditional future that would transpire in the context of the interrelationship between God and humanity. Biblical scholars point out that recorded prophetic oracles did not always come to the originally expected fulfillment. Oracles spoken conditionally did not necessarily come to fruition, especially if they were judgment oracles and God was merciful, so as to relent from the threatened punishment. In some instances the oracles uttered simply did not come true, as when Ezekiel foretold that Nebuchadrezzar would take the city of Tyre (Ezek. 26:7–14). Because God was viewed by the prophets as free to change the divine intent in response to human behavior, an absolute prediction of the future could not be made. All prophetic "predictions" were conditional; hence, they were really

---

[8]Ford, "Biblical Recital," 206, and "Divine Curse," 81–87.
[9]Fretheim, *Suffering,* 153.
[10]Ford, *Lure,* 24.

anticipations. Prophetic oracles that spoke of the future had to be subject to change or cancellation by God if the appropriate responses were forthcoming from people.

Oracles were conditional because they were provided by a deity who was part of the human process. God was free to change the divine intent by forgiveness, and God also could be thwarted by human lack of response or disobedience. In either case, God would render a new message through the same prophet or prophets in a later generation. The sum total of prophetic oracles reflects the image of a deity who persistently attempts to obtain an appropriate response from people. Eventually, the total course of fulfilled, partially fulfilled, broken, and altered oracles leads to what is perceived by Christians as an ultimate form of fulfillment in the life of Jesus.

Ultimately, the fulfillment of so many prophetic expectations by the Christ event includes many ironic fulfillments that originally referred to something else when first spoken by the Hebrew prophets, but came to be connected with the experiences of Jesus by the early Christian community in symbolic fashion. The images that spoke of a great Jewish kingdom or empire especially came to be equated with a "kingdom not of this world," and the new Jerusalem came to refer to Christian believers and not the actual restored and glorified city.

Oracles that remained unfulfilled or become fulfilled only in a symbolic or ironic sense might appear to challenge our process paradigms at first, but process theologians have suggested categories for this phenomenon. An oracle given in the process of human development at a particular moment may be seen as contingent divine interaction with that moment that has meaning for that culture in a particular time and place, regardless of its ultimate fulfillment. For example, a judgment oracle that brings about human repentance, such as Jonah's harsh message in Nineveh (Jon. 3:4), need not be fulfilled in actuality to achieve its real purpose. Rather, its true intent is really not to be fulfilled, but to bring about the avoidance of the dire predictions by a human response of repentance. The oracle has a purpose beyond its literal prediction of the future. This conforms to the process perception of divine interaction with human history, which feels no obligation to maintain the concept of divine omnipotence.

Traditional biblical theologians who adhere to classical theology and the notion of divine omnipotence must feel a twinge of pain when dealing with unfulfilled oracles originating from an all-knowing deity. Process theology can accept the unfulfilled or only partially fulfilled oracle as contingent on and part of the greater process of God's interaction with the world much more effectively than traditional systematic theology can. Process thought sees each oracle as an expression of the divine intent, or a divine lure and enticement, for a particular moment in the human historical process. The truth or falsity of prophecy is determined by whether it reflects God's intentions for that particular situation, not whether it came true.[11]

VII

The clarion cry of the classical prophets was for justice in their age, especially justice for the poor and oppressed highland Yahwists of Israel and Judah. The classical prophets, and especially Amos, spoke of the conniving tactics used by the rich and powerful in Samaria and Jerusalem to manipulate the economy and thus put the peasant farmers at economic risk. Their goal was to obtain the land of the peasants and make debt slaves out of many of those once free highland peasant farmers. The details of this oppressive process have been outlined elsewhere and need not claim our attention here.[12]

The prophets called for economic justice in society that would protect the peasants and grant a degree of economic equality, and certainly legal equality, for all. Their dramatic appeal for justice has inspired many in the Judeo-Christian tradition over the years, and most especially social reformers in the Western European Christian tradition in the last two centuries. Social encyclicals in the Roman Catholic tradition often have quoted passages from the prophetic corpus. As of late, we have observed a worldwide emergence of liberation theology in Christendom, which taps deeply into the rhetoric of the classical prophets.

The theme of justice emerged in the prophetic tradition when significant economic change affected the entire Syro-Palestinian coast, much of which was set in motion by the emerging Assyrian Empire. Trade flourished, and it brought great wealth to some people in urban centers, who then used it to gain more wealth. Their activities elicited a new, dramatic prophetic response, which we have come to recognize as the classical prophetic movement. These prophets called for exclusive devotion to Yahweh and a just society by boldly stating that ethical behavior in social relationships was more important than sacrifice or cultic activity. Such moral behavior, which conformed to the social expectations of the laws, was the most pleasing thing one could offer to Yahweh. Isaiah declared:

> Bring no more vain offerings;
> incense is an abomination to me…
> Your new moons and your appointed festivals
> my soul hates;
> they have become a burden to me,

---

[11]Ibid., 133.

[12]Gnuse, *You Shall Not Steal: Community and Property in the Biblical Tradition* (Maryknoll, N.Y.: Orbis Books, 1985), 67–85.

> I am weary of bearing them...
> Wash yourselves; make yourselves clean;
> remove the evil of your doings
> from before my eyes;
> cease to do evil,
> learn to do good;
> seek justice,
> rescue the oppressed,
> defend the orphan,
> plead for the widow. (Isa. 1:13–17)

Amos sternly declared:

> Thus says the LORD:
> For three transgressions of Israel,
> and for four, I will not revoke the punishment;
> because they sell the righteous for silver,
> and the needy for a pair of sandals—
> they who trample the head of the poor into the dust of the earth,
> and push the afflicted out of the way. (Am. 2:6–7)

Perhaps Micah most eloquently summarized prophetic beliefs:

> He has told you, O mortal, what is good;
> and what does the LORD require of you
> but to do justice, and to love kindness,
> and to walk humbly with your God? (Mic. 6:8)

Quotes like these could be multiplied endlessly. Needless to say, the prophetic corpus has become an impressive repository of images and rhetoric statements to be used by Jews and Christians to speak of human dignity, basic equality, and justice in society.

Such language is near and dear to the hearts of process theologians. Whitehead was critical of the Hebrew Bible because he was not familiar with many of the texts found therein, especially those that spoke of social reform and human rights. Whitehead stressed in his system the great inter-relatedness of all things. Translated into social and political terms, the implications are that humanity should live in a truly meaningful "social harmony." Charles Hartshorne, John Cobb, and others picked up on this theme of social harmony in process thought and developed it in their theological writings. They are aware of how significant biblical themes converge with process metaphors. Social harmony occurs when justice prevails. The Hebrew prophets have contributed to Western European culture and the Judeo-Christian tradition a vital urge toward the creation of justice and equality in society. Process thought affirms this and sees such social values as one of the significant implications of biblical thought.

Furthermore, a process theologian would invite us to observe the demand of the prophetic call for justice and help for the poor as another classic example of a divine lure into the future. Prophets called people to move forward in their social values toward an ideal society in which the dignity of all would be protected. Although their vision was idealistic, the lure they provided has been effective. The prophetic imperative has inspired social reformers over the ages to engage in social, political, and economic reform. We must admit that the lure proclaimed by the classical prophets more than two thousand years ago functions effectively as an ever-living lure into the future for many Jews and Christians. It is a lure still worth heeding by us today.

VIII

There are found within the prophetic corpus oracles that we would term eschatological. These, too, are worthy of our attention. When the prophets began to speak to the Israelite and Judahite masses from the eighth century B.C.E. onward, they increasingly spoke of the corporate and national future of the people. They warned of future destruction that would come upon them if they did not heed the laws and ethical requirements of Yahweh. These oracles, which spoke conditionally of the future, often in terms of judgment, probably developed what we have come to recognize as their sense of history. Discourse about Yahweh's guidance in the past combined with anticipation of the divine response to human behavior in the future created the image of a temporal or historical sequence in which Yahweh was actively relating to the people of Israel. This gave rise to the imagery that we have termed *Heilsgeschichte*. It is legitimately there, even though we may have stressed its significance too much in the last generation.

Part of this vision of a God who acted in the past to save and who could act in the future to either punish or save was the metaphor of the "Day of the Lord." The motif is a touchstone by which to measure the eschatological imagery of the entire prophetic movement. Perhaps Amos (Am. 1–2) may have been the first to take the once nationalistic motif of divine deliverance of Israel from national enemies and transform it into an image of divine judgment on Israel for disobedience to the Law. Later prophets such as Isaiah could add imagery about a lucky "remnant" that would survive and live in an age of peace, probably referring to the Assyrian wars of Judah from 710–701 B.C.E. and their aftermath. Zephaniah and Jeremiah transformed the day into one of international warfare and ultimate judgment on the nations. Postexilic prophets went full circle and made the motif into a day of national salvation and restoration for oppressed Jews, a day when the Messiah would come and bring the great age of peace and glory for Jews and faithful believers who constituted the "righteous remnant." Finally, for Christians it became the "new age" inaugurated by Jesus, and its images became associated with the second coming of Jesus.

A process theologian would observe this metaphor and declare it to be a superb example of symbolic religious discourse about the primordial body of God. The Day of the Lord motif is the ultimate lure into the future, which calls on people to make a significant decision to heed the words of the prophets and obey the law of Yahweh. Rather than seeing the Day of the Lord exclusively as a threat, we might sense the image of promise. If the Law is obeyed, then the dangerous destruction of the judgmental Day of the Lord can be avoided. In this way the motif can be seen in process categories as an effective divine lure proclaimed by the prophets.

The motif is more than a lure, however. It contains the promise of a significant future unveiling, the unfolding of tremendous potential, which might be either good or bad. The course that this unveiled future will take is dependent on human response in the present, at least to avoid the evil. In the later prophetic movement the great hope that the image portends really relies on the grace of God in bringing a glorious age to fruition. In this latter respect, the Day of the Lord motif really looks more like the promise that the primordial body of God offers to humanity in its totality—the grace of endless potential. The very dramatic and grand nature of the Day of the Lord betokens more than the lure of God into the future; it sounds like the fuller potential of the endless possibilities offered to humanity by the gracious deity. In particular, when Christians take the motif and associate it with the new age of Jesus, they universalize it. They proclaim that the new age is available to all people, and that it is the ultimate symbol of divine grace for the entire universe. At this stage the dramatic metaphor may be equated closely with the overall hope that is offered by the primordial body of God as a whole.

IX

In conclusion, the message of the prophets and the literature of the prophetic corpus may offer a rich mine of ideas for process theologians to develop. In turn, process theologians may provide instructors of introductory courses on biblical literature and theologians of the sacred text some new ways to discuss old topics. The common theme that process thought seeks to integrate into discourse is a note of optimism and a significantly stronger emphasis on the graciousness of God. Judgment oracles are perceived more as a lure for people to lead them to moral behavior, a just society, and the social harmony that is willed by a God.

This is not out of line with past theological assessments of judgment oracles. Commentators have observed that judgment oracles written down in the literary prophetic corpus actually serve as a foil for the hope oracles. Judgment oracles are seen as having been fulfilled in the past, while hope oracles may be fulfilled yet again in the future. The prophetic corpus speaks not of a God of judgment but rather of a God of hope, whose promise to bring a glorious future can be trusted because the word of judgment has been fulfilled already. The judgment oracles serve to make the hope oracles more significant in the minds of the listeners or readers; they become the foil for the hope that is truly the final word of the prophetic literature.

Process theology seeks to reinforce that message today for the readers of the prophetic corpus. Too often people read their Bibles and conclude that the God of the Hebrew Scriptures is a deity of wrath and judgment. They have not read the text in its proper context. The judgment imagery is but a foil for the ontologically prior and more important promise of salvation from God. We speak of hope, grace, or salvation being ontological prior, for the metaphors used by the prophets that God is parent or jealous spouse (Hosea especially) imply that God becomes angry only because God loves the chosen people in the first place. Process theology combined with prophetic theology can dynamically reinforce that primary message of divine love and compassion. Because the prophetic literature is such an important part of the greater Hebrew Scriptures, this is not an inconsequential contribution to the overall biblical theological task.

10

God in the Process of Justice and Law

I

A significant portion of the Hebrew Scriptures is composed of laws. For Jews that portion of the Hebrew Scriptures becomes existentially the most important, for it lays the foundation and guidelines for everday life. For Christians the Pentateuch is narrative material with the laws inserted into historical narratives, but for Jews the Pentateuch is the Law with narratives serving as a literary foil for this venerable Torah, which had its origin with Moses at Sinai. The significant Pentateuchal laws are located in Exodus 20–23, 25–31, 34–40; Leviticus 1–27; sporadically found in Numbers 1–36 among narratives of Israel in the wilderness; and Deuteronomy 5, 12–26. Christians view the laws as abrogated by the new covenant that came with the resurrection of Jesus, and pious Christians who read the Bible from over to cover often skip these sections because they are so boring. Most people read the laws and see a rather thorough, even systematic, set of guidelines for the life and existence of ancient Israel and modern Jews, and it is a common temptation to view these laws as fixed and static.

To perceive these laws as a static and unchanging set of eternal guidelines would be a mistake, however. Critical scholars, both Jewish and Christian alike, recognize that in these chapters we have a legal repository that developed in preexilic Israel and among exilic and postexilic Jews for many centuries. The texts give testimony to a grand legal evolution. The inclusion of several legal codes from a centuries-long process actually testifies to the sacredness of the process that generated the laws as well as the laws themselves. This is evident in the later Talmudic exposition of the Hebrew

141

Scriptures from 100 C.E. to 600 C.E., which articulated further guidelines by which pious Jews might live. We have in the Hebrew Bible a living and dynamic legal tradition, not just a set of fixed laws.

Introductory textbooks generally point out the existence of separate legal codes in this Pentateuchal tradition: (1) The Ten Commandments are found in Exodus 20 and Deuteronomy 5, and they often are attributed to the time of Moses in some simple oral form, which developed over the years to become these two variant written traditions. Exodus 20 in written form is dated to 550 B.C.E. in the Babylonian exile, and Deuteronomy 5 may come from the time of King Josiah of Judah in 620 B.C.E. (2) The Ritual Decalogue, or Dodecalogue, in Exodus 34 may date from the pre-monarchical period (1050 B.C.E.) at the earliest or the early years of the monarchy. (3) The Book of the Covenant in Exodus 21–23 likewise may be dated as early as 1050 B.C.E. or to the time of King Hezekiah in Judah (700 B.C.E.). (4) The Holiness Code in Leviticus 17–26 may be dated as early as the time of Hezekiah also or anywhere down to the time of the Babylonian exile in 550 B.C.E. (5) The Deuteronomic laws in Deuteronomy 12–26 are sometimes projected in simpler form back to 750 B.C.E. in the northern state of Israel, or they are placed in the time of Josiah around 620 B.C.E., or they are attributed to the Babylonian exile. (6) Miscellaneous Priestly laws located in Exodus 25–31 (which are repeated in Exodus 35–40), Leviticus 1–16, 27, and laws throughout Numbers 1–36 are usually situated in the Babylonian exile and the years thereafter until 400 B.C.E. (or the time of Ezra, which is either 458 B.C.E. or 398 B.C.E.).

At this point, process theologians have significant observations to make. The fact that the sacred text incorporates not one legal code from a specific era but a host of laws developing in an oral and written tradition from the time of Moses to the time of Ezra bespeaks process. Jewish piety saw all laws emanating from Moses, even those in the Talmud, because their roots were to be found in that primordial Sinai experience. The legal process of centuries is written down in the biblical text, not a fixed set of laws given at one point in history. For the process theologian this becomes an image of a God active in Israelite and Jewish legal life. Even the testimony of ancient rabbis that the legal tradition of the Talmud still emanated from Moses in their own day can be adduced to reinforce this image. The laws of the Hebrew Bible are a processual historical phenomenon perceived as the manifestation of the divine will.

II

There are other themes connected to the understanding of the Torah that may be available to the process theologian. The process theologian may focus on the theologoumena that the laws are an expression of the divine will. Here again we have the image of a deity deeply involved in the world and interacting with conscious human beings. The Law is the great self-manifestation of God to Israel at Sinai, and for Jews this is the most important self-disclosure of God, in the same way that Christians view the incarnation of Jesus. Torah reveals the deepest aspects of the divine nature, reflecting the ultimate will of God for the chosen people.

The divine will attempts to shape the human identity and lure it into the future by offering possibilities for human actions in the form of legal guidelines. The law encourages people to follow the will of God and therein find life and happiness. The Torah lures people into obedience, a closer relationship with the deity. Biblical and Jewish traditions speak of how obedience to the Torah brings people closer to God and creates a fuller and happier life. As a lure into the future, the Torah could be metaphored as part of the primordial body of God.

Israelites and later Jews saw the Law as a gracious gift of God and an attempt to provide an identity to the people of God. Obedience to the Law shaped the adherents as devotees of God, and it brought them closer to God. In addition, obedience to the laws brought about social harmony by creating peace and justice in society. The concept of social harmony is near and dear to the hearts of process theologians such as Charles Hartshorne. Later rabbis asserted that if the Torah were kept by Jews perfectly, if only for a day, the great messianic age would come. Obedience to the Law could bring not only harmony into society but also the golden messianic age.

Finally, obedience to the laws distinguished Israelites and Jews from other peoples in the world, who did not keep those laws. They then became bonded as a people even more closely. It was this bonding that prompted Priestly editors to finally create the entire corpus of laws in written form as we now have them. Obedience to the laws in the Babylonian exile separated Jews from neighboring Babylonians and led to the creation of a cohesive and distinct Jewish people, which exists even to this very day. Again, the process theologian would characterize this as an intimate form of social harmony and love between people.

Hence, there are a number of aspects available to the process theologian by which to speak of the nature of the Law as a manifestation of the values of process theology. This way of viewing the laws in the Hebrew Scriptures should be stressed in opposition to those who simply view the biblical laws as an oppressive burden placed on people by a tyrannical God. Our Christian perspective too often leads us to see the Law as oppressive, and we miss the truly gracious and liberating aspects of the laws that those pious Israelites and Jews felt. The expositions of process theologians might alleviate these misunderstandings.

III

There is yet another way for process theologians to focus on these legal traditions. In the developing legal process there are instances where a particular law or set of laws is repeated in a new and expanded fashion, often reflecting the reform impulse of a later generation to create a more effective guideline to protect people in more complex economic circumstances. This image of legal development in specific laws testifies to a process that is confessed to be the manifestation of God's will among people. The best examples of such laws are those that address rights for poor and oppressed people. This coincides with process theology's concern with social harmony and the images of divine love for humanity and love of people for one another.

We can observe attempts to create justice for people in the Book of the Covenant (Ex. 20:23–23:19). These laws have been attributed to the pre-monarchic period (1050 B.C.E.) by textbooks in the past, but increasingly they are dated by critical scholars to a later period, such as the social and religious reform of King Hezekiah in Judah around 700 B.C.E.[1] This tendency to date such legal material later probably reflects the awareness of the later dates for monotheism and other aspects of Israelite belief and literature. The Deuteronomic laws (Deut. 12–26) were hypothesized as being eighth century B.C.E. in origin as an oral legal tradition, and their precipitation into writing was associated with Josiah's reform of religious and social practices in Judah after 622 B.C.E. and the discovery of the Book of the Law in the temple. Naturally, it was assumed that Deuteronomy 12–26 was that Book of the Law with some editorial additions provided by the reformers around 620 B.C.E. Now critical scholars assume it is more likely that the vast bulk of the laws arose in the time of Josiah, and perhaps additions continued to be made to the legal corpus throughout the Babylonian exile and beyond. The laws in the book of Leviticus were considered to have precipitated from oral tradition to written form during the exile, with additions made by the Priestly editors. The oldest laws were said to be in a section called the Holiness Code in Levitcus 17–26, which might have been at least two centuries old in oral tradition before their precipitation into written form by 550–400 B.C.E. Some scholars suggest a more well-defined Priestly legal tradition in Leviticus, perhaps in written form as early as the reign of Hezekiah of Judah around 720–700 B.C.E. Others have suggested that the Holiness Code may be later, and more secular, than some of the other Priestly laws, which then are projected back to the time of King Hezekiah instead.[2] Newer critical theories provide a complex debate.

Regardless of these recent debates, I believe that we still can work with a basic sequence of laws that suggests that the laws in the Book of the Covenant are the earliest, the Deuteronomic laws are subsequent, and the Priestly laws in Leviticus are the latest. This acknowledges that some of the

---

[1]Frank Crüsemann, *The Torah,* trans. Allan Mahnke (Minneapolis: Fortress Press, 1996), 109–15.

[2]Israel Knohl, *The Sanctuary of Silence* (Minneapolis: Fortress Press, 1995), 1–230.

laws in Leviticus, either the Holiness Code or the other Priestly laws, may actually be very old. But in their early and oral form these Priestly laws were not public; rather, they were in the possession of an elite group of priests. Their impact on the wider Jewish populace was not truly felt until the exile, and therefore after the time of the other two legal corpora.

Scholars who study the relationship between the laws of these various codes observe an initial breakthrough in human rights with some of the early laws in the Book of the Covenant, but a fuller explication and application of these laws appears in the Deuteronomic legislation, which was produced by a prophetically inspired reform movement in Judah that came to some position of authority under Josiah around 622 B.C.E. A comparison of the two law codes indicates that Deuteronomy 12–26 shares so many parallels with Exodus 20:23–23:19 that it must have been a revised and expanded version of it.[3] The assumptions of those who expanded the laws reflect the impact of prophetic preaching and probably other aspects of Yahwistic, proto-monotheistic reform. One senses that in diverse agenda behind this Deuteronomic revision there is a clear attempt to provide more rights for poor and marginal people. Frequently the reader encounters the refrain in Deuteronomy 12–26 that there is a great moral imperative for Yahweh's chosen people to care for the poor, the widow, the orphan, and the sojourner in the land. Deuteronomy also has a much stronger emphasis on monotheism, for the call for social justice and monotheism appear to be organically connected in the laws and sermons of Deuteronomy as well as the ensuing Deuteronomistic History of Joshua, Judges, Samuel, and Kings.

IV

Deuteronomy's reform-oriented legislation seeks greater protection for the poor and marginal by developing the trajectory established in the old legislation of Exodus. The best examples may be drawn from those laws that address interest on loans, debt slaves, and the status of women. Herein we may observe the trajectory for evolutionary development that is generated in the biblical tradition and continues to blossom in our modern age. There is no fixed set of timeless laws in the Hebrew Scriptures, but rather several law codes from different eras build on each other in regard to certain issues. As we observe the development in these laws, the message is that the literal meanings provided by the laws is not what is binding on modern believers. Rather, the spirit of the laws should inspire us, or more properly stated, the direction in which the legal tradition is evolving should be our source of inspiration. Laws evolve in order to provide justice for all, protection and hope for the poor, and a society that lives with dignity. For

---

[3]Dale Patrick, *Old Testament Law* (Atlanta: John Knox Press, 1985), 97–98, provides a good summary chart for comparison of the law codes.

us to truly keep the spirit of the biblical laws, we must be inspired by the ongoing trajectory of evolution to which the laws testify. To this end, let us consider the development of selected laws that provided protection for the poor and thus attempted to maintain a healthy society.

Interest laws protected middle-class highland peasants and the poor by preventing the rich from devouring the land of those who were economically marginal. Predecessor laws in the ancient Near East likewise sought to protect debtors and those at potential financial risk. We can observe this as early as the third millennium B.C.E. in the legal reforms of Sumerian city-state rulers like Urukagina and Gudea of Lagash, in the later Sumerian law code of Ur-Nammu (or his succesor Shulgi) of Ur III (twentieth century B.C.E.), in the Amorite law code from Eshnunna (nineteenth century B.C.E.), and in the Amorite law code of Hammurabi (eighteenth century B.C.E.). All provided for fixed interest rates to protect debtors, as well as laws to protect widows and orphans of debtors who had died.[4] Mesopotamian rulers also practiced debt release. Most notable are edicts from early second millennium B.C.E. Amorite Babylonian kings called *mishnarum* and *anduraru,* edicts issued at irregular intervals to release debts and slaves.

We might suspect that kings sought to reinvigorate the economies of their societies by releasing large numbers of people from crippling indebtedness. Indeed, that was the result when such wealth was released from the control of temples and returned to the people, or the private sector (as we would say). However, the ancient Near Easterners had little or no sense of economic systems. The ancient kings released debts and debt slaves sporadically because it brought them tremendous popularity in the eyes of their subjects. Maybe even more importantly, this release hurt those potential opponents of the king by eroding their bases of wealth.[5] Even if this was true for Israel, nonetheless, we must respect the idealism of those who first generated the laws, regardless of their motivations. In Israelite legal corpora the laws connected to debt easement are better developed and more regular in implementation than their sporadic ancient Near Eastern counterparts. If regularly enforced in Israel, laws pertaining to debt easement would have benefited the poor and the oppressed much more.

Israelite law built on these previous ancient Near Eastern humanitarian assumptions with comparable laws concerning interest on loans and debt release. But in theory the Israelite legal tradition went further in its attempt

---

[4]Isaac Mendelsohn, *Slavery in the Ancient Near East* (New York: Oxford, 1949), 26; Hillel Gamoran, "The Biblical Law Against Loans on Interest," *JNES* 30 (1971): 127; and R. P. Maloney, "Usury and Restrictions on Interest-Taking in the Ancient Near East," *CBQ* 36 (1974): 1–20.

[5]Marvin Chaney, "Debt Enslavement in Israelite History and Tradition," in *The Bible and the Politics of Exegesis,* ed. David Jobling et al. (Cleveland: Pilgrim Press, 1991), 127–39.

to protect the poor and outlaw interest altogether. Because ancient Near Eastern laws generally were legislated for well-developed economic systems in comparison to Israel's economy, those laws had to legitimate some form of interest for the sake of commercial purposes. Because most Israelites were predominately simple highland villagers functioning in a pastoral, barter economy, the bulk of the loans were given by individuals to others to assist in times of personal economic distress. Israelite communities were founded on a kinship model, and so your neighbor was theoretically seen as part of your extended family. Loans were provided to reduce poverty and to keep the extended family from experiencing economic degradation. Thus, in theory, a loan was an attempt to help a "family member."

With the economic development that came to Israel in the eighth century B.C.E., many individuals saw an opportunity to become wealthy at their neighbor's expense. In this context, the prophetic critics and legal reformers reiterated traditional beliefs about the nature of loans and interest in a new legal fashion. In all eras interest was condemned because it could reduce borrowers and their families to debt slavery. In a pastoral society such as Israel's, the bulk of the debtors were simple peasants, whereas in a more sophisticated economy debtors would have included merchants, who could reap great profit from their economic activity. The possibility of a simple peasant's repaying a loan with interest was significantly less than that of a merchant's.

The earliest prohibition of interest appears in the Book of the Covenant, or the Covenant Code, which has been variously dated to the pre-monarchic period or the late eighth century B.C.E.[6] If the latter date is accepted, the Book of the Covenant may be seen as an attempt to legislate economic reform in the face of social change in the eighth century B.C.E. The law of loans and interest reads in Exodus 22:25 as follows: "If you lend money to my people, to the poor among you, you shall not deal with them as a creditor; you shall not exact interest from them."

Human nature, however, led people to circumvent this law by clever ruses. Scholars have suggested that a loan could be given and a certain amount taken out of the sum before the debtor received it. For repayment the debtor had to give back the full amount to the creditor, including the initial sum or "bite" taken out by the creditor. This "bite," or *neshek*, was not considered interest by the creditor, but it ensured that the debtor paid back the loan with profit for the creditor. The later law in Deuteronomy condemned this form of interest:

> You shall not charge interest on loans to another Israelite, interest [*neshek*] on money, interest [*neshek*] on provisions, interest [*neshek*]

---

[6]Crüsemann, *Torah,* 109–15.

on anything that is lent. On loans to a foreigner you may charge interest, but on loans to another Israelite you may not charge interest, so that the LORD your God may bless you in all your undertakings in the land that you are about to enter and possess. (Deut. 23:19–20)

Interest may be charged to a foreigner (*nokhri*), since the foreigner was probably a merchant who lived by the rules of finance with all the appropriate guidelines for loans and interest.[7]

Loopholes still could be found. If scholarly suggestions are correct, creditors could request an unspecified added amount, called a *tarbith* (or *marbith*), on a loan extended to a debtor. Of course, there is much discussion about whether there is a difference between *neshek* and *tarbith,* and we shall never have the final answer. Nevertheless, if *tarbith* is yet another form of circumventing the laws against interest, then Leviticus attempts to close this loophole.[8] In Levitical legislation against interest both the *neshek* and the *tarbith/marbith* are condemned: "Do not take interest [*neshek*] in advance or otherwise make a profit [*tarbith*] from them, but fear your God; let them live with you. You shall not lend them your money at interest [*neshek*] taken in advance, or provide them food at a profit [*marbith*]" (Lev. 25:36–37).

One can sense a trajectory here through these three texts. Reform-oriented lawgivers legislated on behalf of the poor, and in each generation the laws were expanded to cover new loopholes. Although this reflects the process that many laws go through over the years, we can observe that the spirit behind these three laws is one designed to protect the poor.

V

As we turn to slave laws, we observe an even better example of how the impulse to reform social customs evolved. Whereas the development in the interest laws was designed throughout the process merely to stop the charging of interest, in the slave laws increased rights are given to slaves with each subsequent legal articulation.

Ultimately, slave laws came to their complete fruition as legal formulations only in our modern era with the total abolition of slavery worldwide by the United Nations. We might add that the spirit of that biblical legislation will be fulfilled only when human slavery of all types is abolished. The evolution of the biblical laws on slavery is a classic example

---

[7]Edward Neufeld, "The Prohibitions Against Loans at Interest in Ancient Hebrew Law," *HUCA* 26 (1955): 359–62, 375–410; and Peter Craigie, *The Book of Deuteronomy,* NICOT (Grand Rapids, Mich.: Eerdmans, 1976), 302.

[8]Robert North, *Sociology of the Biblical Jubilee,* AnBib 4 (Rome: PBI, 1954), 177; Neufeld, "Prohibitions," 357–74; Gamoran, "Interest," 129–32; and Samuel Loewenstamm, "Neshek and m/tarbith," *JBL* 88 (1969): 78–80.

of a trajectory that may take centuries to unfold completely. Only in the modern era have the full implications of those laws been unveiled in movements to abolish slavery. Alfred North Whitehead noted this with the biblical laws on slavery when he observed that it took the humanitarian movement of the eighteenth century to bring to fulfillment the old beliefs of Judaism, Christianity, and the ancient Greeks regarding the dignity of all human beings.[9]

In both Israel and the ancient world, slavery, especially debt slavery, and interest were very closely connected, for the failure to repay loans due to high interest rates led many people into debt slavery. This was true throughout the ancient Near East, but particularly in Mesopotamia, where economic stagnation sometimes occurred because so many people fell into debt slavery. Amorite Babylonian kings, including Hammurabi, issued *mishnarum* and *anduraru* proclamations to release debts and debt slaves in order to rejuvenate the economy and alleviate social discord. Biblical legislators may have been inspired by these Mesopotamian traditions in their own attempts at reform, especially with the laws on Sabbath Year in Deuteronomy and Jubilee Year in Leviticus.

Slavery existed in Israel, but compared with the rest of the ancient world, Israel attempted to provide greater protection and more opportunity for release. This was rooted not only in the prophetically inspired reform legislation but also in the popular memory that their ancestors had been slaves in Egypt. The classical prophets excoriated against debt slavery. Amos spoke of how debt slaves became so common that one could purchase a slave for the cost of a pair of sandals (Am. 2:6). Israelites could become slaves in several ways: Children might be sold (Ex. 21:7–11); children might be seized for debts (2 Kings 4:1; Neh. 5:5); and adults could be enslaved for debts involuntarily (1 Sam. 22:2; Am. 2:6; Isa. 50:1) or voluntarily (Ex. 21:5–6; Deut. 15:16–17).

Biblical laws challenged the assumptions of debt slavery, and the Bible appears to be the first document in the ancient world to do this.[10] Slaves had to be treated with respect. They were permitted to share in the family religious life—sabbath (Ex. 20:10; 23:12), sacrificial meals (Deut. 12:12, 18), festivals (Deut. 16:11, 14), and Passover (Ex. 12:44). Provisions were made to release the slave if brutal beating occurred (Ex. 21:20, 26–27) or if young slave girls were not treated properly by becoming wives when they reached adulthood (Ex. 21:7–11). Particularly dramatic is the law that demands the death penalty for whomever kidnaps a person to sell him into slavery (Ex. 21:16; Deut. 24:7). A comparable law commending capital punishment for kidnapping was decreed by the Code of Hammurabi (Law no. 14),[11] but it

---

[9]Whitehead, *Adventure*, 35; and Cobb and Griffin, *Process Theology*, 32–33.

[10]Mendelsohn, *Slavery*, 123; and Severino Croatto, *Exodus* (Maryknoll, N.Y.: Orbis Books, 1981), 36.

[11]Chilperic Edwards, *The Hammurabi Code and Sinaitic Legislation* (Port Washington, N.Y.: Kennikat, 1904), 30.

applied only to the young male children (minors) of free citizens of Babylon. The Israelite law applied to people of all classes. These protections emerged already in Israel's earliest legal traditions, the Book of the Covenant.

In the later legislation of Deuteronomy even more radical guidelines are found. According to Deuteronomy 23:15–16, a slave who escapes from a foreign land is not to be returned to his master, but should be allowed to live in Israel in a place of his choosing. By saying this, Israelites violated established international laws for escaped slave return.[12] No comparable legislation is to be found anywhere in the ancient world. Ancient Near Eastern fugitive slave laws were harsh. Sumerian law would fine a person twenty-five shekels of silver for hiding a fugitive slave; Nuzi laws in the late second millennium B.C.E. also imposed fines; and in Hammurabi's law code the penalty for hiding or helping an escaped slave was death.[13] Slave laws epitomize the biblical assault on the assumptions of the institution of slavery in the ancient Near East.

The most significant legislation to observe is the slave release legislation, which continued to evolve throughout the history of Israelite legal development. Exodus 21:2–6 provides the earliest norms for the release of a debt slave:

> When you buy a male Hebrew slave, he shall serve six years, but in the seventh he shall go out a free person, without debt. If he comes in single, he shall go out single; if he comes in married, then his wife shall go out with him. If his master gives him a wife and she bears him sons or daughters, the wife and her children shall be her master's and he shall go out alone. But if the slave declares, "I love my master, my wife, and my children; I will not go out a free person," then his master shall bring him before God. He shall be brought to the door or the doorpost; and his master shall pierce his ear with an awl; and he shall serve him for life.

The male slave should be released in the seventh year of his service, for the assumption is that no debt is greater than six years of bonded service. There is no provision for female slaves under this guideline. The slave may leave with his family if they came into slavery with him. But if the slave's family came into existence during his servitude, they belonged to the master. One could suggest that a crafty master might match a slave girl with his debt slave in hopes that the resulting wedded couple (with children) would remain permanent slaves for him. Also, the law could be abused by slave masters who simply failed to count the six years properly, and then the debt slave was strangely mired forever in year four or five of his servitude. Perhaps, if the family of the debt slave appealed to the courts,

---

[12]Craigie, *Deuteronomy*, 300–301.
[13]Edwards, *Hammurabi Code*, 30–31.

they might find themselves before a relative of the affluent slave owner or at least a judge easily bribed by the rich and powerful. Thus, manipulative slave masters could create a large number of permanent slaves for themselves.

In the face of such loopholes, later legislation expanded protective legislation for debt slaves. In Deuteronomic laws an institution called the Sabbath Year Release was generated, which combined debt release and guidelines for debt slave emancipation. The Sabbath Year is described in Deuteronomy 15:1–18; selected portions of that text read as follows:

> Every seventh year you shall grant a remission of debts. And this is the manner of the remission: every creditor shall remit the claim that is held against a neighbor, not exacting it of a neighbor who is a member of the community, because the LORD's remission has been proclaimed. Of a foreigner you may exact it, but you must remit your claim on whatever any member of your community owes you…If a member of your community, whether a Hebrew man or a Hebrew woman, is sold to you and works for you six years, in the seventh year you shall set that person free. And when you send a male slave out from you a free person, you shall not send him out empty-handed. Provide liberally out of your flock, your threshing floor, and your wine press, thus giving to him some of the bounty with which the LORD your God has blessed you.

This law attempts to solve several problems that had emerged. The dishonest counting of years of servitude is eliminated by making the year of slave release a universal seventh year. Scholars suggest that the Deuteronomic legislators did this by a clever literary ruse. They connected the law of slave relase to the law of debt release, which clearly was a debt release designed to occur every seven years nationwide. The reference to the six years of debt slavery in verse 12 then becomes a reference to the fixed cycle of six years mentioned in the previous passages concerning debt release.[14] If all slaves were released at the same time, no dishonest master could keep his debt slaves permanently.

The legislation also addresses other issues. Women debt slaves also may leave in the seventh year of debt and slave release. Presumably, these would have been the wives and daughters of householders who fell into deep financial distress. Previously, they simply were not covered by the laws. Furthermore, the slave master is encouraged to provide the newly freed slave with provisions to enable the former slave to begin anew without the fear of falling back immediately into debt and subsequent debt slavery. Hence, Deuteronomic laws expanded debt slave legislation in view of the

---

[14]North, *Jubilee,* 33; Julian Morgenstern, "Sabbatical Year," *IDB* 2:142; and Ben Zion Wacholder, "Sabbatical Year," *IDBSup,* 762–63.

years of economic development and social abuse they had observed after the creation of the Book of the Covenant.

Levitical legislation goes even further in addressing loopholes in debt slave release guidelines. Leviticus combines debt slave release with land restoration, an even more dramatic economic reform. The institution generated by Levitical legislation was called Jubilee Year, the "most vigorous act of hope in the law of Israel."[15] The passages germane to debt slave release are in Leviticus 25:39–55, and the following selected portions are noteworthy:

> If any who are dependent on you become so impoverished that they sell themselves to you, you shall not make them serve as slaves. They shall remain with you as hired or bound laborers. They shall serve with you until the year of the jubilee. Then they and their children with them shall be free from your authority; they shall go back to their own family and return to their ancestral property. For they are my servants, whom I brought out of the land of Egypt; they shall not be sold as slaves are sold. You shall not rule over them with harshness, but shall fear your God.

This passage states that the family, particularly children born while their parent was a debt slave, may come out of servitude with their parent. This new legislative twist ends the practice of matchmaking by masters who tempted their debt slaves into permanent servitude.

The Jubilee Year release described in Leviticus 25:1–55 was designed to occur every forty-nine or fifty years.[16] It was the most thoroughgoing attempt to restore economic equality to society by canceling debts, freeing slaves, and, most importantly, restoring land to the original owners. This law moves beyond the Book of the Covenant and Deuteronomic laws by adding land restoration to the process. If people can be resettled on their original farm lands, then their economic future is much more secure than if they merely received provisions, as Deuteronomic law suggested. Perhaps this legislation betokens the failure of previous slave release laws, for it compromises for a longer period of time—fifty years instead of six.[17] On the other hand, the theoretic inclusion of such drastic reform as land restoration may have required that this happen with less frequency. In return for the longer period of time proposed for Jubilee Year, the Levitical laws sought to make slavery less degrading by improving the treatment received by debt slaves.

---

[15]Walter Brueggemann, *Old Testament Theology,* ed. Patrick Miller (Minneapolis: Fortress Press, 1992), 80.

[16]S. B. Hoenig, "Sabbatical Years and the Year of Jubilee," *JQR* 59 (1969): 222–36; and Robert Gnuse, "Jubilee Legislation in Leviticus," *BTB* 15 (1985): 43–48.

[17]Hinckley Mitchell, *Ethics of the Old Testament* (Chicago: n.p., 1912), 263; and North, *Jubilee,* 135, 153.

In the evolving law codes of Israel one clearly sees an attempt to alleviate the oppression caused by the institution of slavery, especially debt slavery, the most common form of enslavement in the ancient world. Herein is a clear evolutionary trajectory in the legal tradition.

VI

We can observe this trajectory in a different manifestation in the New Testament. In Jesus' teaching all of humanity is embraced by Jesus and told to prepare for the coming kingdom of God in which distinctions such as race, gender, age, class, purity status, and free or slave status would be abolished. In the gospels no specific sayings are recorded concerning slavery. However, in the later writings of the New Testament there are references to slaves and the nature of their relationship to owners. Most notable is the saying in Ephesians 6:5–9:

> Slaves, obey your earthly masters with fear and trembling, in singleness of heart, as you obey Christ; not only while being watched, and in order to please them, but as slaves of Christ, doing the will of God from the heart. Render service with enthusiasm, as to the Lord and not to men and women, knowing that whatever good we do, we will receive the same again from the Lord, whether we are slaves or free. And, masters, do the same to them. Stop threatening them, for you know that both of you have the same Master in heaven, and with him there is no partiality.

One is tempted to say that the New Testament has compromised the reform rhetoric of the Hebrew Scriptures, but this New Testament passage must be placed in context. In the barbaric age of cruelty spawned by the Roman Empire slaves were chattel, the property of their master, who could be killed indiscriminately by their masters. The second half of the imperative (v. 9), addressed to the masters, is revolutionary for that age. To call on masters to be kind to their slaves would have been extremely offensive to the Roman authorities, who demanded oppressive control of slaves, lest a slave uprising destroy all slave owners. We fail to appreciate how liberal such statements were for that age and how dangerous it was for the author of Ephesians to encourage such kindness from masters. It also must be remembered that early Christians lived with the expectation of Jesus' imminent return, so they did not see it necessary to reform society, for this age was passing away.

What we should focus on is that early Christians sought to abolish distinctions between slave and free in their worshiping communities. Even though Christians recognized the institution of slavery, it is remarkable that slaves could become clergy, and in the second century C.E. there is evidence of slaves who even became bishops. One such bishop is said to have excommunicated his master over a particular issue, and the master relented. The early Christian understanding of slavery is best summarized by Paul's statement in the letter to the Galatians (3:28), "There is no longer Jew or Greek, there is no longer slave or free, there is no longer male and female; for all of you are one in Christ Jesus."

Paul is sometimes criticized because in the letter to Philemon he encourages a slave to return to his master, which appears to violate the spirit of the law in Deuteronomy that encourages Jews not to send slaves back to their masters. But Paul's sending Onesimus back to Philemon was different, for both were Christians, and both would live with certain moral guidelines that set them apart from the everyday ways of the world. Pauline churches were composed primarily of the poor (with a few rich benefactors), and many were slaves, or women and children, who were equally powerless groups in the Roman Empire. To encourage these people to oppose the institution of slavery would have gotten them all killed. Paul encouraged the effective abolition of the distinction between slave and free in the church, as the passage in Galatians indicates.

There is, however, an aspect of the letter of Philemon that we often overlook. According to Roman law, escaped slaves had to be punished on their return, usually by whipping. In some parts of the empire a slave who escaped might be put to death as a warning to other slaves. Roman law decreed that whatever punishment a slave merited, it would be visited on the master if the master were remiss in administering the appropriate punishment. In Philemon 16–18 Paul encourages Philemon not to punish Onesimus, but to receive him as Philemon would receive Paul himself. In effect, he is telling Philemon to break Roman law and thus engage in an act of civil disobedience on the slavery issue. We fail to appreciate how radical this advice of Paul's was for its era. One can hardly say that Paul supported the institution of slavery as it was practiced in the Roman Empire. It simply was not part of his "busy agenda" to instigate a well-organized abolitionist movement in the first century C.E. However, had he lived in another era, when Christians were not the weak and oppressed, he might have said things differently.

To appeal to these laws in the Hebrew Scriptures or to Paul in order to justify slavery, merely because the laws and Paul recognize the institution, as was done by some Christians in the nineteenth century, is most incorrect. This interpretation misses the entire spirit of the Hebrew Bible's legislation, which was designed to lessen the impact of this evil institution. Furthermore, such an interpretation overlooks the nature of the evolutionary trajectory in these laws, which seeks with each new age and each new law code to lessen the impact of slavery. The laws in the Hebrew Scriptures are designed to alleviate the suffering of the debt slaves, provide them greater rights, and make their access to freedom more certain. The biblical laws really tell us that slavery ought to be abolished in all forms, physical, financial, or psychological, for such abolition would be the culmination of the trajectory set in motion by those biblical reformers. Ancient Christians had no power to shape the institutions of their age, and if they could see what Christians have done in regard to slavery over the years, they would hang their heads in shame. For they would see Christians with the power to change their societies, and too many of them choosing not to by referring to texts from that bygone age when Christians were powerless to change those forces that beat people into the ground.

VII

Finally, the same observations may be made about laws concerning the rights of women. Here, too, there is a trajectory of evolution not only within the biblical tradition, but one that implicitly continues into our own modern age. In the Book of the Covenant women are provided with rights and dignity by laws that protect female slaves (Ex. 21:7–11, 20, 26–27) and widows (Ex. 22:21–24). Laws in Deuteronomy offer further protection by instituting divorce papers, which enable a divorced woman to remarry legally without the accusation of bigamy or adultery by her previous husband (Deut. 24:1–4), by advancing guidelines to protect women prisoners of war (Deut. 21:10–14), by expanding the laws to protect widows (Deut. 24:17–22), and by creating the Levirite Law, which ensures a widow the support of a future son someday (who also can inherit the family land legally) through the agency of her deceased husband's brother (Deut. 25:5–10).

Some scholars express a manifest disappointment with the biblical legislation because it still partakes of the cultural assumptions of that age wherein women are unfortunately subordinate to men in a patriarchal society. Naomi Stern, for example, points to legislation in Deuteronomy where women could be cruelly executed for lack of virginity (Deut. 22:13–31), and women had to defend themselves from complicity in cases of rape in ways that men were not required to do.[18] To these observations we must respond by saying that we are part of an evolving trajectory created by the biblical literature. We should not glorify the contemporary culture and the mores of the biblical authors; rather, we must observe in what directions they were moving with their legislation. As the biblical legislators sought to improve the rights of poor and oppressed people, especially women, we must continue the same course of reform. The biblical authors lived in a patriarchal age; we should not expect them to have been able to reform their society according to our modern expectations. We must not ossify ourselves in their social-cultural mode of existence or seek to return to it,

---

[18]Naomi Stern, "The Deuteronomic Law Code and the Politics of State," in *The Bible and the Politics of Exegesis,* ed. David Jobling et al. (Cleveland: Pilgrim Press, 1991), 168.

as some bible literalists have advocated. We must move forward, inspired by the spirit of biblical reform. It is at this point that the intellectual presuppositions we use when interpreting the biblical text may be influenced significantly by process theology. Process thought demands that we view the world as an organic, evolving phenomenon and see that in the dynamics of the biblical texts, especially those dealing with law and morality. We are on a trajectory set in motion by the biblical authors; we are faithful to the spirit, not the letter, of the laws.

VIII

Deuteronomy expanded the legislation of the old Book of the Covenant by plugging the loopholes in those old laws, which originated in a much simpler society. These loopholes became problematic for society in Israel and Judah during the economic and political changes of the eighth century B.C.E., when the rapacious greed of the rich and powerful victimized highland peasants. Inspired by the oracles of the eighth- and seventh-century B.C.E. classical prophets, Deuteronomic reformers expanded the older laws. This was an evolutionary development stimulated by the social, political, and economic forces of that age. This legal development unfolded latent ideas found in the earlier laws, but the fuller manifestation of the legal and social implications came only in the crucible of human cultural experience of Israel and served to develop concepts of monotheism and social-economic justice.[19]

Christians believe that Jesus further developed the religious and social teachings of the Hebrew Scriptures in his radical ethic of love and total obedience to God. His message built on the Israelite and Jewish intellectual and religious values; he advanced the "monotheistic revolution," or the evolutionary process. His imperative to go beyond the basic requirements of the law accorded well with the spirit of the classical prophets and the Deuteronomic reformers, and he preached these insights with a profound clarity that would inspire millions of people for thousands of years. He was the one through whom the Jewish prophetic vision transformed Western culture. His radical call to love one's enemies and to embrace a common humanity in its pain and suffering was an evolutionary breakthrough in the human cultural experience.[20] The Sermon on the Mount contains teachings that still await a fuller implementation in human culture, especially the message of love of enemies and nonviolent resistance to evil. For centuries the vast majority of Christians felt that this imperative could be

---

[19]Christopher Wright, *God's People in God's Land* (Grand Rapids, Mich.: Eerdmans, 1990), xiv–xx, 1–265; and Albertz, *Israelite Religion*, 1:1–242.

[20]Cobb, *Pluralistic Age*, 98; Walter Brueggemann, *Prophetic Imagination* (Philadelphia: Fortress Press, 1978), 80–108; and Theissen, *Biblical Faith*, 82–128.

fulfilled only on an individual level, that it was not practical as a guideline for relations between peoples. Then Mahatma Gandhi and Martin Luther King, Jr., applied the principle of nonviolent resistance on a large social scale, and the results were independence for colonial India and greater rights for minorities in the United States. This was accomplished without revolution and bloodshed, which so often come with great social change. Christian intellectuals who considered the sayings of Jesus too ideal for the "real world" were put to shame by these accomplishments of the twentieth century.

Christians have proclaimed the message of Jesus, Paul, and the other New Testament authors for centuries, stressing the spiritual or psychological dimension of that message. While forgiveness and salvation have been preached with varying degrees of clarity, too often the church has forgotten the social dimension of the sayings of Jesus. In great measure this has resulted from the fact that for many centuries the church was the political, as well as religious, custodian of barbarian Europe. These custodial responsibilities created a mentality of order and stability rather than reform and egalitarianism in the minds of Christian leaders. Occasionally, Christian religious orders and dissident movements proclaimed the spirit of reform, justice, and equality. But not until the modern era, after the Enlightenment, did the church became disenfranchised from political power, Catholic and Protestant alike, and realize the fuller message of the Christian gospel and the social responsibilities it entailed. Only then did we see the proclamation of a Christian social message in the theology and preaching of the church. Attempts to aid the poor, the abolition of slavery, well-intentioned though misdirected efforts for temperance, campaigns for racial equality, the drive for women's rights, the call to end world hunger and eradicate certain diseases around the world, and many other movements have been inspired by Judeo-Christian teachings. It was centuries after Jesus' earthly ministry before such campaigns arose, yet Jesus directed his first listeners to undertake these activities. It takes time for the fuller implications of an intellectual breakthrough to become fully manifest, because the social-historical conditions have to be right for people to undertake such actions. But such is the nature of the human process that is lured onward by a gracious God.

In conclusion, a study of the legal materials in the Hebrew Scriptures leads the reader to see an evolving trajectory from the Hebrew Bible through the New Testament and Western society up until our own age. Our inadequate perception of this trajectory in years past, and our tendency to ossify the social values of the past with no desire for reform, may be overcome by our conscious perception of the biblical text as a dynamic corpus of literature that inspires an ongoing process of social and religious reform. This may be actualized in an intense and dynamic fashion if we accept the intellectual assumptions of our own age, including process theology.

11

Heilsgeschichte
God in the Process of Human Life

I

If you read the Bible from the book of Genesis onward, you cannot avoid the perception of how the first fifteen books, Genesis through Nehemiah, provide a unified historical narrative from the beginning of time down to the late fifth century B.C.E. If you subsequently read the prophetic books, the oracles found within often date to events and periods of time recalled in the earlier narratives. This leads you to overlook the ahistorical nature of the poetic materials (Job, Psalms, Proverbs, Ecclesiastes, and Song of Solomon) between the narratives and the prophets. The Hebrew Scriptures then appear as a great religious history. In the New Testament, the Gospels record the life and teachings of Jesus and do not seem to constitute a history. But the book of Acts recalls the events of Christian missionary expansion, and you unconsciously connect the stories in the Gospels and Acts together as a short history of the ancient church. Paul's letters, like the prophetic corpus, can be correlated with the narratives of Acts. With the momentum provided by the Hebrew Bible, you are inclined to see the New Testament also as a sacred history. The two testaments together speak of God's interactions with people throughout history. As you ignored the poetic sections in the Hebrew Scriptures, you ignore the General Epistles and Johannine letters in the New Testament. Finally, Revelation provides the capstone by speaking of the eschatological end of time. Hence, you have a sacred history.

This view of the biblical text not only has provided a significant approach to Bible study in the popular and educational literature of

159

Christians, it also has exercised the minds of serious biblical theologians.[1] The biblical testimony to the revelation of God and religious experiences of human beings over many generations has been called a *Heilsgeschichte* tradition, or a history of salvation, by biblical theologians in this century. Theologians spoke not only of a God active in the historical arena, but they also sought to develop the theological and philosophical implications of this insight. They saw the divine activity in the exodus event and the resurrection of Jesus to be paradigm events around which to organize all biblical literature. They not only spoke of God's being present in the history of Israel and the ancient church, but in the later years of this theological movement theologians even began to talk of history itself as revelation.

These biblical images of *Heilsgeschichte* were used by Christian theologians from 1945 to 1970 in what has been called the "biblical theology movement," a movement influenced greatly by early twentieth-century European neoorthodoxy, which also reacted negatively to nineteenth-century idealistic liberal theology and simple evolutionary paradigms.[2] Biblical theologians in this movement relished the rhetorical contrast of monotheistic and ethical Israelite religion to the fertility religions of Canaan and the rest of the ancient Near East, and they emphasized the radical ideological and social break undertaken by the Israelites. In the last generation, however, the *Heilsgeschichte* model has undergone a significant demise, and with it the biblical theology movement.[3] Elsewhere, I have attempted to characterize this movement, the critique it received, and some possible ways in which insights from the movement may be revitalized in the light of our contemporary critical understandings.[4]

Furthermore, since 1965 scholars in the Hebrew Scriptures have sensed that our lack of attention to the theology of legal, cultic, and didactic biblical texts has left our biblical theology too narrow. This was one of the reasons for the increasing dissatisfaction with the traditional biblical theologies, especially those built on a *Heilsgeschichte* model, such as the work of Gerhard von Rad.[5] Von Rad's theology drew from the Pentateuch and the Prophets, and when he finally wrote a book on the wisdom literature, it was not part

[1]Wright, *God Who Acts,* 11; and Wright and Reginald Fuller, *The Book of the Acts of God* (Garden City, N.Y.: Doubleday, 1957), 15–360.

[2]Reventlow, "Die Eigenart des Jahweglaubens als geschichtliches und theologisches Problem," *KD* 20 (1974): 199–200; and F. L. Hossfeld, "Einheit und Einzigkeit Gottes im frühen Jahwismus," in *Im Gespräch mit dem dreieinen Gott,* ed. Michael Böhnke and Hanspeter Heinz (Düsseldorf: Patmos, 1985), 57.

[3]Bertil Albrektson, *History and the Gods* (Lund: Gleerup, 1967), 7–122; Brevard Childs, *Biblical Theology in Crisis* (Philadelphia: Westminster Press, 1970), 13–87; and H. W. F. Saggs, *The Encounter with the Divine in Mesopotamia and Israel* (London: Athlone, 1978), 64–92.

[4]Robert Gnuse, *Heilsgeschichte as a Model for Biblical Theology,* College Theology Society Studies in Religion 4 (Lanham: UPA, 1989), 1–151, and *No Other Gods,* 23–128, 229–73.

[5]Von Rad, *Theology,* 2 vols., passim.

of his two biblical theology volumes; it was a separate work, because he could not integrate it into his theological system.[6]

There were also other reasons why the critics assailed the *Heilsgeschichte* theology, or the biblical theology movement. I do not wish to go into that rather complex debate at this time, but rather I seek to address the relationship of *Heilsgeschichte* concepts, including more nuanced contemporary views, to process thought.

II

Several theologians maintain that such perceptual categories of God active in social or historical events may be understood better by process modes of thought rather than by static, theological categories.[7] This would be a logical assumption, since process philosophy is very interested in explaining the temporal flow and how development occurs. Such a system, concerned with time and development, would relate naturally to biblical theological themes that stress the ongoing relationship of God with a chosen people throughout the vicissitudes of history, especially when divine actions call forth a human response and the Divine subsequently reacts to those human responses.[8] Process thought would correlate well with biblical theology, which assumes a development of religious thought in the divine-human relationship.

Gerald Janzen pointed out a significant insight in regard to the so-called historical perspective of the Bible. The concern of the text may not be so much with history as it is with people in the historical arena. The myths of surrounding nations emphasize the lives of the gods and the relationship of the gods with the greater cosmos. Although we do not wish to engage in the stark contrast of biblical literature with ancient Near Eastern literature that was typical of scholarship in a previous generation, there is nonetheless a difference in the biblical literature with its greater emphasis on people and the social arena in which they functioned as opposed to many of the texts from the ancient Near East. Janzen maintained that the perception we should have of the biblical literature is not that it so strongly emphasizes the historical dimension, but rather that it emphasizes the human dimension, and in particular the relationship between humanity and God. Yahweh's interactions with other theoretic gods in the divine realm becomes irrelevant compared with the interactions with humanity. Janzen notes, "Humankind has been drawn into the myth and now shares the stage with divinity. The sphere of power is no longer...on the summit of the cosmic mountain or at the sources of the double deep: it is that public and present

---

[6]Gerhard von Rad, *Wisdom in Israel,* trans. James Martin (Nashville: Abingdon Press, 1972), passim.

[7]Janzen, "Process Perspective," 496–97.

[8]Ford, "Biblical Recital," 208.

world which humans inhabit."[9] Classical theists might read the biblical text and say that the narratives function as a sacred history, for history is an abstract category worthy of philosophical reflection. Process theists read the same texts and say that the narratives speak of an ongoing relationship between God and people, because they see things from the perspective of interpersonal relationships and dynamic process. If we sense that by *Heilsgeschichte* we really mean the relationship over time between God and people, we may correct many of the intellectual weaknesses for which *Heilsgeschichte* theology was criticized.

Process thought can be integrated with biblical themes of history, development, and a God who relates to people in a changing role over many years. This is particularly true of Pentateuchal traditions, which are designed to proclaim the great acts of Yahweh for Israel in lives of the patriarchs, the exodus, the Sinai revelation, the wandering in the wilderness, and the entrance into the arable land. This is a theological tradition that functions as a recital to the community of faith of God's great acts, and it "concentrates not on what God necessarily is but on what he has contingently done."[10] The Pentateuch, Prophets, Gospels, and the New Testament book of Acts are those special portions of the biblical text that testify to the actions of God in the lives of people, both as individuals and as corporate entities, be they ancient Israel or the Christian church. Discourse about divine interaction in the social realm or history is something that comes more naturally to process categories of thought than to classical theism.[11]

As mentioned at the outset of this chapter, we now acknowledge that *Heilsgeschichte* categories do not provide an overarching paradigm by which to apprehend the entire canon; nonetheless, the imagery of God active in history is still appropriate as a characterization for large portions of the text. Although modern scholars have critiqued aspects of the *Heilsgeschichte* paradigm, the fact remains that the story line in much of the Bible presents itself as a great historical drama. At this point the language of process thought can become useful in the discourse of biblical theology. The God of the Hebrew Bible is portrayed very organismically in the texts, often in many diverse ways. God is not viewed as timeless, but rather God has entered into the historical and social experience of people.[12]

As process thought is introduced into the task of biblical theology, it must be used to craft paradigms that include, but also go beyond, the *Heilsgeschichte* imagery. The Bible speaks of God as active not only in the social and historical arena but also in nature, the cult, human reason, and

---

[9]Janzen, "Metaphor," 23.
[10]Ford, *Lure,* 27.
[11]John Macquarrie, *Thinking about God* (New York: Harper and Row, 1975), 113.
[12]Fretheim, *Suffering,* 35, 43–44.

other aspects of physical existence. Biblical theology must not limit itself to *Heilsgeschichte,* and biblical scholars are well aware of this. This has led many in the last generation to speak disparagingly of *Heilsgeschichte.* Even process theologian Lewis Ford speaks of "the ghetto of sacred history" in biblical theology.[13] Cobb and Griffin speak of how process thought can overcome the overly unilinear thinking of *Heilsgeschichte* theology.[14] These statements might be a little bold, since it is possible to retain *Heilsgeschichte* themes in a modified form, as I have formerly proposed.[15] We must strive for a biblical theology that includes *Heilsgeschichte* themes and yet encompasses the other aspects of biblical thought. Process thought may provide the helpful insights for a new biblical theology, for by its very nature process thought integrates the entire spectrum of human experience in the historical, natural, cultic, and intellectual realms as arenas in which the Divine has become panentheistically involved.[16]

Used in the creation of biblical theology, process thought will produce a healthy synthesis. Process thought complements the historical recital by speaking of a God capable of relationships, interaction, change, and growth in relationship to human beings. It is this dynamic portrayal of God that *Heilsgeschichte* theologians were most interested in affirming in the first place. They, too, stood in critique over against the static portrayals of God and salvation that were found in traditional, classic Protestant thought, and they sought to affirm that God is portrayed in a very personal and dramatic fashion in the Bible. The Hebrew Bible concentrates not on what God is but rather on what God does, and they saw the historical sphere as the arena in which God was most powerfully, though not exclusively, involved in human affairs.[17] The original biblical authors, modern biblical scholars, and process theologians all wish to speak of God as personally involved with the created order, especially with human beings. The paradigms and language of all three can be brought together in a profitable intellectual synthesis.

Classical theology placed the abstract God of systematic theology in tension with the deity who became incarnate in the life of Israel or the person of Jesus Christ. In actuality, the concept of incarnation may be found in implicit form already in the Hebrew Scriptures with the frequent discourse of God's very physical-like presence among people in the early epic traditions. Herein we find anthropomorphic and anthropopathic portrayals of God, which characterize God in a dynamic fashion even for the modern reader.[18]

---

[13]Ford, *Lure,* 27.
[14]Cobb and Griffin, *Process Theology,* 152.
[15]Gnuse, *No Other Gods,* 229–73.
[16]Janzen, "Process Perspective," 501; and Ford, *Lure,* ix.
[17]Ford, *Lure,* 25–27.
[18]Fretheim, *Suffering,* 23, 35.

Traditionally, in our theologies and our confirmation manuals, we spoke of the tension between divine transcendence and divine immanence, placing passages that spoke of intimate divine presence in a dialectic with those that described the majestic imagery of God the creator. However, in biblical thought that tension may not necessarily be there, for the biblical authors and audience perceived the various portrayals of God as simply affirmations about the wide range of divine activity in the world. Likewise, in process philosophy and theology God becomes involved with the created world more dynamically. As in the biblical texts, process thought does not distinguish between the transcendent or the immanent actions of God, but rather views them holistically as a unified testimony to the presence of God in the universe. This may solve some of the theological dilemmas created for the modern mind by the reading of the Bible. Once the tension in classical theology between the transcendent and the immanent is re-placed by a process metaphor of interaction, the anthropomorphic and anthropopathic descriptions in the Bible are not the embarrassing expressions of a primitive mind but a symbolic way of describing God's natural self-involvement with the world.

Process thought is a modern worldview that enables us to approach the biblical texts in a mode more sympathetic to their original worldview, for both process thought and the worldview of the biblical age are dynamic in their perceptions of God and the divine-human relationship. Lewis Ford notes that process theology complements historical recital by describing the "necessary conditions," a dynamic process view of God, for biblical theologians. In return, the biblical texts complement process theology by giving "concrete historical contours," that is, examples of the divine self-involvement in the human experience.[19] To speak of God as active in human history implies that God can enter into a process of interrelationship involving contingency and change not only for humanity but also for God.[20] *Heilsgeschichte* theological categories, by their very nature, require the assumptions of process thought to undergird their discourse.

In both testaments the contributions of process thought may be significant. In the Hebrew Scriptures God is portrayed as being connected to the human social level, so that "God does change in the light of what happens in the interaction between God and the world."[21] By this we mean that the biblical text portrays God as having an emotional relationship to people. By being in the temporal flow, God has undertaken kenosis, or a gracious self-emptying.[22] This, of course, shares much in common with the New Testament, wherein God is portrayed as undertaking the ultimate kenosis by becoming human and dying.

---

[19]Janzen, "Process Perspective," 502; and Ford, *Lure,* 27.
[20]Fretheim, *Suffering,* 23.
[21]Ibid., 35.
[22]Ibid., 58.

III

Heilsgeschichte paradigms and process thought are both organic and open-ended; they are not neatly organized, systematic, closed theological systems. Process thought does not ignore or diminish the importance of the great symbols of salvation history in the Hebrew Scriptures, such as land, Messiah, and Day of the Lord, and melt them into abstract, systematic, universal truths. It lets them stand with all their historical and cultural particularity, which can be crude sometimes, as the modes by which God is revealed in the human process. Therefore, biblical theologians, especially those in Hebrew Scriptures, resonate intellectually with the themes and categories of process thought, because process thought respects the original social-historical context of the biblical symbols without forcing them to become something else in a systematic theology.

There are several other perspectives in the biblical text that resonate well with process theism. Norman Pittenger notes that the metaphors and myths in the Hebrew Bible present an image of God similar to what process thought seeks to attain. Both systems of thought are open-ended and can acknowledge the scientific theory of evolution and the emergence of new significant possibilities and symbols to inspire humanity in the ultimate quest for the Divine. Additionally, Hebrew Scriptures give testimony to a vision of God that appears to develop over the years in the divine-human relationship. This is an evolutionary process most appropriately theologized by us with the categories of process thought.[23] One has to applaud Pittenger on this evaluation he made in 1977, for he anticipated subsequent Hebrew Bible scholarship that spoke of the more gradual and later development of monotheism in Israel and postexilic Judaism.

The insight that new or novel theological perceptions may arise leads to another connection between biblical thought and process theology: the acceptance and affirmation of diversity. In the theological model of salvation history it is natural for a concept to emerge that may contradict or at least stand in tension with a previous religious belief; such is the nature of progressive revelation implied by a salvation history model. Such phenomena are observed by biblical scholars as they study the various theological trajectories in divergent traditions throughout the biblical text. Such tensions or contradictions naturally pose difficulties for classical systematic theologians. Biblical theologians seek to impress on systematic theologians that this developmental process or trajectory is an important part of the biblical text. This, however, causes tension between biblical and systematic theologians, especially in the more conservative denominations of Christendom. But this conflict with biblical theologians

---

[23]Pittenger, *Process,* 20–22, and *Triunity,* 23–25.

does not exist for the process theologian for whom divergent biblical traditions are natural. For the process theologian such tensions merely reflect different stages in the ongoing process of divine involvement and interaction with the human condition with all its different social-historical settings.

Scripture contains many different testimonies of God and human understandings of the divine will arising over a thousand-year period. Process thought can accept such tensions due to what one author calls the "lack of concern for temporal consistency" in diverse biblical traditions.[24] Process thought affirms diverse pictures of God and religious responses of human beings, because they reflect different stages in an intellectual and religious evolution. Furthermore, these divergent tensions permit and promote growth by their accumulation and interaction in the greater faith community and their ultimate transcription in the Bible. Different viewpoints from different eras and stages of religious development add up to a multi-faceted perspective of the divine-human reality.[25]

Hence, process thought may affirm a presentation of biblical thought that speaks of a personal God active in the lives of human beings, a salvation history throughout the ages, and a traditio-historical development of religious beliefs. This is possible only because process thought is comfortable with the notion of religious development testified to in the biblical text.

IV

Because of the contemporary critique of the *Heilsgeschichte* paradigm, many biblical theologians seek to avoid this paradigm and find others to replace it. That may be an overreaction. Much of the biblical text indeed is a "salvation history," but not all of it fits into that model, as previous advocates of *Heilsgeschichte* theology assumed. Biblical theologians need not surrender the concept; rather, they need to place it in tension with the other theological perspectives found in the biblical text. Such perspectives include the imagery of the Psalms and the wisdom literature, which bespeak a deity present in the order of creation as well as the social and historical arena. Literature in the New Testament, especially the General Epistles, add to this the importance of moral behavior in the social order as a human response to the great acts of God. *Heilsgeschichte* themes need to stand together with imagery that describes the presence of God in creation and human insight, such as wisdom literature. Biblical theologians need to explicate how the text speaks of the divine presence not only in the social affairs of humanity but also in natural and human intellectual phenomena.

---

[24]Ford, "Contingent Trinitarianism," 62.
[25]Ford, *Lure,* 129–30.

Process thought may provide categories for a broader form of theologizing that encompasses the portrayal of a God active in all these arenas. Process thought can accept the appearance of the Divine in divergent phenomena, for it affirms that the creative advance of the Divine moves throughout our universe in manifold ways. A biblical theologian at least somewhat influenced by the categories of process thought would be intuitively more sensitive to explicating themes in psalmic and wisdom thought in conjunction with traditional *Heilsgeschichte* categories.

The emphasis on God's self-revelation in the social or historical experience of humanity appears strongest in the Pentateuch, the Prophets, the Gospels, and the New Testament book of Acts, for in these works the biblical authors endeavor to communicate the feeling of God's guiding presence in the lives of individuals, and most importantly, in believing communities in a corporate way. In Psalms and wisdom literature we sense the human affirmation of divine presence in the created order and the human intellectual quest. When we read the Pauline epistles and the General Epistles, we hear discussion of how God is experienced in an existential mode by individuals and the church as a whole. The unified testimony of the biblical text is to the presence of God in manifold ways, and often that presence is in an opaque or elusive fashion, apprehended only by the faith of individuals and believing communities.

Biblical theology must summarize the biblical text in a way that captures the diverse imagery connected to God's self-manifestation in the world. Perhaps the best theological articulation of this totality of revelation has been provided already by Samuel Terrien's biblical theology.[26] But the influence of process thought among biblical theologians in general may facilitate other theological evaluations in a mode similar to what Terrien has done. If biblical and systematic theologians proclaim the diversity of the various theological traditions in the Bible and recognize that such diversity speaks in many ways of the same truths, they may recognize equally that this diversity results from the historical flow. Different religious symbols and expressions flow from different eras and social settings, but the presence of God panentheistically involved in the human experience renders them all valid. We can recognize the validity of these diverse expressions by mentally acknowledging that they emerge from an evolutionary process. The real intellectual breakthrough is to recognize that there is an evolutionary process capable of producing diverse truth, and process thought may assist in that reflective insight.

The biblical text proclaims the self-manifestation of the Divine in divergent fashions, and the implication, of course, is that the Divine may be apprehended in faith in similar modes even today. Process thought may be used as a theological idiom to capture the grandeur and significance of

---

[26]Terrien, *Elusive Presence,* 1–483.

this diversity. Process thought does more than simply tolerate divergent theological trajectories; it affirms that diversity is an extremely important ingredient in a fuller understanding of the divine self-manifestation. It would proclaim that, in the unfolding of the divine-human relationship, God chooses different modes of self-disclosure in the complexity of the human experience to speak to different people at different times with significant messages to actualize the divine-human relationship. Process thought accepts the radical diversity of this divine self-disclosure. It can lead Christians to accept the diversity of piety among themselves in different denominations and even within the various Christian denominations.

If we sense that within the Bible there are diverse truths originating from different social and historical settings in a great religious evolutionary process, we may recognize that out of the biblical tradition have grown two great and valid religions, Christianity and Rabbinic Judaism. We are sister religions, planted in the same soil, and we have grown in two different but equally valid directions. Paul, in Romans 11:11, 26–32, implies that, despite their rejection of Jesus, the Jews remain God's people and heirs of the old covenant. Christians, too often, have ignored these words of Paul, thinking that if Christianity is true, then all other religions are false. Process thought can lead us to understand the dynamics of valid diversity of belief produced by the historical flow.[27] This, in turn, can lead us to see there are two great covenanted peoples of God with a valid message and relationship to the divine presence in their midst. There are two trunks in the great tree of God's people, each valid under the terms of its own covenantal relationship. Perhaps we might go even further and admit to the possibility of the same divine presence in the other great religions of the world. Process thought, with its emphasis on the dynamic of the temporal flow and the universal presence of the Divine, can lead us to this understanding.

V

There is also another way to view this discussion of the nature of biblical revelation. In the past two or three generations biblical theologians have moved from talking about divine revelation in history to divine self-disclosure in manifold categories of human experience. Process thought appears to be flexible in changing with new directions in biblical scholarship, for it can accept the notion of diverse categories of divine revelation. That is a significant observation to make, since it implies that process thought may not become dated with the changing directions of biblical scholarship. That is more than may be said for early twentieth-century neoorthodoxy, which was most comfortable with discourse about a God active in human

---

[27]Ford, "Contingent Trinitarianism," 62.

history and tended to resonate with the post-World War II *Heilsgeschichte* theology in the English-speaking world.

It should be mentioned also that process thinkers initially expressed some discomfort with the old biblical theology movement and its strong emphasis on *Heilsgeschichte* theology. This discomfort arose because those older biblical theologians implied that the historical arena was the chief or only dimension for divine self-disclosure. With the decline of the *Heilsgeschichte*, or biblical theology movement, some process thinkers rejoice, for now a new philosophical theology may be permitted to integrate more fully with biblical theology. Biblical texts may be viewed from a wider conceptuality with new process categories of thought that place biblical theology in a wider sweep of history, nature, and human experience.[28]

Biblical theologians grounded in process theological assumptions now may say that God is not one who dramatically intervenes only in history as the old neoorthodox model of the biblical theology movement portrayed it. Rather, God is in the total universal process, thoroughly and completely in every facet of history, nature, and human consciousness. God draws, entices, persuades, and lures the world and the entire evolutionary process onward toward a yet unrealized goal. This coincides well with themes in the Hebrew Scriptures and particularly with the eschatological images of the later prophets. Such was the exciting imagery in the writings of Teilhard de Chardin, a theologian whose ideas were related closely to process thought; his theological vision, which combined religion and evolutionary theory, is still very relevant.[29]

The biblical tradition testifies to people who are drawn forward by the interaction of the divine lure and human free will. Lewis Ford characterized the biblical tradition nicely:

> God has no fixed, inalterable plan here, but everywhere seeks inexorably to urge creation beyond itself. We may interpret the biblical record as God seeking to further this aim first with all mankind, then with his chosen people Israel, then with the faithful remnant, finally with that individual person willing to embody in his own life the meaning, hopes, and mission God has entrusted to Israel.[30]

---

[28]Pittenger, *Process,* 5; Janzen, "Process Perspective," 502, 506; and Ford, *Lure,* ix.

[29]Pierre Teilhard de Chardin, *The Phenomenon of Man,* trans. Bernard Wall (New York: Harper and Row, 1961), 31–313, *The Future of Man,* trans. Norman Denny (New York: Harper and Row, 1964), 11–323, *The Divine Milieu,* trans. Bernard Wall (New York: Harper and Row, 1965), 13–155, *Man's Place in Nature,* trans. René Hague (New York: Harper and Row, 1966), 13–121, and *Toward the Future,* trans. René Hague (New York: Harcourt Brace Jovanovich, 1975), 7–215.

[30]Ford, *Lure,* 76.

Process theologians in the future may affirm not only a biblical theology that speaks of salvation history, but one that resonates the wider theological concerns in the biblical text. This may be most significant for theologians of the Hebrew Bible who synthesize themes of a God active in the social and historical arena (narratives in Genesis through Chronicles) with the testimony of divine revelation in worship and cult (Psalms), the viable quest for God exerted by human reason (wisdom literature in Proverbs, Job, Ecclesiastes, Sirach, and Wisdom of Solomon), and the experiences of everyday life (legal material and fictional postexilic novels such as Ruth, Jonah, Esther, Daniel, Tobit, and Judith). Their attempts to generate more broadly based theological expositions[31] will produce models that accommodate an intellectual framework provided by process thought. Process theism affirms that the Divine is manifest in many ways in human culture, and now biblical theologians stress that the Hebrew Scriptures made very comparable observations more than two thousand years ago in the breadth of the entire canonical witness.

---

[31]Terrien, *Elusive Presence,* 1–483, and *Till the Heart Sings* (Philadelphia: Fortress Press, 1985), 1–223; Brevard Childs, *Old Testament Theology in a Canonical Context* (Philadelphia: Fortress Press, 1985), 1–247, and *Biblical Theology of the Old and New Testaments* (Minneapolis: Fortress Press, 1993), 1–727; Paul Hanson, *The People Called* (New York: Harper and Row, 1986), 1–546; Levenson, *Creation,* 3–156; and Brueggemann, *Theology,* 1–307.

12

Process Categories and the Intellectual Advance of the Hebrew Scriptures

I

Process theological categories may be used not only to explicate themes found within the Hebrew Scriptures; they may be useful in a scholarly attempt to characterize the religious and intellectual development that occurred among the ancient Israelites and Jews. As indicated in our second chapter, contemporary scholarly theories now envision the development of the Israelite ethos as a phenomenon that emerged later and more gradually than heretofore has been emphasized. Critical scholars now stress the continuities that Israelite and Jewish belief had with the contemporary ancient world more than the differences. Israelite beliefs are seen to have emerged out of ancient Near Eastern beliefs, as the later classical prophets, Deuteronomic reformers, Priestly editors, and the various authors of the Hebrew Scriptures articulated their own particular worldviews in contradistinction to the views of those peoples around them. Although the biblical authors wished to make their views concerning Yahweh appear much more distinctive, there were obvious connections between them and their predecessors, which modern scholars have observed.[1] Hence, we may speak of both the continuities and the discontinuities that biblical authors shared with the religious beliefs and customs of peoples who preceded them.

---

[1]Peter Machinist, "The Question of Distinctiveness in Ancient Israel," in *A Highway from Egypt to Assyria,* ed. Israel Eph'al and Mordechai Cogan (Jerusalem: Magnes, 1990), 420–42.

Process theology at this juncture would offer its paradigm of prehension as a way to understand this entire intellectual process. As one actual entity prehends the data from the actual entity that preceded it, there are both positive prehensions and negative prehensions. Something of the past entity is preserved through a process that we could call "feeling," and something is rejected, though it is ultimately remembered in the consequent body of God.

The way in which Israelite belief emerged out of previous ancient Near Eastern thought, yet at the same time sought to move beyond or differ from it, might be compared with prehension. Prehension might be a form of reconfiguration or modification, terms that several biblical scholars have used to describe how Israelite faith redefined the beliefs of the ancient world.[2] Prehension draws forth data from what preceded it, but essentially that data is reorganized in a new way so as to create a new and unique actual entity. On an intellectual level Israelites and Jews might be said to have prehended ideas and placed them together in a new matrix to create an intellectual breakthrough. This intellectual and religious reconfiguration of ideas by the biblical authors can be imagined as a large-scale process of prehension.

If one wishes to draw the analogy even further, one might suggest that the subjective aim provided to the process is the guiding direction of God in the intellectual development of the ancient Israelites and Jews, which modern Christians and Jews would confess by faith to have been part of that ancient process. As in process thought, one would acknowledge the freedom of the intellectuals who crafted the biblical text by saying that God, as the ground of religious feeling, directed the process by inspiring these intellectuals without determining the particular direction this religious evolution would take.

One of the critical scholarly models proposed by biblical scholars is the dialectic of "convergence" and "differentiation," which has been advocated so well by Mark Smith.[3] Although not exactly the same as the process of prehension, the paradigm evokes a similar perception of the religious evolutionary process. As Israelites began to confess the identity of Yahweh, according to Smith, they began to merge other deities with Yahweh's persona (such as El), and they began to reject certain characteristics (such as the fertility imagery of Baal) in a process of divergence. This is comparable to prehension, which accepts certain data from the past while rejecting others, as the selected data are put into a new structure. So also Israelites took certain images from various deities to apply to Yahweh,

---

[2]Brueggemann, "A Shape for Old Testament Theology," *CBQ* 47 (1985): 28–46; and Shmuel Eisenstadt, "The Axial Age Breakthrough in Ancient Israel," in *The Origins and Diversity of Axial Age Civilizations,* ed. Shmuel Eisenstadt (Albany: SUNY Press, 1986), 127–34.

[3]Mark Smith, *Early History,* passim.

while they rejected others. Thus, process thought not only dovetails with the paradigm advocated by Smith, it may enable the reader of Smith's work to be more receptive to the scholarly model he proposes.

I might advocate comparable but different language in this regard. One might say that Israelite thinkers took from the ancient world a great deal of religious insight, both in a conscious and an unconscious fashion. They engaged in an intellectual process by which they either critiqued or embraced certain images, metaphors, vocabulary, and general ways of viewing reality. Once the process of critiquing and embracing was underway, it was inevitable that the resultant perceptions appeared to be new and different despite their origin in the thought that preceded them. For to selectively draw forth religious insights while rejecting others means that you will reconstruct those ideas you have adopted in a new matrix of thought.

II

Although we cannot strive for a comprehensive evaluation of biblical themes that have been drawn from the ancient world and developed by biblical theologians, we may attempt a brief overview of some central themes. Biblical scholars have noticed the similarity of language and thought that connects certain images and literary formulas found in particular biblical texts with literature found in the ancient Near East. Form critics, in particular, found that not only language but the sequence of material or the outline of various biblical texts was so parallel to ancient Near Eastern sources that the biblical authors had to be using these older texts consciously and revising them for their own religious needs. Special attention was given to creation accounts, covenantal texts, ancient Near Eastern references to prophets, wisdom literature, and general portrayals of the gods or the Divine. Let us focus our attention on these themes.

Genesis 1, the creation account, appears to be inspired by and a reaction to previous creation accounts in the Near East, and it may have been generated in the sixth century B.C.E. during the Babylonian exile by priests. Early attention was drawn to the similarities between Genesis 1 and the "Enuma Elish" of Babylon. Later scholarship also took other texts into consideration, including the Sumerian account, "Enki and the World Manor"; the Akkadian version of creation and the flood, "The Atrahasis Epic"; and other fragmentary creation myths, including Egyptian cosmogonies involving the god Ptah.[4]

When considering the similarities or positive prehensions the biblical authors undertook in their use of predecessor texts, we might observe the

---

[4]A good contemporary analysis of these is provided by Simkins, *Creator and Creation,* 41–81.

following: (1) The sequence of creative acts in both the biblical and the ancient Near Eastern accounts are rather similar: water, sky, bodies in the heavens, plants, animals, and humanity. (2) As there are eight creative acts in an account such as "Enki and the World Manor," so also there are eight creative acts by God in six days (two creative acts occur on the third and sixth days). (3) A very significant creative act by Marduk in the "Enuma Elish" is the separation of the waters, which God undertakes on both the second and the third days. (4) As God creates by the spoken word or command, so also Ptah creates by his command or spoken word. (5) In "Atrahasis" and "Enuma Elish," a goddess is assigned to create humanity by hand out of the mud of the earth combined with the blood of a defeated, evil god. (6) Allusions to kings and the affairs of royalty are found in Mesopotamian and the biblical accounts; in the latter they are attributed to the first couple. Although not comprehensive, this list highlights the key images that led scholars to conclude that the biblical authors were familiar with older creation accounts and deliberately used their formats.[5]

More significant are the differences, those points at which the biblical authors consciously departed from the earlier accounts, presumably to make some significant point to their audience. We would call these their negative prehensions. Key points of divergence include the following: (1) The biblical narrative debunks polytheism and specific gods in particular. Word plays on the names of the Babylonian goddess Tiamat, the symbol of chaos in the "Enuma Elish," are parodied in the biblical account with reference to how the earth was without form (*tohu*), how God separated the waters (*tehom*), and how God made the sea beasts (*tannin*) to swim where commanded. All these words are either translations for Tiamat's name or an allusion to her function (like the biblical *tannin,* Tiamat also had seven heads). The reference to the "lesser light" and the "greater light" on the fourth day are expressions designed to ridicule the worship of the sun (Shamash) and the moon (Sin) gods, both of whom were important for sixth-century B.C.E. Chaldean Babylonian kings. The woman, who is later called Eve, is said to be the "mother of all living things" in Genesis 3, an obvious allusion to fertility goddesses, such as Inanna and Ishtar, who are now portrayed as pagan confusions of the human mother, Eve. (2) In Genesis 1 the world order is created without combat, a motif very important in "Enuma Elish" and "Atrahasis," wherein the good god Marduk must defeat, kill, and split in half the body of the evil water goddess, Tiamat. God is so powerful that no combat is necessary, only a command. Such characterizations appear to indicate a strong monotheism on the part of the author(s) of Genesis 1. (3) In "Enuma Elish" and "Atrahasis," people are made of clay and the

---

[5]Bruce Vawter, *On Genesis* (Garden City, N.Y.: Doubleday, 1977), 37–63, is one of several excellent texts that analyze the biblical materials in light of antecedent ancient Near Eastern ideas.

blood of an evil god, Kingu, and therefore they are meant to be slaves of the gods, work on the land, which is owned by the gods (the Temple Manor), and provide sacrifice for the gods. However, the biblical author has man, who is both male and female, created in the image and likeness of God. The terms *image* and *likeness* are expressions used in both Babylon and Israel to talk about the king. The man and the woman are to "rule" (*radah*) over creation, and this term is usually reserved to describe the actions of a king. The man and the woman in Genesis 1 are not slaves, but kings, who stand as wise rulers over the created order in the stead of God. (4) Moreover, Genesis 2 carries the image of human freedom and nobility further by having Yahweh create the first man out of dirt and the breath of the good creator God, not the evil defeated god, which also bespeaks a high place in creation for the human beings. Not only are people ennobled by this biblical version, but the biblical author may be undercutting the authority of both priests and the Babylonian king, who are legitimated by the Babylonian creation accounts and the accompanying rites, which are performed on New Year's Day. Much more could be said about the differences, but these aspects highlight the significant theological observations made by commentators on Genesis 1–2.

III

Covenant is a very significant biblical concept in both the Hebrew Scriptures and the New Testament. It, too, is a concept drawn from the ancient world, as our discovery of second-millennium B.C.E. Hittite and first-millennium B.C.E. Assyrian treaties has impressed on us.

When we read Hittite and especially Assyrian covenant texts, we are impressed by the structural similarities and the use of similar vocabulary: (1) In all covenant reports there is a similar outline: A preamble identifies the parties involved in the pact. A historical prologue describes what the suzerain, or superior nation, has generously done for the vassal, or conquered nation (usually this is blatant propaganda). The stipulations that the vassal must keep are listed. Blessings and curses are mentioned that will occur with either obedience or disobedience by the vassal. Oaths are sworn to the gods of both nations, which call for punishment by all the gods if the treaty is broken. Provisions are made for the deposit of copies of the treaty in both nations and for their periodic public reading. Biblical scholars immediately saw structural similarities with the Ten Commandments in Exodus 20: the exodus is the past gracious action of the suzerain deity; the commands are stipulations; curses and blessings are recalled in the second commandment; the tablets are deposited in the ark; and so on. The entire book of Deuteronomy was seen to be in covenantal format: Deuteronomy 1–11 recalls the past acts of Yahweh; the laws in Deuteronomy 12–26 are stipulations; blessings and curses are in

Deuteronomy 27–28; and provisions are made for the oath, the treaty deposit, and periodic reading. (2) Beyond the tremendous similarities of outline and structure, other parallels drawn from the covenant tradition of the ancient world were found in biblical texts. Specific treaty curses in ancient Assyrian texts, such as the Sefire texts, were found scattered throughout the biblical text in Deuteronomy 27–28 and the Prophets.[6] (3) Some commentators suspected that prophetic judgment formulas, such as the Lawsuit or *Riv* formulary, which appeals to classic judicial imagery, may have been rooted in the notion of a covenant treaty made with Yahweh. If the treaty was broken, then Yahweh could take the people to court, as the prophet formulas implied.[7] Of course, this theory assumed the early use of covenant language, prior to the Deuteronomic Reform of the seventh century B.C.E., which not all scholars accept today. Nonetheless, the use of Mesopotamian covenant language by biblical authors became clear to scholars once these ancient texts were observed.

Despite the great similarities between the form and language of the biblical and the ancient Near Eastern treaties, some significant differences, or what we call negative prehensions, were observed: (1) Unlike the tyrannical rulers of the Assyrians, Yahweh was portrayed primarily as a gracious suzerain, especially in the election of the Israelites. Israel was saved at the sea from the Egyptians, protected in the wilderness, and brought into a fertile land. These were very significant and gracious gifts provided by Yahweh, the suzerain. The corresponding response of obedience to the stipulations then became portrayed much more as a thankful response by grateful people. (2) This image of Yahweh as suzerain, the only true suzerain in the world, tended to undercut the agenda of the political arena. Deuteronomic reformers, who used covenant imagery more than any other tradition did, called on the Israelites not to create covenants with foreign nations, since that entailed the acknowledgment of their foreign gods. The very nature of the biblical covenant language proclaimed that Yahweh was the only true suzerain in the world, and foreign nations could offer only a bogus suzerain-vassal treaty. The kings of nations were humans; they were tyrants; and they could not offer the real blessings that Yahweh could. (3) The stipulations provided in the biblical texts, by their very nature as religious texts, provided religious and ethical guidelines rather than political and economic terms, as were found in the Hittite and Assyrian treaties. This, too, carried a different message to the audience: that moral behavior was more important than politics and economics. Thus, the biblical authors

---

[6]Delbert Hillers, *Treaty Curses and the Old Testament*, BibOr 16 (Rome: PBI, 1964), passim.

[7]Herbert Huffmon, "The Covenant Lawsuit and the Prophets," *JBL* 78 (1959): 286–95; and F. C. Fensham, "Common Trends in the Curses of the Near Eastern Treaties and Kudurru-inscriptions Compared with the Maledictions of Amos and Isaiah," *ZAW* 75 (1963): 155–75.

took over a significant formulary from the ancient world and turned it into a dynamic way of portraying the relationship of God to the people.

IV

Prophecy as a phenomenon was found throughout the ancient Near Eastern and Hellenistic world, and in both the ancient world and in Israel there was development, although scholars have disagreed over the particulars of this evolutionary process. Also, critical scholars have observed that there appear to have been differences between the early prophets of Israel down to the time of Amos (750 B.C.E.) and those prophets whom we call the classical prophets, Amos to Malachi. Whether significant differences differentiated the early and classical prophets, or whether we are simply confused by our literary sources in the Bible, we cannot say. An author like John Bright[8] sees great differences, and another author, such as Johannes Lindblom,[9] sees great continuity with all these prophets. Thus, if an author suggests that there is an evolutionary trajectory from the ancient Near Eastern prophets through the early prophets (including Samuel, Nathan, Gad, Ahijah of Shiloh, Elijah, Elisha, and others) down into the classical prophetic movement, then immediately he or she becomes involved in a long-standing, complex scholarly debate. In light of this, our suggestions must remain highly tentative.

Hebrew prophets shared certain common features with their ancient Near Eastern contemporaries, especially those prophets that we know something about at Mari:[10] (1) All prophets spoke in the name of the deity and proclaimed a message given from the deity to them to communicate to a greater audience. Sometimes the prophets spoke of receiving the message in ecstasy, sometimes not. Sometimes the prophets testified to receiving the message at a shrine, sometimes not. At Mari, prophets referred to divine messages that came to them in dreams. All these characteristics are reminiscent of prophets in the Hebrew Scriptures. (2) Prophets often used a common set of formulaic expressions, which are similar to those used by diplomatic messengers who carried official messages from one king to another. Expressions like "Thus says the deity, XX" were used in many prophetic settings. Oracles could be terminated with the formula "Thus it is said of the deity, XX." In similar fashion, prophets in Israel would utter "Thus says the Lord" and "Thus it is said of the Lord" in conjunction with their oracles. (3) Prophets believed that once they had received the message from the deity, they were obligated to proclaim this

---

[8]John Bright *Jeremiah*, AB 21 (Garden City, N.Y.: Doubleday, 1964), xxii–xxiv.
[9]Lindblom, *Prophecy*, 47–219.
[10]Joseph Blenkinsopp, *A History of Prophecy in Israel* (Philadelphia: Westminster Press, 1983), 53–60.

message either to the king, priest, or public audience. Assyrian political envoys developed the practice in the eighth century B.C.E. of proclaiming the message of the Assyrian kings to city populaces at large, even though, in theory, they were speaking to the king. Often these envoys spoke words of dire threat and warnings of brutal war atrocities that would come to rebellious vassal cities, and proclaiming the messages aloud to the people was a tactic designed to intimidate the local king by threatening and terrifying his entire populace. Perhaps Hebrew prophets beginning with Amos spoke to public audiences more frequently because they were inspired by the Assyrian diplomatic strategy.[11] (4) Messages in all cultures could be either a warning or a promise of hope. Often in the ancient Near East kings were told that they ought to do something, such as repair a cult site or offer sacrifice to a neglected deity. If they failed to do this, the deity would be angry and punish them. If they accomplished the assignment, they would be blessed. The Hebrew prophets likewise spoke words of judgment or hope, depending on the circumstances of the audience. Hence, in all cultures future results were predicated on the actions of the human beings who heard the message. This is an eschatological function of the messages—the future would bring divine actions appropriate to the deeds of the human listeners.

Israelite prophecy grew out of ancient Near Eastern roots, but the debate rages as to the degree of difference that emerged among Israelite prophets. The following have been suggested as ways in which Israelite prophecy evolved in new and different directions: (1) Perhaps with Israelite prophets there was less use of divinatory practices and techniques, at least with the later classical prophets. Ancient Near Eastern prophets, such as those at Mari, refer to the cultic actions and divinatory activity in which the original divine message was received or to such activity that may have been undertaken subsequently to verify the message received from the god(s). No such actions are mentioned with Israelite prophets, save for some vague allusions to possible dreams in which Yahweh may have spoken (2 Sam. 7:4), and these dreams might have been deliberately incubated by the prophets. However, the omission of such details by the later authors of the written biblical text indicates that the biblical theologians at least wished to portray the prophets as distinct from their ancient counterparts, even if the actual historical experiences of the prophets had continuity with foreign prophets. (2) It appears to us that, increasingly in the evolution of the prophetic movement, ecstasy as a means by which to receive or to incubate a divine message fell into either disuse or disfavor. In general, biblical prophets appear to have had less recourse to ecstatic experiences, or the practice of singing, dancing, incubating dreams, using drugs or alcohol,

---

[11]Huffmon, "Covenant Lawsuit," 286–95.

and self-inflicted pain to induce a revelation from God than their ancient Near Eastern counterparts. Although such actions (except for self-inflicted pain) seem to have characterized the disciples of Samuel and Elisha, among the later classical prophets there is no indication of such activities. Furthermore, Isaiah and Jeremiah explicitly condemn the reception of revelation through dreams (Isa. 29:7–8; Jer. 23:25–32; 27:9–10; 29:8–9), and presumably other comparable practices were scorned likewise. But we tread on thin ice, for perhaps we simply have not been told that the later prophets used these same techniques, or perhaps at all times there simply were different types of prophets, some ecstatic and others calm, and our sources are too limited to reflect this. (3) Classical prophets in Israel appear to have been less subservient to the king and less likely to have served in the court of the king than the prophets of the ancient world and even earlier prophets in Israel. Samuel, Nathan, and Gad appear to have been in the royal court, and others who did not live in the court, such as Ahijah, Elijah, and Elisha, nevertheless put in frequent appearances before kings to give them rather discomforting messages. However, again we must be careful in our generalizations. Isaiah appears to have served Ahaz and Hezekiah in the court of Judah, and perchance others may have put in quite regular appearances at the court (including, so it seems, Jeremiah). Or perhaps there were always both court prophets and peripheral prophets, critical of the court, who coexisted in society together, and our sources are simply too limited for us to see this clearly.[12] (4) Later classical prophets seemed to have developed a more comprehensive social message with strong moral overtones for the audience to whom they spoke. If, indeed, the later prophets were more inclined to speak to the people than the king, this could explain the evolution of a more developed theological and moral prophetic message. Addresses to the king more likely treat matters of dynastic concern or national and international politics. But messages to the people more comprehensively speak of those social and economic concerns that are affected by religious values, and the nature of these messages will lead to a reflective and sophisticated worldview of prophets who thus speak over the years. Caution is once more advised, for it has been suggested that the sophistication of the prophetic oracles proclaimed by those later classical prophets might have been rendered intellectually and religiously reflective for us by the scribal intelligentsia who wrote the oracles down during the Babylonian exile and in the subsequent years. (5) In a related way, it has been suggested that classical prophets developed an insightful sense of history and eschatology from the days of Amos onward. If so, it would be the result, once more, of spokespersons addressing a corporate group of people and speaking to their concerns. When

---

[12]Robert Wilson, *Prophecy and Society in Ancient Israel* (Philadelphia: Westminster Press, 1980), 21–308.

addressing the entire populace, the prophets not only began to speak more of ethical and social matters, they also projected the future destinies of the people in light of either continued sinfulness or penitent obedience. Such concerns led the prophets, as the theory suggests, to develop a sense that linear and temporal references were significant categories by which to understand reality, and so eschatology and a historical sense gradually evolved.[13] Again, we must remember that this sophisticated worldview might be attributed to the authors of the written prophetic corpus, who recalled and very creatively rearticulated the oracles of the old preexilic prophets. In conclusion, one must say, however, that if these differences have any merit, then most certainly we are looking at new developments in the prophetic movement from the eighth century B.C.E. onward. If so, then consciously or unconsciously negative prehensions were made by those prophets of the phenomena that preceded them in the prophetic movement—most particularly the emphases on divination, ecstasy, royal service, and a simple, two-dimensional concern with the agenda of the royal family. In its place came the great themes of classical prophecy, which were built on the points of shared continuity with previous prophets, the positive prehensions.

V

That which we call wisdom literature (Proverbs, Job, Koheleth or Ecclesiastes, Sirach or Ecclesiasticus, and Wisdom of Solomon) in the Bible appears to have been a common literary phenomenon in the ancient world, for we have excellent parallels with biblical passages among the literary texts of Egypt and Mesopotamia especially. The Egyptian text "Wisdom of Amen-en-ope" (1200 B.C.E.) shows great similarity with, and perhaps even inspired, the passages in Proverbs 22–24. Many other collections of Egyptian and Babylonian wisdom sayings parallel what the authors of the book of Proverbs were doing. The dialogue of a righteous sufferer with his friends, the book of Job, has antecedents in Babylonian texts, such as the Sumerian "A Man and his God," the Akkadian "Babylonian Theodicy," and the Akkadian "Ludlul-bêl-nêmeqi" ("I Will Praise the Lord of Wisdom"), all of which may have inspired the author of the book of Job. Koheleth, likewise, has parallels in the Egyptian "Song of the Harper" and other texts.[14]

A number of significant literary and intellectual assumptions connect Israelite wisdom literature with comparable literature in the ancient Near

---

[13]Gerhard von Rad, *The Message of the Prophets,* trans. D. M. G. Stalker (New York: Harper and Row, 1965), 77–99.

[14]James Pritchard, ed., *Ancient Near Eastern Texts Relating to the Old Testament,* 3d ed. (Princeton, N.J.: Princeton University Press, 1970), 421–25, 434–37, 467, 589–91, 596–604.

East[15]: (1) Such literature primarily seeks to address concerns of everyday life, especially providing advice on how to succeed in business, the royal court, or the normal matters of life faced by everyone. (2) Everyone's literature has a strong sense of causality, or the perception that certain human actions lead to certain results. That wise behavior or hard work leads to success and foolish behavior or laziness leads to self-destruction is the common assumption that undergirds the collections of sayings in Egypt, Mesopotamia, and Israel. (3) The literature appears to have been created by scribes in every culture, and it appears to have been addressed to those intelligentsia with what we might call a middle-class work ethic, or the desire to get ahead in life and advance one's social standing and wealth. (4) Some of the wisdom texts are very concerned with the order of creation, or how things work in nature. There is an assumption on the part of the authors that there is unity, structure, and purpose in life, and this order may be observed both in the natural and social realms. Observing the natural order gives insight into the social order and further provides direction to a person on how to live a successful life. One may observe frequent allusions to natural phenomena in Proverbs, Job, and Koheleth especially. (5) The wisdom literature in all these societies also gave expression to the other side of human existence: that not all life was fair. Sometimes the world, and human society especially, did not grant success to those who were righteous, hard working, and wise. Wisdom literature in all the societies plumbed the depths of human suffering, misery, and the injustice of life in literary-theological works that we would call theodicies. (6) The god or gods portrayed in wisdom literature tend to be more distant than the god or gods worshiped in cult and revered in hymnody in the ancient Near East and Israel. This deity seems to be portrayed as a principle of cosmic order that brings appropriate reward and retribution for human actions via the logical and rational order that is found in the world. Or again, the same deity might be challenged in theodicies that lament the unfairness or lack of proper retribution that might be found in the world. In biblical books, such as Proverbs, Job, and Koheleth, we do not observe the traditional themes of Israelite faith, such as talk about the exodus, Sinai, the Law, covenant, prophets, sacrifice, purity, or the typical divine portrayals of Yahweh, which are found elsewhere in the Pentateuch and the Prophets. This literature looks very much like the generic intellectual or philosophical discourse, if you will, of the ancient world in general. In conclusion, we might observe that Israelite wisdom literature not only shared common assumptions with the rest of the ancient world, but apparently particular works in the Bible even have direct ancient Near Eastern antecedents. In fact, it is with wisdom literature that Hebrew Bible scholars are most prone

---

[15]James Crenshaw, *Old Testament Wisdom* (Atlanta: John Knox Press, 1981), 55–65, 212–35.

to talk about continuity between the biblical texts and the predecessor literature in the ancient world.

Nevertheless, we may still speak of ways in which biblical wisdom literature expresses a degree of particularity. We may say that biblical authors positively prehended the literature and values of the ancient world in this corpus of texts, but some negative prehensions still occurred: (1) The later wisdom tradition in Israel, especially in the books of Sirach and Wisdom of Solomon, reintegrated the traditional religious themes of the rest of the biblical tradition into an organic synthesis with wisdom literature. Sirach speaks of the Law as the "fear of God," uses much of the traditional language, and has a sense of sacred history in the discourse about the great believers of the past (Sir. 44–50). Wisdom of Solomon integrates wisdom, traditional biblical values, and middle Platonic philosophy in a very sophisticated fashion. (2) The later wisdom tradition seems to have placed Yahweh back into focus as the deity who presides over the cosmos. The earlier literature tended to use the more generic word for God, Elohim, but the later literature, especially Sirach, reverts to the traditional name and traditional portrayal of Yahweh, the deity of Israel, instead of a deity who could be seen as the cosmic deity worshiped by all peoples. (3) The personification of Wisdom as a deity, or as a goddess in particular, which may be observed in the other cultures, is nuanced in all the biblical texts. Wisdom is personified as feminine in Proverbs 8, but clearly subordinate to God as either an abstract principle or an extension of the divine nature. Other wisdom hymns in Job 28, Sirach 24, and Wisdom of Solomon 7 all show the desire to maintain the monotheistic faith of Israel clearly by personifying Wisdom without turning her into a separate deity. Other cultures with their assumed polytheism could deify wisdom without complication, even though some authors, such as the wisdom thinkers in Egypt, seemed monistic at times. Biblical literature may have drawn on the Egyptian images of the goddess Isis, who was the patron deity of wisdom. But in so doing, they reformulated the imagery associated with this goddess to turn it into attributes of the didactic principle of wisdom. Sirach, in particular, equated Wisdom with the Law or the "fear of God," which would be a thorough form of debunking for the Egyptian goddess, Isis. (4) Finally, one might suggest that the tragic vision of Job differs from the prior texts in Mesopotamian literature, which might have inspired the biblical author. In those other texts there is more of a sense of resolution: The deity comes to the sufferer and sets things right. The drama in Job indeed does end with a divine appearance of God, but one is still left with a pained feeling that all is not right. The biblical author has created this feeling by the prolonged absence of God, as the debate between Job and his friends dragged on for so many chapters (Job 3–31). And the response of God to Job does not really answer the question of why Job suffers, but rather has God overwhelm Job with creation imagery. One feels that the author tells us that no answer can be given for the existence of suffering, and the rebellious and defiant Job seems to be affirmed precisely because he has cried out against God in language very comparable to the lament hymns in the book of Psalms.[16] At any rate, here again one senses that the biblical authors were rooted in the thought and literature of the ancient Near East, and yet they advanced the intellectual and religious trajectory with their own peculiar insights.

VI

The final motif worthy of consideration by us is the biblical portrayal of God, or Yahweh, certainly the central theological theme of the biblical tradition. Mark Smith has provided us with an excellent survey on the evolution of the imagery associated with Yahweh in his book *The Early History of God,* and we shall not be able to improve on it here. Nevertheless, some critical observations ought to be made to demonstrate again how religious thought among the Israelites and Jews built on and yet went beyond the categories of ancient thought.

The portrayal of Yahweh in the biblical texts has much in common with the portrayal of gods throughout the ancient Near East. These shared themes too often have been overlooked by biblical theologians in the past, who stressed the distinctive character of Yahweh. Scholars overlooked legitimate similarities that were there, and thus the perception that there was a dramatic evolutionary process among the Israelites in reconfiguring the image of their God was lost. In the light of our recent critical understandings, we not only perceive that the image of Yahweh developed among the Israelites, but we may observe, as does Smith, that this was a process of accepting some themes and rejecting others. Smith speaks of "convergence" and "differentiation" in describing this process,[17] but a process theologian might characterize the process as one in which positive prehensions and negative prehensions occurred in the development of a new, creative image of God.

The biblical text gives witness to common characteristics Yahweh shared with other deities, especially as recalled in some of the older texts and poetry in the Pentateuch: (1) In the ancient poetry Yahweh is portrayed as a male storm deity, perhaps coming from "his" (masculine gender is appropriate for a storm god) mountaintop home on Sinai, or the wilderness of Seir (Edom) or Paran, both of which are archaic names reflecting an early origin of the imagery. This imagery gives the impression of a regionalized or local deity, perhaps a deity of the wilderness. Critical scholars suggest that the vast majority of Israelites were people already in the land

---

[16]Norman Habel, *The Book of Job,* CBC (Cambridge, U.K.: Cambridge University Press, 1975), 151–234.

[17]Mark Smith, *Early History,* passim.

who evolved from being Canaanites, but they acknowledge that worship of the deity Yahweh probably came in from the outside, most likely from Edom and perhaps with the small Joshua group. If so, the portrayal of Yahweh is no different from that of other storm gods in the ancient world. In fact, his portrayal would be so similar to Baal that there would be natural conflict between them (or more properly speaking, their adherents). This is what is most surely portrayed in the biblical narratives: conflict between Yahweh and Baal, in which Yahweh pre-empted Baal by swallowing up some of his characteristics and disowning the rest. (2) Yahweh is portrayed in many old biblical poems as leading his people in war, especially in the triumphal march into the promised land.[18] This, too, is a traditional way of portraying a god of war in the ancient Near East, which could be attributed to any patron deity of a conquering pharaoh or king. In particular, certain deities, such as Marduk and Ishtar in Babylon, Ashur and Ninurta in Assyria, Baal and Anat in Canaan, and various deities in Egypt, could receive this kind of ascription. Yahweh's portrayal was very traditional in this regard. (3) Yahweh is said to be surrounded by the "heavenly host" or "Sebaoth." These are the lesser deities that serve any great high god in the ancient world. In particular, the "host" follows the high god into war, and they function in the combative process by which the people of that deity prevail over their enemies on the battlefield. One may find this imagery in the old poetry of the Pentateuch and indirectly permeating the book of Joshua. Yahweh comes to fight accompanied by the heavenly host. The metaphor continued into the prophetic corpus, where it was used with "Day of the Lord" imagery, and most notably we can observe it with the prophet Amos.[19] As monotheism emerges, the "heavenly host," or the "sons of the gods," have to be converted slowly into benign messengers or angels of God, so that they are no longer deities in their own right. (4) Although overlooked by biblical theologians in years past, the image of Yahweh's rule over both the natural order and the social order, clearly found in the Hebrew Scriptures, is also to be found in the texts of the ancient Near East (perhaps to a lesser degree). Recent scholars have documented the images of Babylonian gods (Marduk) and especially Assyrian gods (Ashur and Ninurta), who are portrayed as being social deities who have a sense of historical destiny for their devotees.[20] Thus, the portrayal of Yahweh as both a god of nature and a social deity may be one of the continuities that the biblical text shares with ancient Near Eastern literature, not a unique

---

[18]Patrick Miller, *The Divine Warrior in Early Israel* (Cambridge, Mass.: Harvard University Press, 1973), passim; and Choon-Leong Seow, *Myth, Drama, and the Politics of David's Dance*, HSM 46 (Atlanta: Scholars Press, 1989), 104–31.

[19]Gerhard von Rad, *Der heilige Krieg im alten Israel,* 5th ed. (Göttingen: Vandenhoeck und Ruprecht, 1969), passim.

[20]Albrektson, *History,* 7–122; Saggs, *Encounter,* 64–92; and Gnuse, *Heilsgeschichte,* 53–71.

difference. The language of the ancient world often spoke of the destiny willed by the deity for the patron people, and this translated into language about victory in war, imperial conquest, and the eventual spread of respect for the deity. One would think of the vision of manifest destiny and success in battle promised to Joshua in the Deuteronomistic History. (However, there are some obvious differences here with the biblical literature in prophetic texts, where conquest of enemies is not a concern.) (5) Finally, there is election language in both Israel and the ancient Near East. In the past, biblical theologians too often spoke of this language as though it were unique to Israel. But again, critical contemporary scholars have shown that Egyptian and Mesopotamian texts also speak of a deity electing a land and a people who live in that land and promising them fertility and national success. The classic portrayals of Yahweh, both in the early archaic poetry and the later Deuteronomistic and prophetic texts, share much in common with the ancient Near East. Such characteristics again may be termed the positive prehensions of the biblical authors.

However, there are nuanced differences that appear in the biblical texts that may lead us to clarify each of the above-mentioned points. The ways in which biblical authors redefined or reconfigured some of these motifs may be described as a process of prehension that involved exclusions, or negative prehensions: (1) Although the early poetry described Yahweh as a god of nature, and a storm god in particular, this imagery faded in time (though it did not disappear completely), and increasingly the emphasis was placed on the social aspects of Yahweh's relationship to the Israelites and Jews, especially on themes of law, covenant, and election. Although not a dialectical difference with ancient texts, the degree to which biblical authors stressed these themes was proportionally greater than what their ancient Near Eastern counterparts did. As a monotheistic portrayal of Yahweh emerged, the nature imagery was transcended, for Yahweh could no longer be associated with one natural force (the storm) but rather had to be associated with all. If Yahweh is associated with all forces, Yahweh then transcends them, and the imagery associated with Yahweh moves into the social categories. We have here a difference in degree, though not in kind, between the literature of the ancient Near East and Israel. (2) Early poetry portrayed Yahweh as a god who led people to success on the battlefield. Increasingly in the prophetic literature this portrait gave way to a theme that spoke of Yahweh's punishing Israelites in war and using those very same foreigners to do it. This undercut the image of Yahweh the warrior and replaced it with the image of Yahweh the universal judge of all people and the one deity who controls all human destiny, as well as armies. We see the roots of this image already in Amos in 750 B.C.E. with his use of the "Day of the Lord" motif. Thus, Yahweh gradually transcended the battlefield to become the judge and the one who calls for cosmic conflict over the whole world in the later apocalyptic literature. Yahweh as warrior subtly evolved into Yahweh as universal judge, and eventually the specific warrior imagery disappeared or was used more loosely in symbolic form (as in apocalyptic literature). (3) Yahweh was served by a "heavenly host," or the "sons of the gods," and in polytheistic terms these beings are the lesser deities who serve the high god, presumably Yahweh. With the emergence of monotheism, these beings are converted into angels, or beings who are neither human nor divine. The motif of powerful minor deities in war becomes transformed into one in which servants obey the will of the one supreme God in bureaucratic fashion. (4) Although one may find testimonies to the societal rule of Ashur, Ninurta, and Marduk in Mesopotamia, the extent to which biblical authors projected this imagery onto Yahweh cannot be matched in the ancient world. (5) Some commentators acknowledge that although election of a people may be found in the ancient Near East, the way in which Yahweh elects Israel appears different. In the texts of other nations the emphasis is on the election of the land and the people who live on it. Such would be natural in a polytheistic system of thought, for each deity has a land over which he or she is patron, and people who reside in that land belong to the deity and share the deity's vision of destiny. However, an emerging monotheistic faith speaks more directly of the election of the people, and those people are the servants of that God, even though they may be in exile. Such was the dynamic of election in the biblical text, wherein the Israelites or Jews remained the people of Yahweh even in the Babylonian exile, for their deity was the only God in the cosmos.

VII

This chapter was not meant to be a thorough review of the ways in which biblical thought was rooted in and yet diverged from ancient Near Eastern thought. That needs to be reserved for a separate monograph. It is hoped that this chapter provides insight into the dynamics of how modern critical scholars understand the evolution of Israelite and Jewish thought in relationship to the intellectual matrix out of which it arose. Modern critical scholars no longer emphasize the uniqueness of Israel and the Hebrew Scriptures or the ways in which Israelites stood in contrast to their neighbors. Now we express the relationship of the Israelites and their thought to the rest of the ancient world in a more nuanced way. There are continuities and discontinuities. More importantly, we see Israelite and biblical thought growing out of the beliefs of predecessor cultures. In previous works I characterized this advance as both an evolutionary and revolutionary advance, because although it was an evolutionary process that took six hundred years, it was an intellectual mutation with significant social and religious implications that are still unfolding for us today, and in the long course of human evolution six hundred years or two thousand years is still a relatively short period of time, a revolution.[21]

For our purposes in this volume, the goal is to observe the congruence between this new understanding of the biblical texts by critical scholarship and the theological paradigms proposed by process theologians. The examples given on five theological and literary themes in the Hebrew Scriptures, I hope, will demonstrate how the concept of prehension can be useful in our intellectual articulation of what occurred not only in the biblical text but also in the intellectual and religious development of that age. Biblical authors positively prehended certain basic aspects of the ancient Near Eastern way of thinking either consciously or unconsciously, but in other respects they negatively prehended other aspects of thought. With the Whiteheadian model of an actual entity or an actual occasion, we observe how in a moment of becoming for one entity certain data are taken over and other data are left behind. In the articulation of religious ideas the biblical authors, in effect, reconfigured notions and images in ways reminiscent of the Whiteheadian diagrams of concrescence and creative advance in the moment of becoming. Ultimately, in the creative advance that was Israel and the postexilic Jews we may observe the process of concrescence as it pertains to an entire intellectual system.

---

[21]Gnuse, "Evolutionary Theory," 405–31, and *No Other Gods,* passim.

13

Process Thought and the Formation of Scriptures and Canon

I

Inspiration has been an attribute used to describe the scriptures since their initial reception by Christians. Previously, I summarized and critiqued the various models used by Christians over the centuries to define inspiration.[1] In the past two centuries, biblical scholars and theologians have debated whether inspiration resides in the actual writings or only in the original speakers, whether inspiration extends to the ideas or both the words and the ideas, and what the implications for the truth content of the biblical text are. (Is it infallible in matters of faith and morals only or does an inerrancy extend to questions of history and science also?)

One particularly interesting theory advanced some forty years ago by Roman Catholic theologians was a paradigm called "social inspiration." It suggested that because the scriptures were the result of a long process of development involving oral tradition, written authorship, and editorial redaction, it might be best to describe the entire process as inspired. The theory fell on hard times with an ensuing Roman Catholic debate concerning the nature of the relationship between the scriptures and the authority of the Magisterium, and discussion faded. In the subsequent generation, several Protestant theologians, including this author, attempted to resuscitate the theory with different categories of discourse.

---

[1]Robert Gnuse, *Authority of the Bible* (New York: Paulist Press, 1985), 14–101.

189

With the introduction of process thought into the discussion of biblical theology, it may be time to refashion the concept of social inspiration in process theological categories. Hence, this chapter may serve as a conclusion to the discussion of themes in the Hebrew Bible by addressing the larger issue of scriptures and canon and the theological significance of the Hebrew Scriptures as part of the canon. In order to theologize with the model of social inspiration, it is first necessary to review briefly the discussion that brought the term to the fore. Then we may suggest the understanding of this model in process theological categories.

II

Although a few authors used the term initially, Pierre Benoit and Karl Rahner developed the concept in greater detail.[2] Benoit stressed that inspiration must be attributed in different ways to many individuals involved in the generation of the biblical text. Rahner spoke of how inspiration of the scriptures was a communal function in the ancient church. John McKenzie combined their ideas to articulate the model in its classic form.[3] Critical response from Dennis McCarthy and others fine-tuned the model even more.[4]

Pierre Benoit seriously laid the foundation for the discussion even before the term *social inspiration* was coined. He defined inspiration as the impulse from the Holy Spirit to act, speak, or write, so that inspiration should extend to all these functions, especially in light of the complex transmission history of the biblical text. In his early writings he spoke of dramatic, prophetic or apostolic, and hagiographic forms of inspiration. In later writings he spoke of cognitive, oratorical, and scriptural (writing) modes of inspiration to describe the phenomena of initial insight, speaking, and writing by either a single person or several people in the scripture-generating process. Although Benoit's three forms of inspiration were artificial, they were helpful categories to stress that inspiration was a process. His most significant observation was the stress on the charisma of inspiration as a gift to many

---

[2]The contributions of Benoit and Rahner were assessed by John Topel, "Rahner and McKenzie on the Social Theory of Inspiration," *Scripture* 16 (1964): 34–44; Wilfrid Harrington, *Record of Revelation* (Chicago: Priory, 1965), 119–28; and John Scullion, *The Theology of Inspiration,* Theology Today Series 10 (Notre Dame: Fides, 1970), 36–44.

[3]John McKenzie, "The Social Character of Inspiration," *CBQ* 24 (1962): 115–24.

[4]Dennis McCarthy, "Personality, Society, and Inspiration," *TS* 24 (1963): 553–76; Harrington, *Record,* 131, and *Key to the Bible,* vol. 1: *Record of Revelation* (Garden City, N.Y.: Doubleday, 1976), 41, 47–49; and Scullion, *Theology,* 48–49.

individuals, but he rejected the idea of "collective inspiration," which attributed the gift to the community as a whole rather than to individuals.[5]

Karl Rahner provided the theological basis for continued discussion of social inspiration, and he focused attention on the community as the locus of inspiration. He characterized God as the author of the apostolic church, which in turn authored the scriptures through the agency of individual authors. He viewed oral tradition as "The Tradition of the Church," and he opined that the church could be understood to be the Magisterium. Once these equations were made, he spoke of the Scriptures/ Tradition and the Magisterium as the theological foundations created by God. The church, created by God, then created the scriptures.[6]

Needless to say, Protestants and many Roman Catholics would not be happy with his facile redefinition of oral tradition as The Tradition and the apostolic church as the Magisterium. The oral tradition or gospel proclamation behind the New Testament is really foundational for the later Tradition of the church, and the Magisterium is only part of the greater Christian church. Rahner really sought to address the question of the relationship between Scripture, Tradition, and the Ecclesiastical structures of the church rather than to talk about inspiration. Biblical theologians dependent on him stressed the corporate nature of social inspiration and moved away from Benoit's careful nuances. Rahner's emphasis on the apostolic church as the origin of inspiration also led him to relegate the Old Testament to a very subordinate or dependent status to the New Testament; it was not scripture until the church received it into the fuller canon. John McKenzie synthesized the views of Benoit and Rahner. He observed that because biblical works were authored anonymously by many persons in a process of oral tradition and literary transmission, we cannot speak of individual inspired authors. Inspiration worked within the community to generate scriptures; God worked through the commmunity to affect individuals so that they would express certain beliefs. Inspiration was not a charisma of books or individuals, but it was a charisma of Israel and the ancient church as a whole. Authors wrote as representatives of

---

[5]Paul Synave and Pierre Benoit, *Prophecy and Inspiration,* trans. Avery Dulles (New York: Desclee, 1961), 84–168; Benoit, "Inspiration," in *Guide to the Bible,* ed. André Robert and A. Tricot, trans. Edward Arbez and Martin McGuire, 2 vols., 2d ed. (New York: Desclee, 1960), 1:9–52, "The Analogies of Inspiration," in *Aspects of Biblical Inspiration,* trans. Jerome Murphy-O'Connor and S. K. Ashe (Chicago: Priory, 1965), 13–35, "Inspiration and Revelation," in *Human Reality of Sacred Scripture,* trans. David Connor, Conc 10 (New York: Paulist Press, 1965), 6–24, and numerous other articles.

[6]Karl Rahner, *Inspiration in the Bible,* trans. Charles Henkey, QD 1 (New York: Herder and Herder, 1961), 6–80, "Exegesis and Dogmatic Theology," in *Dogmatic vs. Biblical Theology,* ed. Herbert Vorgrimler (Baltimore: Helicon, 1964), 31–65, *Theological Investigations,* vol. 6: *Concerning Vatican II,* trans. Karl and Boniface Kruger (New York: Seabury, 1969), 89–112, and other essays.

religious communities, not as isolated individuals, and their work edified the entire community.[7]

McKenzie was criticized on several issues:[8] (1) He submerged the identity of individual biblical authors into the greater community far too much. (2) He overlooked the fact that some biblical authors expressed very critical attitudes toward previous traditions in the scriptures. For example, Job in the Hebrew Bible reacts against earlier concepts of retribution. (3) Individual texts are marked by the personal beliefs and personalities of their authors. Individual prophets in the Hebrew Bible have messages that reflect their own idiosyncratic life experiences, especially Hosea, Jeremiah, and Ezekiel. (4) Individual authors advance the understanding of their religious communities by building on what had been expressed previously. Paul and John in the New Testament, for example, were responsible for a great development in the thought of the ancient church. McKenzie did not give sufficient credit to the religious genius of individuals. After this discussion, the notion of social inspiration no longer interested biblical theologians, and perhaps for them it no longer reflected the categories of biblical thought sufficiently.

III

Despite criticisms of the model, there are a number of strengths in the concept of social inspiration as it first was presented. It places the focus on people as inspired rather than the literature, as old classical models had done. It recognizes the process of oral tradition and literary transmission from which the scriptures ultimately arose. Advocates took more seriously the social and cultural background out of which the biblical text arose. Finally, the model avoids problems associated with other explanations of inspiration: whether inspiration should be described as extending to ideas alone or to the words as well, and whether the final author or the original spokesperson was inspired. Although the model was discussed initially in Roman Catholic circles, over the years Protestant theologians and biblical scholars expressed comparable views. James Barr noted that inspiration by definition must include the entire process, including many nameless individuals who helped to generate our present text, and "it must be considered to belong more to the community as a whole."[9] Paul Achtemeier stressed that inspiration should be attributed to many "nameless people" who "shaped, preserved, and assembled portions of the traditions contained

---

[7]McKenzie, "Social Character," 60–68.

[8]McCarthy, "Personality," 554–56, 569–72; and Harrington, *Record,* 129–32, and *Key,* 47.

[9]James Barr, *Holy Scripture* (Philadelphia: Westminster Press, 1983), 27, *Fundamentalism* (Philadelphia: Westminster Press, 1978), 288–89, and *The Scope and Authority of the Bible* (Philadelphia: Westminster Press, 1980), 124–25.

in the several books," and that inspiration "occurs within the community of faith and must be located at least as much within that community as it is in with an individual author."[10] For him the most dynamic part of the process is the interplay of communal need and individual reflection on the traditions that shape a message to address those needs. Achtemeier spoke of how the process of inspiration embodies a significant criticism of the various traditions and the community that produced them.[11] Among these authors there is more emphasis on the dialectic involved in producing the text and the values that arise by way of strident critique of the community. One might sense that this nuance would be more typical of Protestant authors than their Roman Catholic counterparts. But this motif also might add greater substance to the model of social inspiration by recognizing the dynamic of conflict in the process.

In order to be useful today, some revisions in the concept of social inspiration ought to be made. If inspiration is a community charisma, one cannot overlook the significance of individual contributions, otherwise inspiration is spread thin and rendered amorphous. Great literature is not produced by everyone in the community, but rather by gifted individuals within the group who have superior artistic and theological ability.[12] Using the language of process thought, we would say that God becomes involved in the total life of the group but is especially manifest in the expression of key individuals. Were literature only to reflect the values of the group, how could creative advance occur? The traditio-historical method implies that there is a significant intellectual growth that results from the contributions of creative people, such as the prophets and Paul, who can rise above the values of the group.[13] Nor may the dynamic of dissent be overlooked. The Yahwist crafted the old traditions of Israel in a new creative way; Deuteronomy clarified existing notions of covenant found in the Sinai traditions; Job challenged the traditional views of individual retribution; Koheleth challenged the optimism of Proverbs concerning the human ability to grasp wisdom and find meaning in life; and Paul dramatically challenged the traditional Jewish Christian value system. The books of the Bible arose by a process of challenge and confrontation initiated by brilliant and inspired individuals.

A new model of social inspiration must articulate a healthy tension between the community and its traditions over against the genius of individuals who contributed to those traditions. Individuals arise and stand in tension with the values of the group that nurtured and educated them.

---

[10]Paul Achtemeier, *The Inspiration of Scripture* (Philadelphia: Westminster Press, 1980), 116, 132–33.

[11]Ibid., 90–92, 102–3, 123, 133.

[12]Scullion, *Theology,* 45; and Luis Alonso-Schökel, *The Inspired Word,* trans. Francis Martin (New York: Herder and Herder, 1972), 224.

[13]McCarthy, "Personality," 572; and Scullion, *Theology,* 46–49.

But after they speak, their words are remembered by that very same religious community or part of it. The community will shape or "filter" the message of the new spokesperson and then transmit it to later generations. So in the tension between the words of the individual who spoke and the "filtration" process of the group there exists a two-stage formation process that creates the sacred message, and equal credit must then be given to both the individual and the group.[14] Notice, however, that in this tension the first priority is given to the person who arises to speak, and then the community is said to shape the message subsequently. That paradigm stands in contrast to Rahner's model, which suggests that the community has priority and gives rise to an individual who speaks on its behalf. This sequence gives far more credit to the genius of the individual religious spokesperson.

One also is reminded of the process model of concrescence. As a new actual occasion or actual entity arises, it remembers part, but not all, of the actual entity that preceded it. In the process of prehension there is a selective use of the data, or we might call it an editorial process in regard to traditions and sacred literature. The prophetic spokesperson might be envisioned poetically as an actual entity who comes into being by drawing on what had been taught previously. His or her rearticulation is a creative advance. But then the community subsequently prehends his or her expressions in a new form, often in somewhat tamer and domesticated form, but certainly usable by later generations. This, too, is a new actual entity, which prehends part of the prophet's message, though not all of it, and perhaps not in its original abrasive form.

By attempting to envision both the spokesperson and the religious community rather artificially as actual entities, we are really trying to express the relationship between the two. We acknowledge the spokesperson's creative use, or prehension, of the past, and the equal value of both the spokesperson's contribution and the community's reinterpretation of it. Yet at the same time we recognize the temporal priority and specific value of the spokesperson's original contribution. Overall, the use of Whiteheadian categories reminds us of the organic and evolving nature of this process, which includes past traditions, artistic and creative new spokespersons, and the community that preserves the memories.

IV

A revived model of social inspiration must incorporate concepts from a wider ecumenical perspective and undergird the insights with a newer philosophical model, such as process thought. First, however, we must build on some of the tenets initially expressed by Benoit, such as his emphasis on the many inspired individuals in the process, each of whom is endowed

---

[14]Synave and Benoit, *Prophecy,* 127; McCarthy, "Personality," 553–76; Scullion, *Theology,* 48–49; and Harrington, *Key,* 47–48.

with special charisma. It would be best to include all contributors under the umbrella of inspiration, since all were somehow responsible for the formation of the canonical text. If we truly understood the pyschological mechanism of inspiration, we might speak confidently, as did Benoit, of the different types of inspiration. However, our theological discourse can speak meaningfully of inspiration only as a phenomenon regarded by faith as a mystery. We cannot define the different types of inspiration, nor should we be willing to exclude any one contributor to the sacred text from the category of inspired spokespersons. When we speak of inspiration, we are using symbolic language to confess our respect for the biblical text.

One needs to clearly address the definition of the concept of community, especially in relationship to the individual genius who speaks. One weakness in the Roman Catholic discussion, especially in the writings of Rahner, was a facile equation of community with institutional leaders, or as Rahner called them, "officers of the Church." Institutional leaders in the Jewish and Christian communities were not the source of inspiration; they were too often the targets of critique by those individuals who created the oral tradition and literature. Institutional leaders are part of the religious community of faith, perhaps a most important part, but they are not the community itself. Protestants are less liable to make this unconscious leap from describing a scriptural process to ecclesiastical structures.

A way to avoid this problem is to speak of the community of believers within the greater community of religious adherents. This community within the community produces the context from which the individual genius emerges to speak or to write, and the smaller community of the faithful (such as a circle of prophets) will recall the message of the spokesperson. Eventually, the message has impact on the larger community. Thus, prophets and Deuteronomic reformers were a minority ideological movement in preexilic Israel, but they preserved the message of great spokespersons, and those messages ultimately drew all Israelites toward a monotheistic faith. These reforming communities ought not to be identified with the greater polytheistic worshiping community of all Israel, nor were their theological leaders the institutional leaders of Israel in Jerusalem or Samaria. Rather, they stood in opposition to established royal and priestly leadership. Later, a wisdom circle protested Deuteronomic and prophetic notions of retribution, and out of this circle emerged the author of the book of Job. In the New Testament Paul arose out of theological circles, we assume, within Christianity that stood in dialectic with more traditional Palestinian Jewish Christianity. His writings were preserved in later "Paulinist" circles until they became our text. However, these Paulinists were not the church; they were but part of it. They actually critiqued much of the message of the traditional church at this stage of development in the New Testament era, and eventually their message became part of the total message of the ancient church, just as Paul's letters are part of the New Testament. James, the target of Paul's criticism, also represented a significant segment of earlier

Christians, whose message is represented in our canon in the books of Matthew, Hebrews, and James (all of which reflect the spectrum of liberal Jewish Christian thought). These examples imply that we cannot speak of the community that supports the individual; instead, we have communities within the greater community that generate their thought by standing in dialectic with one another.

At this point we may utilize process thought to explicate our model. All actual entities are defined by their relationships to other entities, especially those that are most proximate to them. Not only does an actual entity prehend the past in the process of concrescence, but it also prehends its relationship to the entities that surround it. This gives each of the entities a distinctive meaning. Likewise, one may speak of the different communities within the greater community of faith, be they the party of Paul, James, or Peter, all of which represented significant theological traditions within the ancient church. Each tradition is an entity that reacts with the other entities and thus formulates its own identity. Each theological tradition prehends those Christian movements in dialectic with it to establish its own identity. In a larger sense, each Christian theological movement also stands in relationship with greater forces within the Hellenistic world. These, too, may be defined as actual entities, which are more distant in the process of prehending the environment. Yet they, too, play a role in the formation of the identity of an actual entity, or in this case, each of the theological movements of early Christianity. If we use this philosophical model to paradigm the ancient church, we stress that the movements (stress the plural, not the singular) of early Christendom not only stood together in tension with each other, but that together they formed a social reality, or a nexus. This nexus of the ancient church was in harmony and tension at the same time, just as Whitehead described the experience of any actual entity. In our modern portrayal it stresses how those communities of belief in the greater ancient Christian church related to each other.

Another problem manifest in the older characterizations of social inspiration was the equation of the oral tradition of the ancient church with the greater Tradition of later Christianity. Herein further clarification is helpful. The oral tradition of the ancient church, or the apostolic preaching or the Kerygma, as various authors have described it, which gives rise to the later written texts, should not be lightly equated with subsequent traditions of the church that seek to elaborate on those earlier traditions, for the later elaborations in the traditions gave rise to the more developed ecclesiastical institutions. Rather, one might more profitably speak of the Tradition of the ancient church, or the gospel, which then gives rise to the scriptures and the later traditions, which include the ecclesiastical structures. So we have two meanings for the word *tradition* or *traditions*. In the foundational sense we have a narrow definition, which refers to the core elements of the gospel, or the Kerygma. In the later sense, we have the broader meaning, which includes the later development of creeds, theology, customs, and institutions of the church. We could call the first the "Tradition" and the second the "Traditions." One could further say that the foundational Tradition is the norm that shapes the scriptures and by which we still interpret the biblical text today, but the later Traditions are actually shaped by both the first Tradition and the scriptures. Clarification of these categories would make the image of social inspiration more viable and acceptable to a wider range of theologians.

Therefore, as we use the model of social inspiration, we ought to speak of the inspired community as only that specific movement that supports the individual genius, for it and not the greater community, be it Israel or the ancient church, provides the ideas for the individual and preserves the contributions of that individual. People within that smaller community engage in the process of transmitting what will someday become sacred literature, and they, as well as their support group, may be said to be inspired. This is then the two-step process, or two phases, of generating inspired literature, that of the spokesperson and also the transmitters. Great literature comes from individuals and the people in the dissenting communities who preserve the memories. Attributing inspiration to the greater community renders the concept of inspiration amorphous and makes it impossible to discern how change truly occurs. Rahner's definition of inspiration residing in the apostolic church might be redefined best as inspiration residing in the spearhead movements of the apostolic church (and similar movements in ancient Israel).

If we are to speak of the role played by the larger religious community, it should be in terms of acceptance. The small group, which supports the critical genius, really promulgates the text; the larger commmunity more passively accepts the text as authoritative after many years and perhaps as a response to a social or religious crisis. For example, the classical prophets and the Deuteronomistic History became sacred text only because the greater community of the Jews had to come to an understanding with the experience of the Babylonian exile. Their acceptance and circulation of this literature should not be considered an act of inspiration. Hence, in the tension between the small group that preserves the words of the prophets and generates the literature on the one hand, and the larger community that accepts this literature on the other hand, we would attribute inspiration only to the former.

V

This leads to another insight about change or religious development. The greater religious community would remain with a static theological position were it not for the challenges produced by inspired spearhead movements and individual spokespersons. A deeper understanding of the concept of tradition in the general sense perceives that the notion really speaks of change or revolution. Faithful to the core of Christian thought, or the Tradition in the foundation sense, Christian theologians proclaim the old message in new form. Early advocates of social inspiration did not stress sufficiently this corollary of the model: "Social inspiration" refers to the creative surge of the Spirit leading Israel, or the church, forward in thought and social values. This affirms the importance of the individual who dissents from the community and challenges their beliefs to grow as well as the community that preserves his or her thought and stands in critique against the larger community. Inspiration as a charisma visited on the small community is a force to promote change and new insight. Inspiration is not a static charisma that leads the genius to summarize the thought of the community in systematic fashion; rather, it causes change, disruption, insight, and above all, creative advance.

The dissenter who speaks under the charisma of inspiration against the community, be it his or her own support group or the larger religious community, is not an outcast, traitor, or heretic. Rather, the dissenter who functions on the periphery and engages in rhetorical conflict with the community is still within the community, for the dissenter speaks from an experience based in the community. When the message is delivered, it may become part of the intellectual interaction of the age and ultimately the received heritage of that community. Conflict is an integral part of any growth process, especially in intellectual movements. To assume this as our evolutionary paradigm implies that each Christian generation must be ready to correct, adapt, or reform the teachings of an earlier generation. This is implied by the development of the biblical traditions as well as the overall history of thought and customs within Christendom.

Herein some of the primary themes of process thought surface. Process thought attempts to give utterance to how the creative advance occurs. It stresses that each new moment of becoming draws from the previous moment and yet is different. Each new moment of becoming produces an actual entity that has prehended part of the previous moment, or actual entity, but not all. Some data are left behind in the process of concrescence. This model stresses the idea of change and evolution. In the arena of human thought there is an advance that changes and transforms old messages into new formats. In terms of Christian tradition we would say that tradition is an ongoing and evolving process of thought, not the collection of individual sacred thoughts to be filed neatly into a collection of ideas called "tradition." Theologians build on the thought of those who went before them, but they must rearticulate anew in every generation the old message. Christian tradition is an organic, evolving process of thought; it is a creative advance. "Tradition" is a dynamic organism that changes; it is not a collection of many small bricks in the form of a great unchanging cathedral. Process thought categories reinforce this dynamic portrayal of inspiration and the tradition process.

VI

Roman Catholic theologians made a significant contribution with the model of social inspiration in the past. It is to be hoped that the model will be revised and will provide a vehicle for meaningful discourse in the future. If the model is to be used, certain nuances must be added: (1) The tension between community and individual must be maintained, lest the contributions of the individual genius be underestimated. (2) The contributions of the many various people in the process of creating scripture must be described with the charisma of inspiration. Separately defined modes of inspiration ought not be assigned for each function according to either quality or degree. (3) The community that supports the individual should not be equated with the entire religious tradition, but it should be recognized as a distinct movement within the greater movement that stands in dialogue with the values of that greater group. (4) The aspect of dissent is most important in the process, for the dialectic of critique enables the entire religious tradition to move forward creatively. (5) "Social inspiration" describes a form of inspiration that promotes a creative advance, not a static preservation of thought in unchanging fashion. (6) Finally, this discourse may be strengthened by the use of process categories, either in direct fashion or in a subtle underlying way, for process thought highlights the whole notion of dynamic evolution. Most importantly, process thought inherently prompts us to think of God as involved in the entire chain of development behind the creation of the biblical text, dynamically involved in the efforts of many individuals over many years. Process thought also encourages us to view the canon itself as a lure used by God to lead us into the future. It offers to us direction into the future in terms of moral choices, individual and group direction, and above all, the promise of hope for a better future, because it provides us insight into the experiences of people in the past. In a sense, the canon illuminates human experience in light of the expectations and choices of the future, as Gerald Janzen once said.[15] With these new insights, the concept of social inspiration might become a meaningful form of discourse among theologians and biblical scholars.

---

[15]Janzen, "Process Perspective," 500.

Conclusion

Why should we undertake a quest to integrate process theology with the study of the Hebrew Scriptures? I believe that there are two truly significant reasons. First, the basic categories of process thought are the intellectual categories of our modern age, the commonsense ways of perceiving reality that most educated people have, whether they know it or not. Process philosophy attempts to give utterance and coherence to our twentieth-century view of the world in concrete and logical terms. In our modern era we see things in a much more holistic and developmental way. This has been impressed on us not only by science, but also by psychology, and even by historical studies, which stress social, political, and economic development in human affairs. We have been influenced by the thought of Georg Hegel, Karl Marx, Charles Darwin, Sigmund Freud, Albert Einstein, and other significant contributors to the modern worldview in the last two centuries in ways that we can no longer recognize. What we call commonsense ways of looking at reality have been affected tremendously by these individuals. Recognizing the validity of process philosophical and theological categories is actually the recognition of how we think in the modern world. It becomes necessary to articulate these categories and use them in our theology and pedagogy. People today no longer resonate with the abstract and idealistic intellectual categories that were the hallmark of intellectual discourse inspired by Greek philosophy. Those ways of speaking have been dying in educated circles, whether we have noticed it or not, since the beginning of the twentieth century. People think in processual categories in varying degrees nowadays, and they call it the normal way of thinking.

I believe there is a second reason, which is even more important, why we should integrate process theology into our discourse about the Bible in general and the Hebrew Scriptures in particular. Process thought redirects our attention to see the divine presence and divine immanence that is found in the biblical texts; it leads us to stress the importance of divine compassion, love, or what Christians would call grace. Too many people in the secular world and even more tragically in church circles view the Hebrew Scriptures as a book that reveals a God of wrath and judgment. Blame a lot of preachers for this too! Those of us who teach introductory courses on the Hebrew Bible find ourselves frequently combating this stereotype. Even then, we teachers still might communicate to our students the image of a judgmental God unconsciously by our use of classic theistic categories. The same holds true for clergy who speak about God on a regular basis in a more popular, personal, and intense way. The study of process theology, like the study of any theological system, assists in our reflection on what we believe and on how we speak to our various audiences. Sometimes good theology tells us not so much what to say, but what to avoid saying, lest we hurt people.

I believe that the conscious use, or at least intellectual acknowledgment, of the validity of process intellectual categories will lead the biblical theologian, Bible teacher, and preacher to articulate images from the Hebrew Scriptures in a way that emphasizes the divine-human relationship in a more meaningful fashion to the audience and in a manner that focuses on the powerful imagery of divine compassion found therein. In particular, process theology helps us to see those images of divine suffering. But also of importance are the conceptual paradigms that speak of covenantal relationships as the dynamic interaction of God and people and the deep divine involvement in total human life—in the realms of history and society, nature, and intellectual inquiry. Furthermore, processual categories may be used to call for the social mandates that the old biblical theology movement called for in the mid-twentieth century. If we perceive that we are part of a grand social and religious advance, we can realize the active role we are called on to take in an advance that is led by the presence of God in our midst. Process thought leads us to realize that we are part of an unfinished monotheistic evolution and revolution. All of this may be abetted by the consideration of, reflection on, and active intellectual use of process philosophical and theological categories.

Process modes of thinking can lead us to view reality in a more unified or holistic manner, and we are led to see God as totally involved in the created order. We may look anew at texts in the Hebrew Scriptures and recognize that God is revealed not only in sacred history, but also in the natural order (Psalms) and in human reflection (wisdom literature). God not only directs the whole human sphere of existence but also experiences the totality of human existence. In this regard, talk about the suffering of God can speak meaningfully to people. It may lead people to envision

God not as the puppet master who pulls the strings while we, the puppets, perform our dance of pain and death below; rather, God may be envisioned as the deity who knows full well what it is like to be human and suffer, for this deity has experienced with us our human pain. If there is a meaningful message that Christianity can proclaim to modern people, this may be the proclamation of our age. Christian discourse about Jesus' death to forgive sin needs to be complemented with talk about the suffering of God in the death of Jesus.

If God is immanent in the gradual pulse of religious change or evolution testified to in the biblical traditions, does not comparable advance still continue today? If we view ourselves as part of that dynamic continuum of change in which God is so intimately involved, we may understand the nature of religious tradition anew. Tradition is a process, not a received set of beliefs that are to be dogmatically defended against supposed change. We then affirm this continuum of religious change and contribute to this creative advance. We are part of the dynamic advance; we are co-creators with God; and we are the agents for unveiling the continuing implications of the millennia-long evolution of religious belief with all its attendant social implications. We are led to see an evolutionary trajectory that originates in the Hebrew Scriptures, carries through the New Testament and the history of Christian thought, and comes to where we are today. We are not a finished product, but part of this ongoing religious and social trajectory, led by a God whom we perceive in faith. Process thought encourages us to think and speak in these categories.

From our study of the Hebrew Scriptures we may perceive unifying themes in other arenas of religious studies. There may be implications for our dialogue with the religions of the world and the cultures in which they are found. We may be led to a greater openness and dialogue with our larger world community, as we sense that the Divine is involved with this world in more ways than heretofore we had recognized and that these divine manifestations may be found outside the Judeo-Christian tradition. God may lure others into a future with a deeper relationship to the Divine. If religious values are seen to emerge in a gradual process in the Hebrew Scriptures, the New Testament, and the history of the Christian tradition, and we no longer speak in terms of contrast and dialectical opposition of the biblical worldview to the values of the ancient world, we may be more inclined to see our own culture and worldview less in opposition to other world cultures. Our feeling for the world community may be enhanced, and this will deepen our sense of real Christian mission to the world. We will be inspired not so much to convert others as to share our beliefs, and we may find our mission more effective. Process theology may lead us to be more open in our dealing with world cultures and other religions, especially when process thought is combined with biblical theology. We may learn to appreciate more our role in a greater religious advance for the human race.

Bibliography

Process Philosophy and Theology

Bacik, James. "Alfred North Whitehead." In *Contemporary Theologians*, 207–19. Chicago: Thomas More, 1989.

Beardslee, William. *A House for Hope: A Study in Process and Biblical Thought.* Philadelphia: Westminster Press, 1972.

———. "Introduction." *Semeia* 24 (1982): 1–6.

Beardslee, William, and David Lull, eds. *Old Testament Interpretation from a Process Perspective. Semeia* 24 (1982).

Bloesch, Donald. "Process Theology and Reformed Theology." In *Process Theology*, edited by Ronald Nash, 31–56. Grand Rapids, Mich.: Baker Books, 1987.

Bracken, Joseph, and Marjorie Suchocki, eds. *Trinity in Process: A Relational Theology of God.* New York: Continuum, 1997.

Christian, William. *An Interpretation of Whitehead's Metaphysics.* Westport, Conn.: Greenwood, 1959.

Clark, Norris. "Christian Theism and Whiteheadian Process Philosophy: Are They Compatible?" In *Process Theology,* edited by Ronald Nash, 219–51. Grand Rapids, Mich.: Baker Books, 1987.

Cobb, John. *Christ in a Pluralistic Age.* Philadelphia: Westminster Press, 1975.

———. *A Christian Natural Theology.* Philadelphia: Westminster Press, 1974..

———. *God and the World.* Philadelphia: Westminster Press, 1969.

———. *Liberal Christianity at the Crossroads.* Philadelphia: Westminster Press, 1973.

———. *Process Theology as Political Theology.* Philadelphia: Westminster Press, 1982.

———. "The Relativization of the Trinity." In *Trinity and Process,* edited by Joseph Bracken and Marjorie Suchocki, 1–22. New York: Continuum, 1997.

———. *The Structure of Christian Existence.* Philadelphia: Westminster Press, 1967.

Cobb, John, and David Ray Griffin. *Process Theology.* Philadelphia: Westminster Press, 1976.

Cobb, John and Widick Schroeder, eds. *Process Philosophy and Social Thought.* Chicago: Center for the Scientific Study of Religion, 1981.

Cobb, John, and David Tracy. *Talking About God.* New York: Seabury, 1983.

Collins, John. "Process Hermeneutic." *Semeia* 24 (1982): 107–16.

Doud, Robert. "The Biblical Heart and Process Anthropology." Unpublished paper. Pasadena City College.

Farley, Edward. *Ecclesial Man.* Philadelphia: Fortress Press, 1975.

Farmer, Ronald. *Beyond the Impasse: The Promise of a Process Hermeneutic.* Studies in American Biblical Hermeneutics 13. Macon, Ga.: Mercer, 1997.

Ford, Lewis S. "Biblical Recital and Process Philosophy." *Int* 26 (1972): 198–209.

———. "Contingent Trinitarianism." In *Trinity in Process,* edited by Joseph Bracken and Marjorie Suchocki, 41–68. New York: Continuum, 1997.

———. "The Divine Curse Understood in Terms of Persuasion." *Semeia* 24 (1982): 81–87.

———. "Hartshorne's Encounter with Whitehead: Introductory Remarks." In *Two Process Philosophers,* edited by Ford, 1–9.

———. *The Lure of God: A Biblical Background for Process Theism.* Philadelphia: Fortress Press, 1978.

———. "Whitehead's Differences from Hartshorne." In *Two Process Philosophers,* edited by Ford, 58–83.

———, ed. *Two Process Philosophers: Hartshorne's Encounter with Whitehead.* Tallahassee, Fla.: American Academy of Religion, 1973.

Gray, James. *Modern Process Thought.* Lanham, Md.: UPA, 1982.

Griffin, David Ray. "Hartshorne's Differences from Whitehead." In *Two Process Philosophers,* edited by Lewis S. Ford, 35–57. Tallahassee, Fla.: American Academy of Religion. 1973.

———. "A Naturalistic Trinity." In *Trinity in Process,* edited by Joseph Bracken and Marjorie Suchocki, 23–40. New York: Continuum, 1997.

Hartshorne, Charles. *Beyond Humanism.* Lincoln: University of Nebraska Press, 1937.

———. *Creative Synthesis and Philosophic Method.* La Salle, Ill.: Open Court, 1970.

———. *The Divine Relativity: A Social Conception of God.* New Haven, Conn.: Yale University Press, 1948.

———. *A Natural Theology for Our Time.* La Salle, Ill.: Open Court, 1967.

———. *Omnipotence and Other Theological Mistakes.* Albany: SUNY Press, 1984.

———. *Reality as a Social Process.* Glencoe, Ill.: Free Press, 1953.

———. *Whitehead's Philosophy: Selected Essays, 1935–1970.* Lincoln: University of Nebraska Press, 1972.

Hartshorne, Charles, and Creighton Peden. "Whitehead in Historical Context." In *Whitehead's View of Reality,* 2–24. New York: Pilgrim Press, 1981.

Hawking, Stephen. *A Brief History of Time.* New York: Bantam, 1988.

Janzen, Gerald. "Metaphor and Reality in Hosea 11." *Semeia* 24 (1982): 7–44.

———. "The Old Testament in 'Process' Perspective." In *Magnalia Dei—The Mighty Acts of God,* edited by Frank Cross et al., 480–509. Garden City, N.Y.: Doubleday, 1976.

Johnson, A. H. *Whitehead's Theory of Reality.* New York: Dover, 1962 (1st ed., Boston: Beacon Press, 1952).

Kraus, Elizabeth. *The Metaphysics of Experience: A Companion to Whitehead's Process and Reality.* New York: Fordham University Press, 1979.

Kuyper, Lester. "The Suffering and the Repentance of God." *SJT* 22 (1969): 257–77.

Lawrence, Nathaniel. *Whitehead's Philosophical Development.* Berkeley: University of California Press, 1956.

Leclerc, Ivor. *Whitehead's Metapyhsics.* New York: Macmillan, 1958.

Lee, Bernard. "An 'Other' Trinity." In *Trinity in Process,* edited by Joseph Bracken and Marjorie Suchocki, 191–214. New York: Continuum, 1997.

Lowe, Victor. *Alfred North Whitehead: The Man and His Work.* Vol. 2. Baltimore: Johns Hopkins University Press, 1990.

———. *Understanding Whitehead.* Baltimore: Johns Hopkins University Press, 1962.

Morris, Randall. *Process Philosophy and Political Ideology.* Albany: SUNY Press, 1991.

Nash, Ronald, ed. *Process Theology.* Grand Rapids, Mich.: Baker Books, 1987.

O'Donnell, John. *Trinity and Temporality: The Christian Doctrine of God in the Light of Process Theology and the Theology of Hope.* New York: Oxford, 1983.

Ogden, Schubert. *Christ Without Myth.* New York: Harper and Row, 1961.

———. *Doing Theology Today.* Valley Forge, Pa.: Trinity Press, 1996.

———. *Is There Only One True Religion or Are There Many?* Dallas: SMU Press, 1992.

———. *On Theology.* San Francisco: Harper and Row, 1986.

———. *The Point of Christology.* San Francisco: Harper and Row, 1982.

———. *The Reality of God and Other Essays.* New York: Harper and Row, 1977.

Pinnock, Clark. "Between Classical and Process Theism." In *Process Theology,* edited by Ronald Nash, 313–27. Grand Rapids, Mich.: Baker Books, 1987.

Pittenger, Norman. *After Death: Life in God.* New York: Seabury, 1980.

———. *Alfred North Whitehead.* Richmond, Va.: John Knox Press, 1969.

———. *Catholic Faith in a Process Perspective.* Maryknoll, N.Y.: Orbis Books, 1981.

———. *The Christian Church as a Social Process.* Philadelphia: Westminster Press, 1971.

———. *Christology Reconsidered.* London: SCM Press, 1970.

———. *The Divine Triunity.* Philadelphia: United Church Press, 1977.

———. *The Holy Spirit.* Philadelphia: Pilgrim Press, 1974.

———. *The Ministry of All Christians.* Wilton, Conn.: Morehouse-Barlow, 1983.

———. *Picturing God.* London: SCM Press, 1982.

———. *The Pilgrim Church and the Easter People.* Wilmington, Del.: Glazier, 1987.

———. *Process Thought and Christian Faith.* New York: Macmillan, 1968.

———. *Reconceptions in Christian Thinking.* New York: Seabury, 1968.

Pollard, T. E. "The Impassibility of God." *SJT* 8 (1955): 353–64.

Price, Lucien. *Dialogues of Alfred North Whitehead.* London: Reinhardt, 1954.

Sessions, William. "Hartshorne's Early Philosophy." In *Two Process Philosophers,* edited by Lewis S. Ford, 10–34. Tallahassee, Fla.: American Academy of Religion, 1973.

Sherburne, Donald. *A Whiteheadian Aesthetic.* New Haven, Conn.: Yale University Press, 1961.

Smith, John. *The Spirit of American Philosophy.* Rev. ed. Albany: SUNY Press, 1983.

Stumpf, Samuel Enoch. *Socrates to Sartre.* New York: McGraw-Hill, 1966.

Sturm, Douglas. "Process Thought and Political Theory: Implications of a Principle of Internal Relations." In *Process Philosophy and Social Thought,* edited by John Cobb and Widick Schroeder, 81–102. Chicago: Center for the Scientific Study of Religion, 1981.

Suchocki, Marjorie. *The End of Evil: Process Eschatology in Historical Context.* Albany: SUNY Press, 1988.

———. *God–Christ–Church: A Practical Guide to Process Theology.* New York: Crossroad, 1982.

———. "Spirit in and through the World." In *Trinity in Process,* edited by Joseph Bracken and Suchocki. 173–90.

Whitehead, Alfred North. *Adventure of Ideas.* New York: Macmillan, 1933.

———. *The Concept of Nature.* Cambridge, U.K.: Cambridge University Press, 1920.

———. *An Enquiry Concerning the Principles of Natural Knowledge.* Cambridge, U.K.: Cambridge University Press, 1919.

———. *The Function of Reason.* Princeton, N.J.: Princeton University Press, 1929.

———. *Modes of Thought.* New York: Macmillan, 1938.

———. *Process and Reality: An Essay in Cosmology.* Corrected ed., edited by David Ray Griffin and Donald Sherburne. New York: Free Press, 1978.

———. *Religion in the Making.* New York: Macmillan, 1926.

———. *Science and the Modern World.* New York: Macmillan, 1925.

Williams, Daniel Day. "Suffering and Being in Empirical Theology." In *The Future of Empirical Theology,* edited by Robert Evans. Philadelphia: Westminster Press, 1971.

Biblical Studies

Achtemeier, Paul. *The Inspiration of Scripture.* Philadelphia: Westminster Press, 1980.

Ackerman, Susan. "The Queen Mother and the Cult in Ancient Israel." *JBL* 112 (1993): 385–401.

——. *Under Every Green Tree.* HSM 46. Atlanta: Scholars Press, 1992.

Ahlström, Gösta. *A History of Ancient Palestine.* Minneapolis: Fortress Press, 1993.

——. "The Role of Archaeological and Literary Remains in Reconstructing Israel's History." In *The Fabric of History,* edited by Diana Edelman, 116–41. JSOTSup 127. Sheffield, U.K.: JSOT, 1991.

——. *Royal Administration and National Religion in Ancient Palestine.* SHANE 1. Leiden: Brill, 1982.

——. *Who Were the Israelites?* Winona Lake, Ind.: Eisenbrauns, 1986.

Albertz, Ranier. *A History of Israelite Religion in the Old Testament Period.* 2 vols. Translated by John Bowden. OTL. Philadelphia: Westminster Press, 1994.

Albrektson, Bertil. *History and the Gods.* Lund: Gleerup, 1967.

Albright, William Foxwell. *From the Stone Age to Christianity.* 2d ed. Garden City, N.Y.: Doubleday, 1957 (1st ed. 1940).

Alonso-Schökel, Luis. *The Inspired Word.* Translated by Francis Martin. New York: Herder and Herder, 1972.

Anderson, Bernhard, ed. *Creation in the Old Testament.* IRT 6. Philadelphia: Fortress Press, 1984.

——. "Introduction: Mythopoeic and Theological Dimensions of Biblical Creation Faith." In *Creation in the Old Testament,* edited by Anderson, 1–24. Philadelphia: Fortress Press, 1984.

Baltzer, Klaus. "Considerations Regarding the Office and Calling of the Prophet." *HTR* 61 (1968): 567–81.

——. *The Covenant Formulary.* Translated by David Green. Philadelphia: Fortress Press, 1971.

Barr, James. *Fundamentalism.* Philadelphia: Westminster Press, 1978.

——. *Holy Scripture.* Philadelphia: Westminster Press, 1983.

——. *The Scope and Authority of the Bible.* Philadelphia: Westminster Press, 1980.

Benoit, Pierre. "The Analogies of Inspiration." In *Aspects of Biblical Inspiration.* Translated by Jerome Murphy-O'Connor and S. K. Ashe, 13–35. Chicago: Priory, 1965.

——. "Inspiration." In *Guide to the Bible,* edited by André Robert and A. Tricot. Translated by Edward Arbez and Martin McGuire. 2d ed. 2 vols. Vol. 1, 9–52. New York: Desclee, 1960.

210 The Old Testament and Process Theology

——. "Inspiration and Revelation." In *Human Reality of Sacred Scripture.* Translated by David Connor. Conc 10. New York: Paulist, 1965.

Biale, David. "The God with Breasts." *HR* 20 (1982): 240–56.

Blank, Sheldon. "Doest Thou Well to Be Angry?" *HUCA* 26 (1955): 29–41.

Blenkinsopp, Joseph. *A History of Prophecy in Israel.* Philadelphia: Westminster Press, 1983.

Bransnett, B. R. *The Suffering of the Impassible God.* Richmond, Va.: John Knox Press, 1965.

Bright, John. *Jeremiah.* AB 21. Garden City, N.Y.: Doubleday, 1964.

Brueggemann, Walter. *Old Testament Theology,* edited by Patrick Miller. Minneapolis: Fortress Press, 1992.

——. *Prophetic Imagination.* Philadelphia: Fortress Press, 1978.

——. "A Shape for Old Testament Theology." *CBQ* 47 (1985): 28–46.

Callaway, Joseph. "A New Perspective on the Hill Country Settlement of Canaan in Iron Age I." In *Palestine in the Bronze and Iron Ages,* edited by J. N. Tubb, 31–49. London: Institute of Archaeology, 1985.

——. "Village Subsistence at Ai and Raddana in Iron Age I." In *The Answers Lie Below,* edited by Henry Thompson, 51–66. Lanham, Md.: UPA, 1984.

Chaney, Marvin. "Debt Enslavement in Israelite History and Tradition." In *The Bible and the Politics of Exegesis,* edited by David Jobling et al., 127–39. Cleveland: Pilgrim Press, 1991.

Childs, Brevard. *Biblical Theology in Crisis.* Philadelphia: Westminster Press, 1970.

——. *Biblical Theology of the Old and New Testaments.* Minneapolis: Fortress Press, 1993.

——. *Old Testament Theology in a Canonical Context.* Philadelphia: Fortress Press, 1985.

Clements, Ronald. *Abraham and David.* SBT 2d ser. 5. London: SCM Press, 1967.

Clifford, Richard, and John Collins, eds. *Creation in the Biblical Traditions.* CBQMS 24. Washington, D.C.: CBA, 1992.

Coats, George. "The King's Loyal Opposition: Obedience and Authority in Exodus 32–34." In *Canon and Authority,* edited by George Coats and Burke Long, 91–109. Philadelphia: Fortress Press, 1977.

——. "The Way of Obedience: Traditio-Historical and Hermeneutical Reflections on the Balaam Story." *Semeia* 24 (1982): 53–79.

Coote, Robert, and Keith Whitelam. *The Emergence of Early Israel in Historical Perspective.* SWBA 5. Sheffield, U.K.: Almond, 1987.

——. "The Emergence of Israel." *Semeia* 37 (1986): 119–42.

Craigie, Peter. *The Book of Deuteronomy.* NICOT. Grand Rapids, Mich.: Eerdmans, 1976.

Crenshaw, James. *Old Testament Wisdom.* Atlanta: John Knox Press, 1981.

Croatto, Severino. *Exodus.* Maryknoll, N.Y.: Orbis Books, 1981.

Cross, Frank. *Canaanite Myth and Hebrew Epic.* Cambridge, Mass.: Harvard University Press, 1973.

Crüsemann, Frank. *The Torah.* Translated by Allan Mahnke. Minneapolis: Fortress Press, 1996.

Davies, Philip. *In Search of "Ancient Israel."* JSOTSup 148. Sheffield, U.K.: JSOT, 1992.

———. "Scenes from the Early History of Judaism." In *The Triumph of Elohim,* edited by Diana Edelman, 145–82. Grand Rapids, Mich.: Eerdmans, 1996.

Day, John. *God's Conflict with the Dragon and the Sea.* Cambridge, U.K.: Cambridge University Press, 1985.

———. *Molech.* Cambridge, U.K.: Cambridge University Press, 1989.

Dever, William. "Asherah, Consort of Yahweh?" *BASOR* 255 (1984): 21–37.

———. *Recent Archaeological Discoveries and Biblical Research.* Seattle: University of Washington Press, 1990.

Dietrich, Walter, and Martin Klopfenstein, eds. *Ein Gott allein?* OBO 139. Göttingen: Vandenhoeck und Ruprecht, 1994.

Drews, Robert. *The End of the Bronze Age.* Princeton, N.J.: Princeton University Press, 1993.

Edelman, Diana, ed. *The Triumph of Elohim.* Grand Rapids, Mich.: Eerdmans, 1996.

Edwards, Chilperic. *The Hammurabi Code and Sinaitic Legislation.* Port Washington, N.Y.: Kennikat, 1904.

Eichrodt, Walther. *Theology of the Old Testament.* Translated by J. A. Baker. 2 vols. OTL. Philadelphia: Westminster Press, 1961, 1967.

Eisenstadt, Shmuel. "The Axial Age Breakthrough in Ancient Israel." In *The Origins and Diversity of Axial Age Civilizations,* edited by Eisenstadt, 127–34. Albany: SUNY Press, 1986.

Eliade, Mircea. *Myth of the Eternal Return.* Princeton, N.J.: Princeton University Press, 1954.

Emerton, J. A. "A New Light on Israelite Religion." *ZAW* 94 (1982): 2–20.

Fensham, F. C. "Common Trends in the Curses of the Near Eastern Treaties and Kudurru-inscriptions Compared with the Maledictions of Amos and Isaiah." *ZAW* 75 (1963): 155–75.

Finkelstein, Israel. *The Archaeology of the Israelite Settlement.* Jerusalem: IES, 1988.

Flanagan, James. *David's Social Drama.* SWBA 7. Sheffield, U.K.: Almond, 1988.

Fohrer, Georg. "Die Gattung der Berichte über symbolische Handlungen der Propheten." *ZAW* 54 (1952): 101–20.

Frankfort, Henri. "Myth and Reality." In *The Intellectual Adventure of Ancient Man,* edited by Henri Frankfort. Chicago: University of Chicago Press, 1946.

Freedman, David Noel, ed. *ABD.* 6 vols. Garden City, N.Y.: Doubleday, 1992.

Fretheim, Terence. *The Suffering God.* OBT. Philadelphia: Fortress Press, 1984.

Friedman, Richard Elliott. *The Disappearance of God.* Boston: Little, Brown, 1995.

Fritz, Volkmar. "Conquest or Settlement?" *BA* 50 (1987): 84–100.

——. "The Israelite 'Conquest' in Light of Recent Excavations at Khirbet el-Mishâsh." *BASOR* 241 (1981): 61–73.

Frye, Northrop. *The Great Code: The Bible and Literature.* New York: Harcourt, Brace, Jovanovich, 1982.

Gamoran, Hillel. "The Biblical Law Against Loans on Interest." *JNES* 30 (1971): 127–34.

Garbini, Giovanni. *History and Ideology in Ancient Israel.* Translated by John Bowden. New York: Crossroad, 1988.

Gerstenberger, Erhard, and Wolfgang Schrage, *Suffering.* Translated by John Steely. Nashville: Abingdon Press, 1980.

de Geus, C. H. J. *The Tribes of Israel.* Amsterdam: Van Gorcum, 1976.

Girard, René. *The Scapegoat.* Translated by Yvonne Freccero. Baltimore: Johns Hopkins University Press, 1986.

Gnuse, Robert. *Authority of the Bible.* New York: Paulist Press, 1985.

—— "Contemporary Evolutionary Theory as a New Heuristic Model for the Socio-scientific Method in Biblical Studies." *Zygon* 25 (1990): 405–31.

——. *Heilsgeschichte as a Model for Biblical Theology.* College Theology Society Studies in Religion 4. Lanham: UPA, 1989.

——. "Jubilee Legislation in Leviticus." *BTB* 15 (1985): 43–48.

——. *No Other Gods: Emergent Monotheism in Ancient Israel.* JSOTSup 241. Sheffield, U.K.: Sheffield Academic Press, 1997.

——. "Tradition History." In *Dictionary of Biblical Interpretation,* edited by John Hayes. Vol. 2, 583–88. Nashville: Abingdon Press, 1999.

——. *You Shall Not Steal: Community and Property in the Biblical Tradition.* Maryknoll, N.Y.: Orbis Books, 1985.

Gottwald, Norman. *Social Scientific Criticism of the Hebrew Bible and Its Social World. Semeia* 37 (1986).

——. *The Tribes of Yahweh.* Maryknoll, N.Y.: Orbis Books, 1979.

Green, Alberto. *The Role of Human Sacrifice in the Ancient Near East.* ASORDS 1. Missoula, Mont.: Scholars Press, 1977.

Habel, Norman. *The Book of Job.* CBC. Cambridge, U.K.: Cambridge University Press, 1975.

——. "The Form and Significance of the Call Narratives." *ZAW* 77 (1965): 297–323.

Hadley, Judith. "The Khirbet el-Qôm Inscription." *VT* 37 (1987): 39–49.

——. "Yahweh and 'His Asherah.'" In *Ein Gott allein?* edited by Walter Dietrich and Martin Klopfenstein, 235–68. OBO 139. Göttingen: Vandenhoeck und Ruprecht, 1994.

Halpern, Baruch. *The Emergence of Israel in Canaan.* SBLMS 29. Chico, Calif.: Scholars Press, 1983.

——. "Settlement of Canaan." *ABD.* Edited by David Noel Freedman. 6 vols. Vol. 5, 1120–43. Garden City, N.Y.: Doubleday, 1992.

Hanson, Paul. *The People Called.* New York: Harper and Row, 1986.

Harrington, Wilfrid. *Key to the Bible.* Vol. 1: *Record of Revelation.* Garden City, N.Y.: Doubleday, 1976.

——. *Record of Revelation.* Chicago: Priory, 1965.

Heider, George. *The Cult of Molek.* JSOTSup 43. Sheffield, U.K.: JSOT, 1985.

Heschel, Abraham. *The Prophets.* 2 vols. New York: Harper and Row, 1962.

Hillers, Delbert. *Covenant: The History of a Biblical Idea.* Baltimore: Johns Hopkins University Press, 1969.

——. *Treaty Curses and the Old Testament.* BibOr 16. Rome: PBI, 1964.

Hoenig, S. B. "Sabbatical Years and the Year of Jubilee." *JQR* 59 (1969): 222–36.

Hopkins, David. *The Highlands of Canaan.* SWBA 3. Sheffield, U.K.: Almond, 1985.

Hossfeld, F. L. "Einheit und Einzigkeit Gottes im frühen Jahwismus." In *Im Gespräch mit dem dreieinen Gott,* edited by Michael Böhnke and Hanspeter Heinz, 57–74. Düsseldorf: Patmos, 1985.

Huffmon, Herbert. "The Covenant Lawsuit and the Prophets." *JBL* 78 (1959): 286–95.

Kaufmann, Yehezkel. *The Religion of Israel.* Translated and abridged by Moshe Greenberg. New York: Schocken, 1972.

Keel, Othmar. "Gedanken zur Beschäftigung mit Monotheismus." In *Monotheismus im Alten Israel und seiner Umwelt,* edited by Othmar Keel, 20–30. Fribourg: Schweizerisches Katholisches Bibelwerk, 1980.

——. "Jahwe und die Sonnengottheit von Jerusalem." In *Ein Gott allein?* edited by Walter Dietrich and Martin Klopfenstein, 269–306. Göttingen: Vandenhoeck und Ruprecht, 1994.

——. *The Symbolism of the Biblical World.* Translated by Timothy Hallett. New York: Seabury, 1978.

——, ed. *Monotheismus im Alten Israel und seiner Umwelt.* BibB 14. Fribourg: Schweizerisches Katholisches Bibelwerk, 1980.

Kitamori, Kazoh. *Theology of the Pain of God.* London: SCM Press, 1966.

Kloos, Carola. *Yahweh's Combat with the Sea.* Leiden: Brill, 1986.

Knight, Harold. *The Hebrew Prophets.* London: Lutterworth, 1947.

Knohl, Israel. *The Sanctuary of Silence.* Minneapolis: Fortress Press, 1995.

Kolarik, Michael. "Creation and Salvation in the Book of Wisdom." In *Creation in the Biblical Traditions,* edited by Richard Clifford and John Collins, 97–107, CBQMS 24. Washington, D.C.: CBA, 1992.

Lang, Bernhard. *Monotheism and the Prophetic Minority.* SWBA 1. Sheffield, U.K.: Almond, 1983.

Lemche, Niels Peter. *Ancient Israel.* Biblical Seminar 5. Sheffield, U.K.: JSOT, 1988.

———. *The Canaanites and Their Land.* JSOTSup 110. Sheffield, U.K.: JSOT, 1991.

———. *Early Israel.* VTSup 37. Leiden: Brill, 1985.

———. "Kann von einer 'israelitischen Religion' noch weiterhin die Rede sein?" In *Ein Gott allein?* edited by Walter Dietrich and Martin Klopfenstein, 59–75. Gottingen: Vandenhoeck und Ruprecht, 1994.

Levenson, Jon. *Creation and the Persistence of Evil.* San Francisco: Harper Collins, 1988.

———. *The Death and Resurrection of the Beloved Son.* New Haven, Conn.: Yale University Press, 1993.

Lindblom, Johannes. *Prophecy in Israel.* Philadelphia: Fortress Press, 1962.

Loewenstamm, Samuel. "Neshek and m/tarbith." *JBL* 88 (1969): 78–80.

Lohfink, Norbert. "Das Alte Testament und sein Monotheismus." In *Der eine Gott und der reieine Gott,* edited by Karl Rahner, 28–47. Munich: Schnell und Steiner, 1983.

———. "Zur Geschichte der Diskussion über den Monotheismus im Alten Israel." In *Gott, der Einzige,* edited by Herbert Haag, 9–25. QD 104. Freiburg: Herder, 1985.

London, Gloria. "A Comparison of Two Contemporaneous Lifestyles of the Late Second Millennium B.C." *BASOR* 273 (1989): 42–52.

McCarthy, Dennis. "Personality, Society, and Inspiration." *TS* 24 (1963): 553–76.

———. *Treaty and Covenant.* AnBib 21. Rome: PBI, 1963.

Machinist, Peter. "The Question of Distinctiveness in Ancient Israel." In *A Highway from Egypt to Assyria,* edited by Israel Eph'al and Mordechai Cogan, 420–42. Jerusalem: Magnes, 1990.

McKenzie, John. "The Social Character of Inspiration." *CBQ* 24 (1962): 115–24.

Macquarrie, John. *Thinking about God.* New York: Harper and Row, 1975.

Maloney, R. P. "Usury and Restrictions on Interest-Taking in the Ancient Near East." *CBQ* 36 (1974): 1–20.

Margalit, Baruch. "The Meaning and Significance of Asherah." *VT* 40 (1990): 264–97.

Mendelsohn, Isaac. *Slavery in the Ancient Near East.* New York: Oxford, 1949.

Mendenhall, George. "Ancient Oriental and Biblical Law." *BA* 17 (1954): 26–46.

———. "Covenant Forms in Israelite Tradition." *BA* 17 (1954): 50–76.

———. *The Tenth Generation.* Baltimore: Johns Hopkins University Press, 1973.

Mendenhall, George, and Gary Herion. "Covenant." *ABD.* Edited by David Noel Freedman. 6 vols. Vol. 1, 1179–1202. Garden City, N.Y.: Doubleday, 1992.

Miller, Patrick. *The Divine Warrior in Early Israel.* Cambridge, Mass.: Harvard University Press, 1973.

Mitchell, Hinckley. *Ethics of the Old Testament.* Chicago: n.p., 1912.

Moltmann, Jürgen. *The Crucified God.* New York: Harper and Row, 1968.

Morgenstern, Julian. "Sabbatical Year." *IDB.* Edited by George Buttrick. 4 vols. Vol. 2, 142. Nashville: Abingdon Press, 1962.

Mozley, J. K. *The Impassibility of God.* Cambridge, U.K.: Cambridge University Press, 1926.

Nelson, Richard. *The Double Redaction of the Deuteronomistic History.* Sheffield, U.K.: JSOT, 1983.

Neufeld, Edward. "The Prohibitions Against Loans at Interest in Ancient Hebrew Law." *HUCA* 26 (1955): 355–412.

Nicholson, Ernest. *Exodus and Sinai in History and Tradition.* Richmond, Va.: John Knox Press, 1973.

Niehr, Herbert. "JHWH in der Rolle des Baalsamem." In *Ein Gott allein?* edited by Walter Dietrich and Martin Klopfenstein, 307–26. Göttingen: Vandenhoeck und Ruprecht, 1994.

——. "The Rise of YHWH in Judahite and Israelite Religion." In *The Triumph of Elohim,* edited by Diana Edelman, 45–72. Grand Rapids, Mich.: Eerdmans, 1996.

Nikiprowetsky, V. "Ethical Monotheism." *Daedalus* 104, no. 2 (1975): 68–89.

North, Robert. *Sociology of the Biblical Jubilee.* AnBib 4. Rome: PBI, 1954.

Noth, Martin. *The History of Israel.* Translated by Peter Ackroyd. New York: Harper and Brothers, 1960.

Olyan, Saul. *Asherah and the Cult of Yahweh in Israel.* SBLMS 34. Atlanta: Scholars Press, 1988.

Patai, Raphael. *The Hebrew Goddess.* 3d ed. New York: Avon, 1978.

Patrick, Dale. *Old Testament Law.* Atlanta: John Knox Press, 1985.

Perlitt, Lothar. *Bundestheologie im Alten Testament.* WMANT 36. Neukirchen-Vluyn: Neukirchener, 1963.

Pritchard, James, ed. *Ancient Near Eastern Texts Relating to the Old Testament.* 3d ed. Princeton, N.J.: Princeton University Press, 1970.

Rad, Gerhard von. *Der heilige Krieg im alten Israel.* 5th ed. Göttingen: Vandenhoeck und Ruprecht, 1969.

——. *The Message of the Prophets.* Translated by D. M. G. Stalker. New York: Harper and Row, 1965.

——. *Old Testament Theology.* Translated by D. M. G. Stalker. 2 vols. New York: Harper and Row, 1962, 1965.

——. *Wisdom in Israel.* Translated by James Martin. Nashville: Abingdon Press, 1972.

Rahner, Karl. "Exegesis and Dogmatic Theology." In *Dogmatic vs. Biblical Theology,* edited by Herbert Vorgrimler, 31–65. Baltimore: Helicon, 1964.

——. *Inspiration in the Bible.* Translated by Charles Henkey. QD 1. New York: Herder and Herder, 1961.

——. *Theological Investigations.* Vol. 6: *Concerning Vatican II.* Translated by Karl and Boniface Kruger, 89–112. New York: Seabury, 1969.

Raitt, Thomas. *A Theology of Exile.* Philadelphia: Fortress Press, 1977.

Reventlow, Henning Graf. *The Authority of the Bible and the Rise of the Modern World.* Philadelphia: Fortress Press, 1985.

——. "Die Eigenart des Jahweglaubens als geschichtliches und theologisches Problem." *KD* 20 (1974): 199–217.

Robinson, Henry Wheeler. *The Cross in the Old Testament.* London: SCM Press, 1955.

——. *Suffering Human and Divine.* New York: Macmillan, 1939.

Saggs, H. W. F. *The Encounter with the Divine in Mesopotamia and Israel.* London: Athlone, 1978.

Scharbert, Josef. *Der Schmerz im Alten Testament.* Bonn: Peter Hanstein, 1955.

Schmid, Hans. "Creation, Righteousness, and Salvation." In *Creation in the Old Testament,* edited by Bernhard Anderson, 102–17. IRT 6. Philadelphia: Fortress Press, 1984.

Schroer, Silvia. *In Israel Gab Es Bilder.* OBO 74. Freiburg: Vandenhoeck und Ruprecht, 1987.

Scullion, John. *The Theology of Inspiration.* Theology Today Series 10. Notre Dame: Fides, 1970.

Seow, Choon-Leong. *Myth, Drama, and the Politics of David's Dance.* HSM 46. Atlanta: Scholars Press, 1989.

Simkins, Ronald. *Creator and Creation: Nature in the Worldview of Ancient Israel.* Peabody, Mass.: Hendrickson, 1994.

Smith, Mark. *The Early History of God.* San Francisco: Harper and Row, 1990.

Smith, Morton. *Palestinian Parties and Politics that Shaped the Old Testament.* New York: Columbia University Press, 1971.

Smith, Robertson. *The Religion of the Semites.* 2d ed. New York: Schocken, 1972 (1st ed. 1889).

Spriggs, D. G. *Two Old Testament Theologies.* SBT 2d ser. 30. London: SCM Press, 1974.

Stager, Lawrence. "The Archaeology of the Family." *BASOR* 260 (1985): 1–35.

Stähli, Hans-Peter. *Solare Elemente im Jahweglauben des Alten Testaments.* OBO 66. Göttingen: Vandenhoeck und Ruprecht, 1985.

Stern, Naomi. "The Deuteronomic Law Code and the Politics of State." In *The Bible and the Politics of Exegesis,* edited by David Jobling et al., 161–70. Cleveland: Pilgrim Press, 1991.

Stiebing, William. "The End of the Mycenean Age." *BA* 43 (1980): 7–21.

——. *Out of the Desert?* Buffalo: Prometheus, 1989.

Stolz, Fritz. "Der Monotheismus Israels im Kontext der altorientalischen Religions-geschichte." In *Ein Gott allein?* edited by Walter Dietrich and Martin Klopfenstein, 33–50. Göttingen: Vandenhoeck und Ruprecht, 1994.

———. "Monotheismus in Israel." In *Monotheismus im Alten Israel und seiner Umwelt,* edited by Othmar Keel, 144–189. BibB 14. Fribourg: Schweizerisches Katholisches Bibelwerk, 1980.

Synave, Paul, and Pierre Benoit. *Prophecy and Inspiration.* Translated by Avery Dulles, 84–168. New York: Desclee, 1961.

Taylor, Glen. *Yahweh and the Sun.* JSOTSup111. Sheffield, U.K.: JSOT, 1993.

Teilhard de Chardin, Pierre. *The Divine Milieu.* Translated by Bernard Wall. New York: Harper and Row, 1965.

———. *The Future of Man.* Translated by Norman Denny. New York: Harper and Row, 1964.

———. *Man's Place in Nature.* Translated by René Hague. New York: Harper and Row, 1966.

———. *The Phenomenon of Man.* Translated by Bernard Wall. New York: Harper and Row, 1961.

———. *Toward the Future.* Translated by René Hague. New York: Harcourt Brace Jovanovich, 1975.

Terrien, Samuel. *The Elusive Presence: Toward a New Biblical Theology.* New York: Harper and Row, 1978.

———. *Till the Heart Sings.* Philadelphia: Fortress Press, 1985.

Theissen, Gerd. *Biblical Faith.* Translated by John Bowden. Philadelphia: Fortress Press, 1985.

Thompson, Thomas. *Early History of the Israelite People.* SHANE 4. Leiden: Brill, 1992.

———. "How Yahweh Became God." *JSOT* 68 (1995): 57–74.

Toews, Wesley. *Monarchy and Religious Institutions in Israel under Jeroboam I.* SBLMS 47. Atlanta: Scholars Press, 1993.

Topel, John. "Rahner and McKenzie on the Social Theory of Inspiration." *Scripture* 16 (1964): 34–44.

Towner, Sibley. *How God Deals with Evil.* Philadelphia: Westminster Press, 1976.

Vawter, Bruce. *On Genesis.* Garden City, N.Y.: Doubleday, 1977.

Vorländer, Hermann. "Der Monotheismus Israels als Antwort auf die Krise des Exils." In *Der einzige Gott,* edited by Bernhard Lang, 84–113. Munich: Kösel, 1981.

Wacholder, Ben Zion. "Sabbatical Year." *IDBSup.* Edited by Keith Crim, 762–63. Nashville: Abingdon Press, 1976.

Weippert, Manfred. *The Settlement of the Israelite Tribes in Palestine.* Translated by James Martin. SBT, 2d ser. 21. London: SCM Press, 1971.

Wellhausen, Julius. *Prolegomena to the History of Ancient Israel.* Translated by Allan Menzies and J. Sutherland Black. Gloucester, Mass.: Peter Smith, 1973 (1st ed. 1878).

Wenning, Robert, and Erich Zenger. "Ein bäuerliches Baal-Heiligtum im samarischen Gebirge aus der Zeit der Anfänge Israels." *ZDPV* 102 (1986): 75–86.

Westermann, Claus. *Creation.* Translated by John Scullion. Philadelphia: Fortress Press, 1974.

——. *Elements of Old Testament Theology.* Translated by Douglas Stott. Atlanta: John Knox Press, 1982.

——. "The Role of Lament in the Theology of the Old Testament." Translated by Richard Soulen. *Int* 29 (1974): 20–38.

Wilson, Robert R. *Prophecy and Society in Ancient Israel.* Philadelphia: Fortress Press, 1980.

Woolcombe, K. J. "The Pain of God." *SJT* 20 (1967): 129–48.

Wright, Christopher. *God's People in God's Land.* Grand Rapids, Mich.: Eerdmans, 1990.

Wright, George Ernest. *Biblical Archaeology.* 2d ed. Philadelphia: Westminster Press, 1962.

——. *God Who Acts.* SBT 8. London: SCM Press, 1952.

——. *The Old Testament Against Its Environment.* SBT 2. Chicago: Regnery, 1950.

Wright, George Ernest, and Reginald Fuller. *The Book of the Acts of God.* Garden City N.Y.: Doubleday, 1957.

Yee, Gale. "The Theology of Creation in Proverbs 8:22–31." In *Creation in the Biblical Traditions,* edited by Richard Clifford and John Collins, 85–96. CBQMS 24. Washington, D.C.: CBA, 1992.

Zevit, Ziony. "The Khirbet el-Qôm Inscription Mentioning a Goddess." *BASOR* 255 (1984): 39–47.

Scripture Index

Author Index

Subject Index

anthropopathism 4, 121, 122, 163
'apiru 14
Aquinas 10
Aristotle 8, 10, 40
Ark Narrative 120
Asherah 19–25, 78
Ashur 21, 184, 185
Assyrian Treaties 112–13, 118, 175–77
Assyrians 131–36, 138, 175–77, 178
Atrahasis Epic 98, 173–75
Augustine 2, 10, 89
Axial Age 50, 54

Baal 19–25, 172, 184
Babylonian Theodicy 180
Balaam 76, 129–30
Bergson, Henri 28
biblical theology movement 160
Bondage of the Will 120
Book of the Covenant 20, 62, 142, 144–53, 155–56
Bronze Age 15, 17
Buddhism 51

Calvin, John 85, 90
Camus, Albert 48
Canaanites 13–25
Chaldeans 46
Chicago School 51–52
"chief exemplification" 36, 47
circumlocution of the Divine 77–80
Clement of Alexandria 90
co–creation 49, 67, 103–7
Code of Hammurabi 149
cognitive inspiration 190
communitarianism 35
"concrescence" 32–35, 57–58, 60, 61, 63
"consequent nature of God," "consequent body of God" 11, 36–39, 42, 46, 50, 65

"continuing creation" 100–103
convergence and differentiation 172–73, 183
Copenhagen School 24
covenant 64, 69–70, 111–23
creatio ex nihilo 12, 55, 97–100
creation of world 97–110
"creative transformation" 50, 51
"cultural symbiosis" 16
Cur Deus Homo 85–86

Daniel 80
Darwin, Charles 201
David 19, 21
"Day of the Lord" 138–39, 184–85
Democritus 28
demythologization 48, 63
Deuteronomic laws 62, 113, 142, 144–53, 155–56
Deuteronomic reformers 18, 21, 25, 52, 114, 117, 118, 144–53, 156, 171, 176, 195
Deuteronomistic History, Historians 21, 22, 56, 69, 77, 112, 113, 117, 119–20, 145, 185
docetism 86
divine judgment and hope 68–70
divine suffering 64, 83–95
dream reports 178–79

Edom 21, 183
Einstein, Albert 201
El 16, 19–25, 172
Elephantine 20, 22
Eli 76, 120
Elijah 19–20, 131, 177, 179
Elisha 19–20, 177, 179
Elohist 62, 77
"emergent monotheism" 19–25, 61
enclosed nomadism 16
Enki and the World Manor 174
Enuma Elish 98, 173–75

227